THE FIVE BOOKS OF MOSES

by the same author

GOSPEL OF JOHN
THE WAY INTO THE HOLIEST
CHRIST IN ISAIAH
TRIED BY FIRE
PHILIPPIANS
EXODUS I AND II
OUR DAILY WALK
OUR DAILY HOMILY
EPHESIANS (KEY WORDS)
SOME SECRETS OF CHRISTIAN LIVING
THE PRESENT TENSES OF THE BLESSED LIFE
THE SHEPHERD PSALM
PETER
ABRAHAM
PAUL
DAVID
ELIJAH
JOHN THE BAPTIST
EXPOSITORY PREACHING
JOSEPH
SAVED AND KEPT
THE FIVE BOOKS OF MOSES

The Five Books of
MOSES

A Devotional Commentary on each Chapter from
Genesis :: Leviticus :: Exodus
Numbers :: Deuteronomy

F. B. Meyer

WIPF & STOCK · Eugene, Oregon

Wipf and Stock Publishers
199 W 8th Ave, Suite 3
Eugene, OR 97401

The Five Books of Moses
A Devotional Commentary on each Chapter from Genesis,
Leviticus, Exodus, Numbers, Deuteronomy
By Meyer, F.B.
ISBN 13: 978-1-5326-1321-0
Publication date 10/24/2016
Previously published by Marshall, Morgan & Scott, 1955

Contents

The Book of Genesis	7
The Book of Exodus	55
The Book of Leviticus	95
The Book of Numbers	124
The Book of Deuteronomy	155
Index	187

The Book of Genesis

THIS venerable Book is unrivalled among the religious records of our race. The Vedas of the Hindoos, the Zendavesta of the Persians, are very ancient: but they consist of hymns and philosophic speculations, or addresses to the elements of nature; and do not profess to be what this Book is—a narrative of man's religious history for more than five-and-twenty centuries; written with devout belief in one God, and in a style of grave, archaic, artless simplicity. In Luther's judgment, there was nothing more beautiful or more useful than GENESIS. It is the befitting portico to the temple of Truth. It is the seed-plot of the Bible; because there is nothing in all the subsequent revelation of which the rudiment or germ may not be discovered here. To master Genesis is to hold the key of Scripture.

As to its name: the Jews called it by its first word—*Bereshith* (in the beginning). The Greeks called it *Genesis* (origination). We may well regard it as the Book of Beginnings; because we may here discover the source of many streams—some turbid; some crystal—which are flowing through the world. (1) The origin of the heavens and the earth; (2) of the human family; (3) of marriage and the home; (4) of sin and death; (5) of sacrifice; (6) of nations and tongues; (7) of the Hebrew race; (8) of the rite of circumcision, and the covenant which it sealed; (9) of the heavenly priesthood.

Amongst the Jews, *its authorship* was always ascribed to Moses—a belief authenticated by Christ (John v. 46, 47). Moses probably wrote it after the name JEHOVAH had been revealed to him (Exod. iii. 14; vi. 2, 3); since he often uses the designation. But he also almost certainly interwove into his story many hallowed narratives of the past, which had been orally transmitted from father to son in the patriarchal tents; which he had learnt in boyhood from his mother; and in which the Almighty was designated as God, *Elohim*, the Strong. This is the explanation of the difference between the Jehovistic and the Elohistic portions, which are clearly marked in the Hebrew, and to some extent in our own version. The first are due to the direct penmanship of Moses; the second to the incorporation of holy tradition; each beneath the Divine inspiration and teaching of the Holy Ghost.

We must not forget *the design* of this Book: to prepare for the story of God's dealings with the Hebrew people, of whom the Saviour of the world was to come. All is made to converge and taper to that fact. Much that would have been interesting, but not relevant, is dropped out of view, or mentioned in the slightest manner. Attention is focused on the Hebrew people, and those incidents which needed to be explained as a preparation for the understanding of all that was to follow. They mistake, therefore, who come to this Book for treatises on geology, ethnology, or archaeology; though, when all the truth is known, nothing in any of these branches of knowledge will have been discovered inconsistent with the general broad outlines of this book.

The divisions of this Book are clearly marked by the recurring phrase, *these are the generations*: of the heavens and earth, ii. 4; of Adam, v. 1; of Noah, vi. 9; of Noah's sons, x. 1; of Shem, xi. 10; of Terah, xi. 27; of Ishmael, xxv. 12; of Isaac, xxv. 19; of Esau, xxxvi. 1; of Jacob, xxxvii. 2: and at each division our attention is fixed on a narrowing area, until from the creation of the heavens and the earth it is left with one sad object of contemplation—an enslaved race, and "a coffin in Egypt."

CHAP. I. **The Creation**

This chapter presents a sublime contrast to the legends of Creation passing elsewhere as current coin. It bears on its front the stamp of Divine inspiration and truth. No attempt is made to prove the existence, or describe the origin, of God. These are assumed as being universally confessed (Rom. i. 20). Without introduction we are brought face to face with Him who, "before the mountains were brought forth, or the earth was formed, from everlasting to everlasting," is God (Ps. xc. 2). Is not this a suitable inscription to put on the forefront of every new enterprise or epoch of time?—"IN THE BEGINNING, GOD" (1).

There is no trace of the doctrine of the plurality of gods which was taught in other religions, and so inveterately held by the Jews themselves. Alone, among its rivals, this Book recognizes the one only living God: though in the plural of the Hebrew word (Elohim), and in the resolve, "Let *us* make man" (26), there are traces of the blessed Trinity, and of the presence of the Son, through whom, as the organ of creation, all things were made (John i. 3; Col. i. 16). Let us pause, and worship!

With pen of unerring truth the Spirit of Inspiration writes God's name on all things, excluding ATHEISM—for *God* created; POLYTHEISM—for *One* God created; THE ETERNITY OF MATTER—for all things began in God; and the word *create* clearly implies to make out of nothing (Heb. xi. 3); and PANTHEISM—for God, the Builder of all, must be distinct from the work of His hands.

The objects of ancient idolatry are specially mentioned in the catalogue of creation—sun and stars; sea-monsters and cattle; as well as creeping things—as if to rebut foolish and ignorant superstition. Creation's progress is described as the eve and dawn of successive days, which are supposed by some to represent vast periods of time (the word *day* is so used: ii. 4). Many scientific men have expressed their belief that the general outlines are in complete accord with the discoveries of recent science.

Here follow a sublime series. The heaving chaos and brooding Spirit (**2**); light shining out of darkness (**3**, and 2 Cor. iv. 6); mists rolled up, and the clear expanse of air separating the clouds from the earth (**6-8**); the waters poured into their beds (Ps. civ. 6-9); earth carpeted with green and covered with vegetation (**11, 12**); the giving of light-bearers for day and night (**14-18**). So the palace stood complete. Then the ocean of air peopled with birds, and that of water with fish (**20-22**); and finally, on the earth, cattle and creeping things, and forest beasts (**24, 25**). Thus the royal retinue was prepared. Lastly, man, the king; moulded of red earth as to his body; made in the image of God as to soul and spirit; appointed to subdue and rule (**26**, and Ps. viii. 4-8). That royalty has been lost; the crown rolled in the dust. But it is restored in Christ (Heb. ii. 9): and we, through faith, being identified with Him, shall get all back and more; for this is the purpose of God (Rom. viii. 29; Rev. v. 10).

CHAP. II. **Paradise**

This chapter brims with interest.

The rest of God (**1-3**): not the rest of indolence or inaction; but of complacency with a finished work. "Behold, it was very good." Christ also rested on the seventh day, lying in the tomb, because His work was done and redemption finished. And, if we believe, we too may share that rest (Heb. iv. 9-11): rest of soul, in His work for us; of heart, in His love to us; of will, in His rule over us. And where God rests, He sanctifies. Wouldst thou be a saint?—then see to it that God rests within!

The story of Paradise (**8**), which has long since vanished from the earth; though its memories, like threads of light, are interwoven in the legends of all peoples. When men point to the vice and misery of our great cities, as a slur on the character of God, point them back to Eden, with its pleasant and wholesome trees; or forward to the City of Gold: these are God's thoughts and ideals. His enemy has wrought the devastation we see around. Man's history begins in a pleasant garden, and ends in a Holy City: but what an agony between!

We hear the murmurs of the waters of *the river* (**10**), of which there is frequent mention afterwards: which flowed in the desert (1 Cor. x. 4); made glad the city of God (Ps. xlvi. 4); issued from under the threshold of the house (Ezek. xlvii. 1), bringing life wherever it came; and proceeds from the throne of God and of the Lamb (Rev. xxii. 1).

Here also (**9**) is the *tree of life*—one of heaven's exotics—which could not flourish in our cold clime; and has been taken back to bloom in perpetual summer (Rev. xxii. 2).

The forming of woman out of man (**22**): which reveals the intimate connection between the two in God's thought; and foreshadows the sacred union between Christ and the Church, which owes her being to His sleep in the tomb. Eve was made, "not from Adam's head, to top him; nor from his feet, to be trampled on by him; but from his side to be his equal; under his arm to be protected; and near to his heart to be beloved." God made the first home.

CHAP. III. **The Fall**

The frequent subsequent references to the story of the Fall forbid us to treat it as a parable or myth (2 Cor. xi. 3; 1 Tim. ii. 11–14). Why should not the devil possess serpents as well as men?

The temptation (**1–5**) followed the same stages as those which are familiar to us—the question about God's dealings; the suggestion that good is to be had outside the fence of His prohibition; the denial that any evil consequences will follow the act of disobedience; and the sly allusion to the advantages that would accrue.

And Eve's sin came about as do our sins (**6**). She listened to the tempter, instead of saying instantly, "Get thee behind me!"; she exaggerated the limits of the prohibition ("neither shall ye touch it"); she looked, and dwelt longingly on the pleasantness and desirableness of the fruit—till desire mastered the protests of conscience, and she took and shared the forbidden spoils.

And instantly *the effects* followed, which follow with ourselves (7–8). Their eyes were opened, and they saw. Temptation blinds us; satiety opens our eyes to see what we have done. And as they hid themselves from one another, so they tried to conceal themselves from God: sin ever breeds fear, which hath torment. Finally, each mistrusted and accused the other; for sin is the great separator of man from God, and man from man.

In the *penal clauses* blessing is marvellously blended with penalty (9–24). The ground is cursed; but it is for man's sake: and arduous toil has often *made* men; taxing inventiveness, and rousing dormant energy, to master difficulty. The woman was to suffer multiplied pain: but pain has been prolific in the discipline of human souls: what a noble progeny is hers! And though the great enemy of man might do his worst, yet the woman's Seed should bruise his head. On the cross of Calvary, and in the grave of Joseph of Arimathea, these words were literally fulfilled.

What pity also was there in God's search for His erring ones; His institution of sacrifice; and His clothing of their nakedness with the victims' skins! And though the flaming sword forbids our return to Paradise Lost, the cherubim point to Paradise Regained for us by the Second Adam, the Lord from heaven (Rom. v. and 1 Cor. xv. 22–45).

CHAP. IV. **Cain and Abel**

We notice: (I.) *The contrast between two different kinds of worship* (3–5).—Cain deliberately refused the Divine appointment of sacrifice, instituted in Eden; and brought fruit which, however fair and ripe, was only a confession of the Divine creatorship; and failed to acknowledge that he was a sinful man, needing sacrifice, atonement, and forgiveness. Abel, on the other hand, realized his sinnership, and brought the goodliest of his flock, confessing, as he did so, that he deserved to die; but pleading for forgiveness in virtue of the lamb's shed blood: emblem of the richer blood, which was one day to bless the world (Heb. xi. 4). Still the distinction holds: the Rationalist may profess religion; but it is the religion of Cain, without blood. How contrary to Heb. ix.!

(II.) *The genesis of sin* (5–9).—When Cain saw the descending fire burn on Abel's altar, the evil of his nature flamed out; for he was of the wicked one. Self-will led to disobedience; that to hatred and jealousy; these to murder; murder to lying, and the imputation of harshness and injustice to God. Beware of the first beginnings of sin!—they are like the first drops of an ocean trickling through a sandbank.

(III.) *The cry of a covered crime* (**10**).—Abel's blood spoke. It cried to God, as all innocent martyr-blood cries, "How long, O Lord, holy and true?" (Rev. vi. 10). And sin which has not been confessed to God always cries to God for vengeance; nor will that cry cease till the sinner has fled to the blood of Jesus, which cries for mercy in sweeter, louder tones (Heb. xii. 24). Shelter yourselves under that blood.

(IV.) *The beginning of the division between the world and the Church.*—Cain founded a city (**17**), where arts, and music, and all that pleased the taste, began to flourish. These were the chief objects sought by his children and their descendants. This was "the way of Cain," brilliant but godless; out from the presence of the Lord (**16**).

CHAP. V. From Adam to Noah

In this chapter we are permitted to walk through one of the cemeteries of the old world, and look at the time-worn monuments on which we can still decipher the ancient names, and the age at which the men died. But only the good people are buried here: those of the line of Seth, who in some degree took the place of the martyred Abel. It is sad, however, to notice that, though they were clearly divided from the Cainites, they were all tinged with Adam's sin, and its results. Adam was made in the image of God; but he begat Seth in his own likeness, after his image (**3**): and so was propagated that bias and tendency towards evil which has passed to every twig in the great tree of humanity. "That which is born of the flesh is flesh" (John iii. 6).

Mark, *The monotony of death.*—Eight times the bell tolls out the solemn words, "And he died." However long the life, it always succumbed at last to the scythe of death. Methuselah himself at last must follow the generations of his race to the darkness of the grave. And there is one reason, amply sufficient: death passed on all, because all sinned (Rom. v. 12). "It is appointed unto men," *and to you,* "once to die" (Heb. ix. 27). Prepare to meet thy God!

The possibilities of faith (Heb. xi. 5).—It enabled a poor, weak man, like ourselves, to walk with God, and please Him, for over three hundred years, amid the growing darkness and impurity of his times. And if he could, surely *we* can. Why not resolve henceforth to agree with God, bringing our thoughts and ways into harmony with His? (Amos iii. 3). Then let it be the aim of our life to do always those things that please Him; and the Father will never leave us alone (John viii. 29). We shall walk with Him in holy and delightful fellowship (1 John i. 3); we shall be able, like Enoch, to give a bright testimony to the world (Jude 14); and we shall be ready to be translated, so as not to see death, if so be that Jesus comes before we die (1 Cor. xv. 51-57).

The disappointment of human hopes.—An aged pair clasped in their arms an infant boy, and called him Noah (rest); but the nomenclature was premature. The Deluge was soon to sweep over the world of men; and the weary generations were yet to wait till One should come who would give forth a universal invitation, "Come unto Me, *all ye* that labour and are heavy-laden and I will give you rest." Our rest cannot come from within: it must come from above.

CHAP. VI. **The Ark Constructed**

God only hastened the results of sin.—Many terms are used to indicate the virulence of the disease (5, 6, 11, 12). So bad was it that ultimately it must have swept the world of men, as small-pox devastates some fair isle in the southern seas. Was it not better to hasten the inevitable result by one sudden act of judgment than let it run out its dismal course of agony? Yet how malignant is sin, that it could send its poison across the Flood in a selected household!

Every means was taken to divert man from his evil way.—God's Spirit strove with man; and though a limit was put to His tender pleadings, yet He plied men with yearning remonstrances, turning away disappointed and grieved at heart (6). There was also considerable delay: for 120 years the long-suffering of God waited (1 Pet. iii. 20), as it waits for you: though it will not wait for ever; there is a limit (Luke xiii. 9). And in the meantime the Ark was a-preparing, and Noah was preaching righteousness (2 Pet. ii. 5).

The character of Noah shines out for our admiration. Just towards man; perfect in wholeheartedness towards God; walking step by step in heavenly fellowship; and yielding implicit obedience to each command (9, 22). This is the man to whom God tells His secrets concerning coming doom; with whom a covenant is established; and who is permitted to pass over into the world of resurrection; saved himself, and a means of salvation to others. Reader, let that character be thine!

CHAP. VII. The Deluge

What a flood was this! Men climbed to the highest storey of their towers in vain; then to the hills; but the greedy waters followed them in their flight, and hemmed them in, driving close together into smaller groups men, women, children, and wild beasts, that crouched with fear, or fought for the highest crag, till this also was covered, and all was still, as the last cry was lost amid the moan of the breakers and the pitiless downpour of rain.

Equally certain and unexpected shall be the final Judgment which shall close the present age.—"AS IT WAS in the days of Noah, so SHALL IT BE in the days of the Son of Man" (Luke xvii. 26). In those days there was no sign of a millennium: sin and lawlessness held undisputed sway; one faithful heart alone beat true to God. Nor shall the Son of Man find it otherwise when He comes. His advent shall startle the children of the world at their wine-parties, their balls, their brilliant theatres, their studios of art and music. Men think this cannot be; they argue from the unbroken course of nature. But the course of nature was broken once by the baptism of water; and it shall be broken again by the baptism of fire (2 Pet. iii. 7).

The safety of the inmates of the ark.—God said, "Come in!" HE was inside. The invitation included all Noah's household. God does not wish us to be saved alone. Seven days before the Deluge came they entered, amid the loud laughter and mockery of the world to which Noah had often preached. But no one, not even of the builders, went with them. And the Lord shut the door behind the last that entered. And when once the Master has shut the door there is no further hope of entrance (Luke xii. 25); neither shall any surge of trouble or judgment break through, though the roar of the billows be heard without (Rev. iii. 7). Are you inside God's Ark? If not, make haste! What saved Noah? The ark?—or his feelings about it? Certainly, the ARK. So are we saved: not by our feelings about Christ, but by His free grace. And in the ark the mouse was as safe as the lion.

Chap. VIII. The Raven and the Dove

Traditions of the Flood are found in every land, from the tablets of Babylon to the rude carvings of the Aztecs. Nothing has ever left so profound an impression on the heart of man as this stupendous act of judgment; and the universal tradition attests the truth of Scripture. Never since then have men been ignorant of the mind of God against sin.

The mindfulness of God (Ps. cxi. 4).—"God remembered Noah." The floods have been descending on your life; but He has not forgotten you, nor can He. He sees the peril, and counts the tears of His saints. Though He tarry long, He will interpose and deliver (Isa. xliv. 21; xlix. 15); and the tossing ark shall at last come to rest.

The mission of the birds.—Noah's window looked upward only, for fellowship; it had no outlook on the world: so he sent forth winged couriers to bear him tidings (7-9). The interval of seven days marks a Sabbath-keeping even in the ark (10). Surely if men kept the Sabbath there, its observance is possible anywhere. The unclean raven found its food and home amid the *débris* of the flood. But the gentle dove found no rest in such scenes; and in this is prefigured the renewed heart which sighs for rest in vain, till the hand of Jesus takes it in unto Himself.

The descent on resurrection ground (18).—Through the waters of death and judgment Noah floated in the ark; and finally, when the face of nature emerged, green and smiling, beautiful as when Eden lay under the blessing of God, he stepped out into the "new heavens and a new earth, in which dwelt righteousness." Then, of the clean animals, which, for purposes of sacrifice, he had taken in larger numbers (vii. 2), he offered a burnt offering (20). We who believe in Jesus have in Him travelled across from the old world that lies under God's curse, the world of the flesh; we have passed to the windward of the storm; we are the "children of the resurrection." Let us live as such!

CHAP. IX. **The Bow in the Cloud**

It is very remarkable to meet here (4) the clear prohibition against the use of blood in food, which, both under the Mosaic economy and in the Christian dispensation, is afterwards repeated on the page of Scripture (Lev. xvii. 11, and Acts xv. 20). And the reason is clearly given—the blood is the life. Is not this what we mean when we speak of the precious blood of Jesus Christ—that He laid down His life for us? "The blood maketh atonement for the soul" (Lev. xvii. 11).

The value of human life (**5**).—If an ox gored a man, or any beast of prey killed him, the animal was to be destroyed (*see* Exod. xxi. 28). The brother of a murdered man was to require the blood of the murderer. The lower creation might be freely used for food* (3); but human life was surrounded by the most solemn sanctions. This would correct any thought begotten by the destruction of the Deluge that God was prodigal of human life. The new law (**6**), so specially protective of human life, was doubtless given to guard against the recurrence of the condition of things which existed before the Deluge, when "the earth was filled with violence" (vi. 11).

The covenant (**11**).—How much grace there was in it! It depended upon no condition on the part of man, but originated in and was maintained by the unmerited mercy of God. Its sign was the rainbow. When you see a rainbow, recall God's pledge, so that you may think the same thing as God; then think of another covenant, true of the spiritual seed of Abraham (Isa. liv. 9, 10). We see only half here; the other half is in heaven, and completes the circle (Rev. iv. 3).

Noah's sin (**21**) reminds us how weak are the best of men; liable to fall, even after the most marvellous deliverances. The love of drink will drag a preacher of righteousness into the dust. Let us see to it that we fall not into this temptation ourselves; and that we tempt not others (Hab. ii. 15). But if one of our brethren sin, let us not parade or tell his fault, but cover it with the mantle of Divine love: hating the sin, but seeking to save the sinner (Gal. vi. 1; Jude 23: *see also* Rom. xiv. 21; 1 Cor. x. 31).

---

* *Verse* 3: "Every moving thing that liveth shall be meat for you." This permission probably only applied to "clean" creatures; as the distinction between "clean" and "unclean" is clearly shown in Gen. vii. 2.

Chap. X. Descendants of Noah

It is very necessary to read this chapter carefully, in order to understand the references to foreign nations made later in the Scriptures; and it will well repay the earnest student to trace, with the aid of Bible dictionary and map, the spread of mankind over the world. Over the whole let us write, "God loved the world."

GENTILES cannot but find a deep interest in this *first mention of their name* (5). And, in these old terms, learned ethnologists have found traces of much that exists around us still. Gomer stands for the Celts; Javan is Greece; Tubal is Tobolsk; Ashkenaz probably points to the Saxons; Tarshish is Spain; Kittim may even be the British Isles. These are those "other sheep" of which the Good Shepherd spake; and it is pleasant to feel that God keeps a list of His prodigal children.

In the enumeration of the children of Ham, we meet *the first mention of Nineveh*, and also of Babylon. From this point to Rev. xviii. the latter name continually recurs; and it always denotes hostility to the people of God. Babylon is Satan's counterfeit of the Church of God. She exists still in the world around us; and Babylonish garments tempt us, as they tempted Israel in the days of Achan; whilst many of God's children are betrayed into worse than Babylonish captivity. Note in **16–18** the progenitors of the seven nations of Canaan, so often referred to in Joshua. Nimrod was a mighty hunter, a fact noticed in contrast to the peaceful shepherd-life around; and in this combination of passions for the chase and war, he is the prototype of the Babylonish kings. It has been said that from being a hunter of beasts he became a hunter of men; and he may possibly have been the first man who made slaves of his fellow-men.

But the main interest centres about Shem and his children: because there we strike the origin of that marvellous line of witnesses for the truth, which gave to the world an Abraham, a Moses, an Isaiah, a Paul; and, above all, Jesus Christ, as to His human nature (Rom. ix. 4, 5).

Chap. XI. Building of Babel

The building of Babel.—Driven by the fear of another deluge, notwithstanding God's distinct assurance to the contrary (ix. 11)—and impelled by a common desire to "make a name" (**4**)—the descendants of Noah began to build on the plain of Shinar. Men seem to be born to be builders. They build houses, or fortunes, or reputations; systems, or societies—but how often atheistically! They reject God's foundation, and build on the sand of the alluvial plain. They think to secure themselves against any flood of misfortune or trouble that may sweep through the world. They are bent on making a name. Some men are always taking brick for stone and slime for mortar; but the work ends in disappointment and confusion. Oh, builders for eternity, get on God's Rock: build according to His plan, and for the glory of His name!

The confusion of tongues.—The whole world had been of one lip and one stock of words (**1**). But God came down: first to see; then to confound. He never confounds in judgment, unless He has carefully examined into the rights of a matter for Himself. He is always coming down to see what we are doing; and nothing can escape His searching eyes. And He can judge us by a very little thing. He touched the lip, and altered the whole method of pronunciation. This disunion prevails in the world: but in the Church God has given the true principle of union in the risen Jesus, and at Pentecost Babel was reversed (Acts ii. 1–11); whilst heaven will give all one lip again (Rev. vii. 9, 10).

The call of Abram (**31**).—We must not forget to compare Acts vii. 2 with the words before us. The movement of that little clan in the grey dawn of history from its original seat was the result of a Divine call to the youngest son. He carried with him the old father Terah, and others of his race; but their presence stayed his march and impeded his obedience, so that the exodus stopped short at Haran or Charran, instead of going forward to Canaan. Only when his father was dead did Abram carry out the Divine programme to the full. "Let us lay aside every weight." Let us do God's will to the uttermost, come what may (Acts xxi. 13, 14; Eph. vi. 13; Ps. xlvi. 2, 3).

Chap. XII. The Call of Abram

God's commands are always linked with promises. Count the six *shalls* and *wills* of this promise. God does not always give His reasons; but He is generous of His promises. The one cry of Scripture is for separation, to which we are graciously allured (Deut. xxviii. 1; Isa. lii. 11; Ezek. xxxvii. 21-28; Matt. xix. 29; 2 Cor. vi. 17, 18; Eph. v. 11). The keynote of Abram's life was SEPARATION; not all at once, but step by step: until country, kindred, Lot, worldly alliances, fleshly expedients—were one after another cast aside; and he stood alone with God.

Abram's obedience.—"So Abram departed" (**4**, and Heb. xi. 8). His obedience was the result of faith in the bare word of God. He was not sure of his destination. The land had yet to be shown. Fierce nations were around. Trackless deserts lay beyond the Euphrates-flood. It seemed impossible that the world could be blessed through a childless man. But it was enough for him that God had spoken. Faith prompted obedience; and obedience reacted on faith (Rom. iv. 13-22). Immediate and scrupulous obedience is the secret of a healthy and useful life.

The tent and the altar.—"He dwelt in tents" (Heb. xi. 9). The tent life is natural to the man whose portion is God, and whose fatherland is the Land of Promise. "Here we have no continuing city; but we seek one to come" (Heb. xiii. 14). The tent is good enough for the pilgrim. God met His obedient child with a new promise, when he reached Canaan. "*This* is the Land" (**7**). And there Abram built his first altar; and afterwards, where he pitched his tent, he reared the altar of praise and prayer and consecration. Wherever we go, at home or abroad, however short our stay, we should rear an altar of testimony.

The famine.—In the way of obedience and faith there always will be difficulties (**10**). By these God tests and teaches us. A famine is no indication that we are wrong; but may imply that God is going to reveal some marvellous deliverance. Alas! Abram failed under the test, and went down to Egypt, which is always the Scripture symbol for reliance on an arm of flesh (Isa. xxx. 1-7). And one sin led to another, in his shameful denial of his wife (**18**). But God did not cast him off: He graciously protected and restored him (Ps. cv. 14, 15).

Chap. XIII. **Abram and Lot**

In the opening verses of this chapter the patriarch seems like a restored backslider. After his grievous descent, he comes up again out of Egypt: and makes his way back to the old spot, on the highlands of Bethel, where his first tent and altar had stood. But all through his wanderings there had been a depressing worldly element in his camp; Lot, his nephew, went with him (5), and Lot was one of those who are swept along by the religious earnestness of others, but are destitute of religious principle and force of character.

Abram's proposal.—He was older and richer; but he took no advantage from either. Feeling that separation was inevitable, he gave Lot the right of choice (9). And it was less difficult to do this; because Abram was sure that, whatever Lot decided, God would do the best thing for Himself. We can afford to waive our rights when God is the portion of our inheritance, and maintains our lot (Ps. xvi. 5).

Lot's choice.—The plain of Jordan was fair as a garden, but steeped in shameful sin. And the young man chose according to the sight of his eyes, with a view to material and worldly gain. He determined to gain the world; "but his choice well nigh cost him his soul." Are there not many still who choose health-resorts, dwelling-places, and schools, irrespective of the religious and moral atmosphere, and only upon such grounds as appeal to the uplifted eyes of human judgment and outward promise?

God's renewed promise to Abram.—It came in the loneliness after Lot's last followers had streamed out of the camp (14). Lot had lifted his eyes for himself. Now God bade Abram lift up *his* eyes—not to choose, but to behold what God had chosen for him. He was first to estimate his treasures: then to enjoy them (17). Let us count up the inestimable wealth stored up in Jesus; and let us enter upon its full and delightful enjoyment. Lot grasped all; and lost all. Abram left all; and won all (John xii. 25).

Chap. XIV. **"Four Kings against Five"**

The little confederate kings of the plain of Sodom thought themselves safe from the kings of the basin of the Euphrates. The desert lay between them; and it was a far cry from Shinar to Sodom. After twelve years' servitude they rebelled. But in the fourteenth year the dreaded Chedorlaomer swept down, and ravaged the neighbouring territories, narrowing the circle closer and closer, till he defeated them on the slippery soil, and marched up the course of the Jordan homewards, flushed with victory, laden with booty, and carrying Lot with him.

Lot's plight **(12)**.—It was a terrible fall from the tent and altar of Abram to the captivity of Chedorlaomer. Men must not expect to get all the sweets of the world, and escape its bitters. The path of separation is the only path of safety and peace.

His triumphant deliverance.—It was an heroic enterprise, that a pastoral chief should dare, with 318 untrained shepherds, to attack a disciplined host. But faith "subdues kingdoms." Here, too, was an example of chivalrous love, which is ever forgetful of injuries and negligent of self. Abram's dispositions were carefully made. His success was complete. He brought back all.

Abram's return.—The moment of success is always one of danger. The king of Sodom insidiously proposed that they should share the spoils: thus ever does the world approach us when we succeed, and attract notice. But Abram had previously met Melchizedec, the royal priest, who had given him bread and wine, and his blessing, and a new title for God (the "Most High"), which the patriarch remembered in the moment of temptation **(19, 22)**. Thus God *prevents* us (goes before) with the blessings of His goodness.

CHAP. XV. God's Great Promise

When temptation has been met and overcome, we may ever expect new revelations **(1)**. Abram might dread retaliation on the part of Chedorlaomer; and therefore God said, "Fear not! I am thy shield." He had not accepted the king of Sodom's offer: therefore came the words, "I am thy exceeding great reward." And all previous promises were excelled by the new great assurance about the seed. Abram was to have a child of his own; and his descendants were to be as numerous as the stars which filled the midnight Eastern sky **(5)**. "And he believed in the Lord." Simple words: but how much they mean! We find them often referred to afterwards. When we reckon God true, He reckons us righteous. Directly we believe, we not only have the seed-germ of a righteous life, but we are accounted judicially righteous before a holy God (Rom. iv. 23, 24).

The covenant.—In olden times, when men bound themselves to each other by solemn oaths, the parts of a victim were divided, and laid upon the ground, and the covenanting parties passed between them; thus Abram divided the appointed sacrifices, and the lamp of the Shechinah fire passed between them, signifying the ratification of the presence of God **(9, 10)**. How much God will do to give a substantial resting-ground for faith! (Heb. vi. 18).

The horror of darkness.—It is hard to wait and watch for God. Abram watched for the whole of a long Eastern day, scaring the vultures from the scorched pieces. Let us be vigilant against aught that might mar our sacrifices. Then, as the sun set, a great darkness fell upon his soul, as he foresaw the sufferings of his posterity: and yet how much mercy was there in it all! God would wait hundreds of years, rather than cut off nations until their iniquity had brimmed to overflowing **(16)**.

CHAP. XVI. **Hagar**

Here we have an example of that energy of our self-life which seeks to fulfil for itself the purposes and promises of God. It is not enough to be sure of God's will: we must wait till He show us how to secure its fulfilment. But Abram anticipated God, and fell in with Sarai's unwomanly proposal that he should marry her slave-girl **(3)**. It was the plan of expediency and policy, which entailed endless misery to all three.

Hagar's flight.—She could bear it no more, and so she fled **(6)**. She had not learnt the meaning of that word *submit*. Yet, what wonder! How few Christians have learnt it!—among servants, and indeed all classes! Remember that even the hard dealings of men are by God's permission, and therefore by His will. Take up the yoke, and carry it, until He says, "It is enough," and bids you go out free (1 Pet. ii. 18–25).

The Jehovah-Angel **(10)**.—Before His incarnation the Lord Jesus often appeared to men in angel-guise; and the peculiar expression of the Hebrew indicates that it was no ordinary angel who spoke to the poor slave-girl, and read the destiny of the "wild ass" man, to whom she was to give birth. She was right, when, in an outburst of mingled awe and joy, she called Him "a God who sees" (2 Chron. xvi. 9; 1 Pet. iii. 12).

Sound advice.—To all who are fretting against God's appointments, and who are fleeing from the path of duty, there is but one word of advice needed: *Return, and submit.* And amid all the hardships of life, let the promises of God ring in your heart, as in that of Hagar, making endurance possible, and life a refrain of sweet music. Oh, listen to God's angel speaking beside the fountains of life!

CHAP. XVII. **The Promise Renewed**

For thirteen years God's voice was still; and then, as if in passing allusion to His servant's failure, He said, "Be thou perfect" (**1**). We must be *whole-hearted.* Our surrender must be without reserve; our obedience implicit. So only will God enter into covenant with us, and multiply us exceedingly. It is ever the wholehearted service which is fruitful service.

The terms of the Covenant.—Investigate them thoroughly: then lay your hands on them, and claim them all. All is yours; if by faith you are one with faithful Abraham (Gal. iii. 9). Fruitfulness in Christian life; the salvation of our households; the inheriting of the land; the abundance of spiritual seed; the "new name" (Rev. ii. 17)— all these are guaranteed to those who can believe God, and walk before Him with an undivided heart.

The new name (**5**).—His name was expanded from Abram to Abraham—from "high father" to "father of many nations": and by this he was henceforth known to Jehovah and to men.

The sign of the Covenant.—The promises of God were made to Abraham, when yet uncircumcised, and therefore are irrespective of any rite (Rom. iv. 11). Still it was a sign and a seal. The counterpart of it, spiritually, is in that purity of heart and life which Christ secures (Col. ii. 11). As to the mere outward rite, that is abolished in Christ. It was the one aim of the Apostle Paul to show that it was temporary and national in its range (Acts xv. 24; Gal. v. 4; vi. 15).

Abraham's reception of God's Covenant.—He laughed with assurance of hope; as he lay humbly in the dust (**17**). He received promises for his wife; for Ishmael; and for the coming child. He obeyed, at whatever cost of suffering, and secured obedience throughout his house (**23**). He quietly waited for the salvation of God.

Chap. XVIII. The Three Angel-Visitors

The Lord Jesus is here giving some anticipation of what He is ready to do for all saintly and separated hearts (John xiv. 23; Rev. iii. 20). And Abraham knew well that "the High and Lofty One, who inhabiteth eternity, whose name is Holy" had come to visit him. Others might only have seen three men; but he recognized his Divine Friend, addressing Him as "my Lord" (3). And when the two angels went forward to do their awful work in Sodom, there arose high converse between the mortal man thus honoured by Divine companionship, and his Almighty Friend, who lingered still.

Entertainment (2-8).—Abraham was prompt. He lost no time. Twice we are told "he ran"; once that he "hastened." Neither he nor Sarah was unaccustomed to perform the common acts of domestic life. And he insisted on this personal service to his august guest. Oh that all we can do were done for Christ our Lord! The very best was chosen: *"tender and good."* And in such a home the Lord found *comfort* and *rest* (**4, 5**). Why should not each heart so open itself towards him? "Abide with us!" "Wash your feet" (*comp.* Luke vii. 44 and John xiii. 3-14).

Communion (**9-12**).—Christ tells His secrets to those He loves (Ps. xxv. 14; John xv. 15); secrets about their domestic life. The promised son was not only to be Abraham's, but Sarah's also. The mother laughed with incredulity, and then denied having done so. And yet the memory that this mysterious stranger had discerned her laugh, through the curtain which concealed the women's quarters, must have assured her of His ability to read the future also. The question of ver. **14**, is answered in Jer. xxxii. 17. Reckon on God's faithlessness and omnipotence. The Lord also can tell His secrets about the world and its destiny to those whom He knows (7-22).

Intercession.—Amid all the mysteries of God's moral government of men, we must cherish the conviction that He is doing what is right. But we must draw near Him to feel so (**23-25**). Abraham's faith grew at each answer to his prayers. Thus God leads on our weak hearts to further and yet further flights of trust, till we ask what we had not dared to imagine; but which we would have asked at first had we known God better. And even then God does "exceeding abundantly."

Chap. XIX. Sodom and Gomorrah

Here is the God of judgment. "With the froward He shows Himself froward" (2 Sam. xxii. 27; Ps. xviii. 26). And yet amid the terrors of the scene there are signs of mercy. He simply did at one stroke what must have been the inevitable result of the sin of Sodom. And the blow did not fall until means had been used, both through the deliverance from Chedorlaomer and the words of Lot (7), to turn them from their evil ways. Moreover, see what Christ said (Matt. xi. 23). It will be well also to turn to the words of Peter (2 Pet. ii. 7–8).

The awful symptoms of depravity.—Before doing anything the Lord went down to hold a solemn inquest (1, and xviii. 21). The angels who had come gladly to Abraham's tent refused Lot's first appeal (2); but were soon made aware that the streets were not safe. When vice walks the midnight thoroughfares, and the sanctity of home is invaded, then be sure that the judgments of God are not far away.

Mercy towards Lot.—How he had deteriorated! At first he only pitched his tent in the vicinity (xiii. 12); then he dwelt in Sodom (xiv. 12); finally he sits in the gate as one of its aldermen (1). But though he had gone up in worldly honour, he had gone back in God's esteem; for the Jehovah-Angel would not come to his home at all: the other two did so only after urgent pressure. Lot was a backslidden child—one in whom the good seed had been choked by the cares of the world, and the deceitfulness of riches, and the lusts of many things. Yet God had mercy on him, and saved him "so as by fire," while the fabric of his life-work was *burnt up* (1 Cor. iii. 15). The angels had four hands, and each was full of work (16). Lot left Sodom; yet he took Sodom with him.

The example of judgment (Jude 7).—God is Love; but he will most certainly punish sin, and we must look upon it from our standing-ground with God. Do not look up at God from the burning of Sodom; but look down on Sodom from the presence of God (27). Jehovah would have saved the lives of Lot's sons, and of his sons-in-law (12–14); but they "would not." Of the whole city-full only four persons came out, and they had to be *dragged forth*. And out of the four one perished within sight of the city of destruction (Luke xvii. 32).

History repeats itself. Such a catastrophe as fell on Sodom and Gomorrah, Admah and Zeboiim (xiv. 8; Deut. xxix. 23; Hosea xi. 8) nineteen centuries B.C., visited the earth and overwhelmed the cities of Herculaneum and Pompeii A.D. 78.

CHAP. XX.   **Abraham at Gerar**

What a terrible fall was here! First, in perpetuating an evil compact entered into years before, and which ought long ago to have been cast off (13). Secondly, in returning to a course of action, which had already proved disastrous (xii. 17, 18). Thirdly, in not believing that nothing could annul the distinct promise of God as to the promised seed. Yet how blessedly did the grace of God step in to avert the evil consequences of the patriarch's fault! And what a delightful assurance there is in the words spoken to Abimelech, "*I withheld thee from sinning*" (6). Let us claim 1 Cor. x. 13; 2 Pet. ii. 9.

See what Abraham was by nature.—The Scripture often draws aside the veil from the character of the loftiest saints, that we may see that originally they were not a whit nobler or greater than ourselves. What they were was due to no native grace, but to the grace of God. Their exploits were entirely due to the power of God, received by faith. And what God did for them He can do for any one of us who yields entirely to Him.

Learn God's shielding care.—Even though Abraham had seriously deflected from the strait path of obedience, yet God did not let the full results of his evil conduct descend upon his head. He said to the King of Gerar, "Thou art but a dead man"; and of His servant Abraham, "He is a prophet; and he shall pray for thee." God may have to chastise His children for their back-slidings; but He will not deliver them wholly into the hand of the oppressor. "The Lord God is a shield" (Ps. xxxiii. 20; lxxxiv. 9, 11). "Who is he that condemneth?" (Rom. viii. 34).

The stringency of God's dealing with secret sin.—He who has eyes as a flame of fire to detect, has a sharp sword to amputate. Never again did the patriarch fail after this fashion. It was needful to take this weak spot out of Abraham's character, that there might be firm ground for the faith which would soon be demanded (xxii.).

CHAP. XXI. **Isaac Born**

The faithfulness of God.—At last the *promise was fulfilled*—at the "set time" (**2**). God never is before His time, or after. As the appointed hour strikes, His messenger stands on the doorstep, the looked-for gift in His hand. Faith may be put to a long test, but never in vain (Ps. xl. 1; Isa. xlix. 23). Meanwhile look, not at circumstances, but at the word and power of the living God (Rom. iv. 20). And God will keep His word. Then comes the happy laughter of fulfilled hope, which wipes out the bitter memories of the past. When God bids you to laugh—laugh (**6**; Ps. cxxvi. 2).

The conflict.—Ishmael represents the covenant of works spoken from Sinai; Isaac the promise of grace in the Gospel (Gal. iv. 23, 24). There always has been, and always will be, conflict between these two principles, whether in the world or in the heart (Gal. iv. 29; v. 17). The law is not sin; but it stirs up our evil propensities, as a pure sunbeam brings out the foetid odour of a pond. We must therefore cast out the legal principle from our heart, as a method of sanctification, as of justification, and give up our nature to the sole indwelling and operation of faith. It is impossible for the two to co-exist.

The tender pity of God.—Are you alone—failing—wondering what will come of your little ones? The bottle of water soon gets spent: you need the fountain of John iv. 10. But if you are on God's plan, as Hagar was (**12**), God will certainly provide. He has heard: He will open sources of supply where all seems desert (Isa. xli. 18). God listens to the voice of lads even when mothers cannot catch a syllable (**17**). Take heart: perhaps the boy of whom you have almost lost hope has already begun to pray. The time of extreme anguish will reveal an earnestness you know not of. Is there not compensation in this?

ISHMAEL. *I will make him a great nation* (**18**).—Little did the slighted and outcast Egyptian woman think, as she sat shudderingly expecting the death of her boy, that from that semi-lifeless stripling (of whom it might have then been said that, like his father Abraham, he was "as good as dead") a vast posterity should come; that in a century and a half a powerful tribe of Ishmaelites would be headed by Isaac's elder son; that under the general name of Edom these descendants of the bondwoman would harry and harass the Jewish people for ages; that in the Herod dynasty they would rule over the land of Israel, the city of Jerusalem, and the chosen people; and that in the Arab tribes there would exist towards the close of the nineteenth century of the Christian era a people more numerous, and more vigorous, than the Jewish race: still, with their "hand against every man" (Gen. xvi. 12).

CHAP. XXII. Isaac on the Altar

In this chapter we have an anticipation of Calvary; and we learn the meaning of those words, "He spared not His own Son" (Rom. viii. 32); though it is clear that God saved His friend from a sorrow, from which He did not spare Himself. Jesus died; whilst Isaac lived. God never tempts to sin (Jas. i. 13); but He puts His children to the test, to bring out into clear daylight the good that is in them, and to force them to take up a position which they had never realized, but from which they shall never recede. So did Jesus test the woman of Canaan (Matt. xv. 27). That which can endure fire must go through fire (Num. xxxi. 23). The branch that bears fruit must be purged (John xv. 2).

Abraham's obedience.—It was *immediate*; God said: Take *now*: and he arose early in the morning. It was *exact*: finding the very place of which God had told him. It was performed in the spirit of *worship* (5). It was *contagious*: for Isaac behaved and spoke to his father, after the same manner as his father did to God: "Here am I." Everything in the way of promise and blessing (**17, 18**) depends on our prompt and exact obedience (Isa. i. 19, 20).

His faith.—He did not for a moment expect to return without Isaac. He knew that Isaac was the link of promise, and indispensable to God's plans. If needs were, he would be raised from the dead (Heb. xi. 19): so he told the young men that he and the lad would return to them (5). And such faith could not be disappointed. In the very moment of direst need, the *Jehovah-Angel* arrested his hand. Do not be surprised if God delay up to the very last moment ere He appears to your help; but He will provide. In the Mount is His deliverance seen (14). JEHOVAH-JIREH.

The obedience of Christ (Phil. ii. 8).—Isaac asked, "Where is the lamb?" That question is answered (John i. 29). That fire and knife had their counterparts in the sufferings of our blessed Lord; but

He shrank from neither, because it was His Father's will. "I delight to do Thy will" (Ps. xl. 8). "They went both of them together" (6). The Lord, like Isaac, bore His own wood; was held fast, not by rope, but by iron; made no resistance, and was quiet in His death (Isa. liii. 7). And out of that has come a seed vast as the sands and numerous as the stars (Gal. iii. 13–25). "He shall see the travail of His soul, and shall be satisfied" (Isa. liii. 11).

CHAP. XXIII. **Death of Sarah**

Sarah was the last relic of that old life beyond the river. It was no common loss when she died. No wonder the aged husband wept.

His confession.—Times of great sorrow remind us of the lightness of our tenure of all things earthly and human (4). A confession doubtless often repeated in after-times (1 Chron. xxix. 15; Ps. xxxix. 12).

His independence of spirit and his habits of business.—Ephron proposed to make a gift of Sarah's burial place; but the patriarch would only take it as a gift from God, and insisted on paying purchase money (9). And his payment was made before proper witnesses, and with great exactitude (16). It becomes us, as Christians, to be specially accurate and careful in all business engagements; because men will judge of our religion by our precision in such things.

His anticipation of the future.—The patriarch might have taken the beloved remains back to Charran. But he felt sure that his children's children would never go thither; and, on the principle that "the graves of the dead mark the homes of the living," he resolved that the burying-place should be in Hebron, in the heart of the land which God had promised to his seed (Jer. xxxii. 8). His faith anticipated the return of his people thither (xv. 16); and until then, in that ancient cave, he and Sarah would await them. Machpelah was the expression of his unwavering belief that Canaan was to become his.

CHAP. XXIV. **Rebekah**

Sarah was dead. And the future of Isaac was pressing on the heart of his surviving parent (3). Daily observation for years had compelled him to form a very unfavourable opinion of the Canaanitish women—the daughters of Heth (of the generation of Ham). Memories of the women of Chaldaea, as he had known them a century before, led Abraham to the conclusion that from among the descendants of Nahor (of the generation of Shem) away in Mesopotamia—probably a thousand miles off—a worthy wife would be found for the child of promise, the son of his old age (7). So he sends his eldest servant on the distant journey, occupying perhaps about fifty days. It is our duty to do what in us lies to secure for our children such life-partners as shall be for them helpers Godward, and not hinderers.

A model prayer (12).—As we enter upon a new day, or a fresh engagement, it is always well to ask for good-speed. Good-speed is God-speed. Praying times are not lost times. The reaper does not lose time when he stops to whet his sickle. The old man had learnt to respect his master's piety, and felt it was a sure plea with God. With how much more confidence may we utter the name of *our* Master, Jesus! (John xiv. 13).

God's answer (15).—Whilst he was praying, the answer was approaching him; and as he finished, Rebekah stood at his side (Isa. lxv. 24). God often gives His waiting children a sign which falls in with the impression made by His Spirit on their hearts, and indicates His will. So the knock of the servants of Cornelius influenced Peter (Acts x. 17). Compare the use of the word *prosper* (21, 40, 42, 56). The sure clue to prosperity is in Ps. i. 3.

The response of the soul to the call of God.—Can we wonder that the old man's visit and invitation sounded as a Divine call to the young girl. Her friends persuaded her to delay. But she insisted on an immediate response; she said, "*I will go*" (58). Then the jewels of her unseen bridegroom hung heavily on her person—the foretaste and pledges of his love, when she should see him, and share his wealth for ever. Thus does the Holy Spirit give us foretastes of our inheritance (Eph. i. 14).

CHAP. XXV. **Death of Abraham**

There is evidently what is known as dispensational truth in the opening verses of this chapter. Isaac's bride comes from a far country; and in this she is a type of the Church, which is so largely composed of those who once were strangers and foreigners (Eph. ii. 12, 13). But after the marriage supper of the Lamb has been consummated (Rev. xix. 7–9), there will no doubt be a wonderful concentration of interest on the seed of Abraham. These things are wonderful, but certain (Rom. xi. 1–36).

Abraham's death.—The aged man, after being for sixteen years contemporary with Esau and Jacob, died without owning a foot of land, which he had not actually purchased (Acts vii. 5). But all was his; and his soul had acquired a property superior to the fairest earthly land that ever invited the quest of a pilgrim. He "died in faith," not having received the promises, but greeting them from afar, and being persuaded of them, and eagerly desiring the city which hath foundations (Heb. xi. 8–17). He was an old man and *full*, satisfied (8). *Gathered to his people:* a phrase which speaks not of dust to dust, for his people were far away across the desert, but of the recognition and welcome of the departed. His two sons met to bury him: whatever our differences, a common sorrow makes us one (9).

Two manner of people **(23).**—In all time there have been these two classes. The Esaus, jovial, pleasure-loving, addicted to feats of endurance and strength, grasping at present gratification and indifferent to spiritual issues (Heb. xii. 16). The Jacobs, quiet, home-loving, deficient in many of those qualities which attract admiration and win love, but devoted to the things of the unseen and future—a curious mixture of worldly cunning and spiritual power. These are both dear to God; but it is only of the latter that He can make princes. This is the meaning of Mal. i. 2, 3.

Sell me this day thy birthright **(31).**—The younger brother took a mean advantage of his elder brother's necessity, thus securing to himself those rights and benefits of primogeniture which should have belonged to the elder. How many a man has for some trifling consideration, or some momentary indulgence, parted with what might have been a life-heritage for himself, and a possession for his children and his children's children! Jacob wronged his brother; but Esau was not blameless—he "despised his birthright." We shall hear more of this.

CHAP. XXVI. Isaac's Failure

There was no harm in Isaac going to Gerar, as he had a distinct command to that effect (2, 3). But he does not seem to have been morally strong enough to stand the test of residence there. Certainly he failed under it; and he failed because he did not realize that God had made Himself responsible for his safety. What could have been more reassuring than "I will be with thee, and bless thee"? They who have the Divine companionship are absolutely safe, and need resort to no earthly expedients.

His faithless cowardice (7).—Isaac repeated Abraham's sin (xx. 2–11); endangering his wife, because so careful of himself. There is a sad deterioration here from the time when he was so willing to die beneath his father's knife. That early dawn had become sadly overcast. But, in spite of this, God kept His word with him, and blessed him (12). A striking illustration of 2 Tim. ii. 13. A man may have outward blessing; but this is no certain proof that his heart is right with God.

Abimelech, King of the Philistines (1–26).—Lest any difficulty should be felt as to the recurrence of the same name at two different eras (xx.; xxvi.), it may be well to explain that *Abimelech* was not so much a proper name as a royal title (The King-father), and was used through one or more dynasties—in this resembling such designations as Pharaoh, Benhadad, Ptolemy, Herod, Caesar, Kaiser, Czar.

Emptied from vessel to vessel (13–23).—These verses are full of strife and removal. Well was it for Isaac that it thus befell, else he might have become too comfortable in Gerar. God has often to break up our nest, and to pour us forth (Deut. xxxii. 11, and Jer. xlviii. 11).

The path of separation is that of communion and blessing (23).— As soon as he took up the right attitude, "the Lord appeared"; there was a renewal of the altar of consecration; Isaac reared his tent to take up again the pilgrim life; water gushed forth to refresh him; and his enemies were reconciled (Prov. xvi. 7).

CHAP. XXVII. Jacob's Sin

Here was a series of those fatal mistakes which issue in years of misery to all concerned. Isaac ignored and sought to set aside the

Divine purpose, clearly revealed (xxv. 23). Esau, notwithstanding his distinct bargain, was now eager to regain the birthright privilege and position which he had despised, and gladly fell in with his father's proposal. Jacob sought to win by fraud what had been promised to him, and which the definite declaration of Jehovah had made secure. And Rebekah was as deeply implicated as any; deceiving her husband; showing evident partiality; and sowing for herself a bitter harvest of pain, in the enforced absence of her darling, and in the division of her house. We dare not attempt to palliate the guilt of one of these offenders. Would that there had never been any other home, professing godliness, but rent by the same sins, and visited by similar woes!

God keeps us to our choice.—Esau could not change the results of his own act in the sale of his birthright. His bitter cries and tears could not reverse its effect. He might be forgiven; but he could not undo (Heb. xii. 15–17).

The raw material of many of God's saints has often been of an inferior quality.—This was the case with this younger son of Isaac. Artful, deceptive, scheming, selfish, "supplanting," he yet eventually became a "prince of God" (xxxii. 28). Who would have thought, looking at Jacob covered by the kid-skins, that one day he would have power with God and men, and bless the mightiest monarch of his time? (xlvii. 10). And if God did so much for him, why should He not do as much for each one who reads these lines, if only each is willing to be as clay in the hand of the Great Potter (Isa. lxiv. 8).

CHAP. XXVIII. **Jacob at Bethel**

This is the Ladder-chapter, in which a wayward, crooked man is seen holding fellowship with the eternal God: that God who loves us, not because of our shortcomings, but in spite of them; and who desires to lift us right away from them into a life of power and victory. Fugitive and erring a man may perhaps be; but he ought never to give up his fellowship with God! From the far country of exile you may cry to Him; even from the fish's belly as did Jonah (Jonah ii. 1). And there is no moorland waste so lonely, so man-deserted, so bare, but that it may be the place from which the ladder may reach to heaven.

Sunset **(11).**—Overtaken by the swift oriental night, Jacob had no resting place but the cold ground, with the hard stone pillows. But he slept both safe and sound, being under Divine protection (Ps. iii. 5, 6).

Night.—"He saw a ladder." There is communication between heaven and earth: the angels come down laden with answers to the prayers which they have borne up. Wait for them. Though they delay, they will come. The circulation of tide, or air, or blood, is not more incessant or multiplied. Oh for opened eyes to see these heavenly activities on our behalf! (Heb. i. 14). How full are these gracious words of God of what He is, and what He will do—"I am with"; "I will keep"; "I will bring"; "I will not leave" (**15**). In his converse with his father, old and blind, Jacob had used the name of the Lord flippantly and wickedly (xxvii. 20); but in this midnight vision on the way to Haran he for the first time realizes somewhat of the majesty of Jehovah, and how solemn a matter it is to have to do with Him. And on awaking he utters the sacred name with an awe and reverence unknown before (**16**). "And he was afraid."

Morning.—The devout soul finds God's house and heaven's gate everywhere. We make our own environment. There was too much bargain-making in Jacob's vow (**20**); and yet the final resolution was good. Well would it be if all readers would resolve to devote a definite part of their income to Him who guards our nights and guides our days. The ladder of Providence is good: but how much better that of Redemption! (John i. 51).

CHAP. XXIX. **Rachel at the Well**

Well might Jacob "lift up his feet" (**1**, *margin*). When we have seen God, we receive strength, which enables us to run (Isa. xl. 31; Heb. xii. 1). "The steps of a good man are ordered of the Lord"; and we have a special claim on Him in all that relates to the most solemn step of our lives—our matrimonial alliances. These ought not to be left to fancy or whim, nor even to the choice of friends (Prov. xix. 14).

There were *many qualities in Rachel*, as a girl, which bespoke her fitness to be a good wife. Her humility and industry; her patience under the oppression of the stronger shepherds; her haste to share her new-found joy with her father, churl though he were (**12**): all these received their reward in the love with which Jacob devoted himself to her, and which made the toil of years seem as a few days (20). Oh that we had such love to Jesus shed abroad in our hearts by the Holy Spirit, that we might consider hard things easy, and rough ones delightful, for His dear sake (Phil. iii. 8).

The deceiver deceived.—"With what measure we mete" it is often "measured" to us again (Matt. vii. 2; Mark iv. 24; Luke vi. 38). Jacob was served as he had served his father; and Leah was substituted for her sister. There is a Nemesis in wrong-doing. Misdeeds come home to roost (Ps. lvii. 6).

The compensations of life (31).—Poor Leah! she was very eager for her husband's love, and reckoned the loss of it as her grief (32). Yet she had a noble family of sons. Whilst Rachel, secure of Jacob's affection, pined for children. So God tempers our joys with our sorrows; and amid them He carries forward our education. The names of Leah's children—Simeon (*Hearing*); Judah (*Praise*)—indicate the inner life of devotion, and the outer life of thanksgiving. In all this how accurately God kept the promises made to Jacob! (xxviii. 15).

CHAP. XXX. **Joseph Born**

The chapter opens painfully. Rachel is envious of her sister; and moreover unjustifiably provokes Jacob to anger. The histories of Bilhah and Zilpah (3, 9) are in some particulars a repetition of the history of Hagar (xvi. 2, 3). These arrangements were *not* according to God. "From the beginning it was not so" (Matt. xix. 4, 8). Rachel (22–24) now has a son, Joseph, "who was sold for a slave," and whose strange, eventful history is recorded farther on (xxxvii.-xlvii.). This boy is Rachel's first-born, and Jacob's eleventh son.

Jacob's longing to return to his native land (25).—Little had he thought when he left Beersheba for a contemplated absence of "a few days" that many years would roll by before he could even venture to speak of a return. How that longing for a sight of the home of their childhood comes over men after years of absence: it touches the Swiss with the *maladie du pays*, and forces him back to his mountain home; and it brings many an Englishman thousands of miles, from the Antipodes to the shores of Britain. "Let me go!" (26). Selfish Laban refuses to part with his valuable "hand," and begs him to remain under new conditions. And Jacob "increased exceedingly" **(43)**.

Chap. XXXI. Departure from Haran

Jacob's worldly possessions had greatly grown. Laban's sons were as greedy and selfish as their father: and their jealousy was excited by the advancement of the one who had brought blessing to their house (xxx. 27), and who was at the same time their cousin and their brother-in-law. They probably biassed the mind of their father against the husband of their sisters. "The countenance of Laban was not toward him as before." Alienation of heart is quickly detected by the one who suffers by it **(1, 2)**. Out in the open, where there could be no eavesdropper, he tells out his mind to his two wives, and takes a retrospect of his uncle's line of treatment through a long series of years **(6–8)**. The man who, under a sense of right which was unusual with him (*comp.* **14, 15,** with xxix. 15), had insisted on paying wages to his nephew, had, in the course of twenty years, changed those wages of his relative *ten times*—not with the view of advancing the interests of his nephew, but just the reverse **(7, 41)**. How different was the conduct of Abraham towards his nephew Lot! (xiii. 1–10). Probably Jacob was wrong in assuming that God approved of the artifice (xxx. 37–41) by which he had become rich in cattle and flocks **(9)**; but the Divine intimation "I have seen all that Laban doeth unto thee," followed by the command, "Get thee out from this land," implies a distinct condemnation of the hard master **(3, 12, 13)**.

Throughout the long sojourn in Haran, Jacob realized that he was watched over, and protected by Jehovah **(5, 7)**.

The secret departure **(20)**.—This was very undignified, unnecessary, and wholly faithless. God had promised to keep Jacob in all places (xxviii. 15). Oh, when shall we realize the perpetual keeping power of God? (Ps. xxxi. 20). Laban meant mischief **(23)** in pursuing Jacob; but He, in whose hand are the hearts of all men, suffered him not to harm his son-in-law **(29)**. How marvellous that the Almighty should undertake the safe keeping of such undeserving ones! But He does it for His own name's sake (Ezek. xxxvi. 22, 32).

Jacob was wroth and chode **(36)**.—If he had only realized that his cause was in the hands of God, he would have been able to hold his peace and quietly wait (Lam. iii. 26). Do we always commit our cause to God, as we should? The exhortations of Rom. xii. 18–21 need to be engraven on our hearts.

The oath (**44**).—Here these families part for the last time, with an armed neutrality, God watching between. Mizpah—"The Lord watch between me and thee!" Laban poured out reproaches upon Jacob; and then, at the close of his harangue, states another grievance —the theft of his gods. We now find that, notwithstanding his acknowledged "experience" of Jehovah's power (xxx. 27), he had his *teraphim* as objects of worship; and that his daughter Rachel, who also had a knowledge of the true God (xxx. 23), had been so led away by evil example that she had actually *stolen* her father's household gods, probably under the belief that they possessed supernatural powers, and could be invoked to exercise them in the interest of herself and those dear to her. And she sinfully retained the idols. Laban returns to his money making; and the pilgrim Jacob goes on his way, freed from the shackles which had bound him, though with idols still in his tents (**34**). He must be delivered from these also; that he may become a vessel meet for the Master's use (2 Tim. ii. 21).

CHAP. XXXII. **Peniel**

Travelling onwards from Laban, Jacob met a troop of angels. This vision was intended to assure him of his safety, and to prepare him for the hostile troop he was soon to encounter. God's hosts are always near us, though we see them not (Ps. xxxiv. 7; 2 Kings ii. 11).

A great alarm (**6, 7**).—It was no small matter to anticipate meeting Esau in a rage; and, in spite of all Divine assurances, Jacob sought for expedients to avert the blow. Obsequiously he speaks of himself as Esau's servant (**18**), and then invents plans by which Esau might be appeased, and something at least be saved from the general wreck (**13–20**). There is no harm in making arrangements against approaching trial, if they are dictated by God. But there is great harm in originating them from our own fears, and relying on their sufficiency. Faith does not plan, but trusts.

A touching prayer (**9–12**).—If only this prayer had come first, and he had entirely trusted God, nothing could have been better. What a strange mixture are we all! His humility (**10**); his pleading of promise *twice*—Thou "saidst" (**9, 12**); his thankful recognition of the past (10); his direct entreaty for deliverance (11). Strange that we need to be put into great straits, ere we learn the true art of prayer!

The mysterious conflict (24).—Alone, and in the dark, amid silence broken only by the murmur of the brook, he was drawn into conflict with a mysterious combatant. The Jehovah-Angel wrestled with him. In the energy of his self-will Jacob held his ground. So do we refuse to yield to God's Holy Spirit, who prevails not till He touches some cherished sinew of strength. Then we leave wrestling for clinging—wrapping our arms in desperation around the person of the unknown Angel. And then we prevail over God and man, and win the blessing, which enriches our lives for ever, and pass from Jacobs into Israels—princes with God.

CHAP. XXXIII. Jacob and Esau Meet

The old nature dies hard. Notwithstanding the wrestle and the blessing of the previous night, we find Jacob still scheming instead of trusting. And he surely abdicated his true position as a Prince with God, when he bowed himself seven times to the ground before his brother. How slow we are to trust God, and to believe that He will literally do as He has said! What could be more explicit than God's guarantees of his safety? (xxviii. 15; xxxi. 3). Unbelief cringes, and schemes, and trembles. Faith is erect and bold, and sings (Ps. lxxi. 14–16, 21–24).

An unlooked-for deliverance (4).—The hearts of all men are in the hand of the Lord (Prov. xxi. 1). He can give us favour in quarters where we least expect it, changing the dreaded foe into a friend (Prov. xvi. 7; Isa. liv. 17). The clouds we dread break in mercy; iron gates open of their own accord; crooked places straighten; mountains sink into the plain.

Prevarication.—Such a blessing as that of Peniel ought to have banished all further misgiving from Jacob's heart; but it seemed impossible to eradicate the subtlety of his crafty nature. He told his brother he would come to Seir, a distance of about 120 miles, which he never for a moment intended to do (14). As soon as Esau was well out of sight, Jacob made for Succoth, and there built a house, as if with the thought of settling.

From Succoth he passed to Shalem. Here, also, was *disobedience*

(17), for he had been distinctly sent to "the land of his kindred"—that is, the district from Beersheba to Mamre or Hebron, called also Kirjath Arba (xxxi. 13: *comp.* xiv. 13; xxi. 14; xxiii. 2, 19; xxvi. 33; xxviii. 10). He "pitched his tent" before the idolatrous city of Shalem. How closely does this resemble the action of Lot in connection with Sodom, about 180 years before! (xiii. 12). Soon after he bought a parcel of a field, in the close proximity of this heathen town. This was worse and worse: it was what Abraham would never have done. Why buy a yard of the land wherein he was a stranger? And why settle so near Shalem, with the memory of Lot's troubles at Sodom, and when all the land was before him? But he had not quite forgotten Bethel or Peniel: for even here he erects an altar to God, the God of Israel (20).

Chap. XXXIV. At Shechem

A sad and mournful story (1, 2). Poor Dinah! she was the only daughter. She went forth to seek companionship and society. How she fell! Was there not in her too much self-confidence, too much dependence upon her own judgment and discretion? She was caught in the outer circles of that fatal whirlpool which has engulphed so many, sinking never to rise again. Curiosity is the parent of mischance.

The results of worldly conformity.—If Jacob had not gone so near Shechem's city, he would never have brought all this sorrow on his home. Alas! professing Christian parents will have a very serious reckoning some day concerning their children's souls, ruined through their own inconsistency. And even though certain young men of the world may be more honourable than most (4, 19), they are not suitable partners for the daughters of Israel. What can be more specious and life-like than Hamor's proposals? (8, 9). This is what the world is ever saying to the Church.

A dreadful retribution (25).—This deed of blood and treachery was never forgotten by Jacob (xlix. 5, 6, 7): it left a terrible memory in the land (30), and it led to a rapid breaking up of the encampment, and a flight to safer and holier dwelling-places. Sin is always followed by disaster. What we sow we reap. It is pitiable to hear Jacob's miserable whine, "*I shall be destroyed*" (xxxii. 7, 11). This for months now had been his one cry. How little did he realize that, though he were faithless and sinful, God would not run back from His exceeding precious promises (xxxv. 5).

CHAP. XXXV. To Bethel!

Arise, go up to Bethel! (1).—Back to Bethel! Hated, fugitive, dreading the consequences of his children's unbridled violence, Jacob knew not what next to do. Then this summons came to him. When we are in straits, God will often take advantage of them to suggest our return to a happier, holier past. The prodigal must have heard that voice, when he said, "I will arise and go to my Father."

Preparations for return (2).—The idols are altogether unfitting at Bethel. There are things in our lives which we permit when we are living at a distance from the Lord, which we feel instinctively are inconsistent with Bethel; with its memories of the ladder, and angel-haunted dreams, and holy converse, and sacred vows. Probably the one thing which keeps you and yours from a Bethel experience is the presence in your tents of idols and strange gods. Remember 1 John v. 21. *He built an altar* (7) and he named the place *El-beth-el*, the God of Bethel, in remembrance of the Divine manifestation there about a quarter of a century before.

The Divine response (9).—It is long since God appeared to you. For long you have lived on an old and threadbare experience. But if you would yield up the accursed thing, He would appear again. You would be recalled from Jacob to Israel (10). Promises of fruitfulness would rejoice your heart (11). And the gifts of God would come thick and fast into your life (12).

Three deaths.—Often a great blessing comes to prepare us for a great sorrow; and the sorrow confirms it, as a kiln burns in some fair colours on the vase. *Of Deborah* (8). How many of us can point to oaks of weeping, hard by altars of deliverance? *Of Rachel* (19). And *of Isaac*, at whose grave the rival brothers buried their differences for ever (29). And then a crime, worse than death, broke in on the home: the crime of Reuben (22), which cost him the birthright (xlix. 3, 4). Instability, weakness of character, may lead to the direst sins.

CHAP. XXXVI. **Esau and the Edomites**

Though the story mostly concerns Jacob, yet here a whole chapter is devoted to Esau and his descendants. This book does not profess to record all God's dealings with the race; but those only which concerned the children of Israel, through whom such great blessings were destined to come to the world. We must ever remember Christ's words about the "other sheep," which did not belong to the Jewish fold; and we must believe that God has followed the wanderings of all mankind with loving interest, noting their very names, supplying them with good things (Acts xvii. 25, 26), and giving them sufficient evidences of His being and law to lead them to Himself (Acts xiv. 17).

Entire deliverance (**6**).—Many a time the proximity of Esau was a menace that filled Jacob with alarm. What a relief it must have been when the elder brother chose to remove further off! So when dreaded evils have served their purpose in the education of our souls, they drop away. God will not always be threshing. "He doth not afflict willingly, nor grieve the children of men" (Isa. xxviii. 28; Lam. iii. 33).

A royal line (**31**).—We have a long line of royal dukes. Esau is a specimen of the men of the world. Bluff, jovial, impulsive, quick equally to resent and to forgive, robust and pleasure-loving. Their portion is in this life (Ps. xvii. 14). What a contrast to the Jacobs, with all their sorrows, their stern discipline, their fiery trials. But, after all, these are the men who become the spiritual leaders of the race, and who conduct the pilgrims of eternity to new acquirements and conquests.

CHAP. XXXVII. **Joseph and his Brethren**

The Hebrew terms indicate that the coat of many colours was not the patchwork garment, which we thought it was in the days of our childhood, but a long-sleeved robe of delicate and beautiful texture, which was worn by the upper classes, the gentry, the men who were not intended to soil themselves with manual labour. What a contrast to the coarse tunic of the other shepherd sons of Israel! It was this that made them jealous. The suspicion was engendered that their father meant to keep the son of his favourite wife from the common toils of the home, and even to make him ruler and heir. This partiality was a mistake, repeating that of Rebekah towards Jacob, and bringing about similar miseries. It may also have induced a tinge of vain-glory and conceit in the lad, which showed itself in his dreams, and aggravated his brothers' hate.

The history of a crime.—Envy (**11**); hatred (**4**); unkind speech (**4**); conspiracy (**18**); deceit (**31**). At first the old man acquiesced in the story; but after a time his suspicions were turned on his sons (xlii. 36). And a terrible Nemesis awaited them. They were destined to hear the piercing cries of that young lad pleading for mercy for many years to come; and, in a moment of supreme anguish, they were to have that scene re-enacted before them (xlii. 21).

There is here the foreshadowing of the Cross.—The Lord Jesus was sent by the Father to His brethren. "He came unto His own, and His own received Him not" (John. i. 11). They said, "This is the heir: come, let us kill Him, and let us seize on His inheritance." He was sold for thirty pieces of silver, and thrown into the pit of death, where He did not tarry. In each case envy lay at the root of the crime; yet all unconsciously the schemes of the murderers were over-ruled to fulfil the purposes of God (*comp.* l. 20 and Acts ii. 22-33).

Chap. XXXVIII. Judah

Another of these dark chapters stained deep with sin! Surely, if crimson and scarlet be fast colours, these might be employed of such a record as this: yet even such sins as these may be forgiven (1 Cor. vi. 9-11). "All manner of sin shall be forgiven unto men" (Matt. xii. 31).

These sins are faithfully portrayed in this chapter, because the Bible is God's looking-glass, held up to human nature, that men may know what is in them (James i. 24, 25). Here is a portraiture of the results, not of religion, but of its lack. It is like a background to show the need for the death of Jesus, and for the advent of the Holy Spirit (Tit. ii. 14; Gal. v. 17).

The record of such sins has not done the harm which some allege; for most read without realizing how much evil is concealed beneath: whilst those who understand the depths of Satan are warned that all who commit such things are "worthy of death" (Rom. i. 32).

Many reading certain verses in the Bible are made to realize, perhaps for the first time, the true nature of practices into which they may have been thoughtlessly betrayed, but which they can never again commit in ignorance of their true nature.

We must be "pure in heart." Without purity the strongest Samsons make shipwreck of their lives (Judges xvi.). And without purity we cannot see God (Matt. v. 8). If we would attain this priceless jewel of personal holiness, we must incessantly claim the purity of Jesus, and trust Him to maintain intact for us the chastity of a pure heart.

Chap. XXXIX. Joseph in Egypt

Egypt was a vast slave mart. In some great market-place Joseph may have been exposed for sale. Ah, what agony for that young heart! But God was in it all. His permissions are His providences. Potiphar was probably chief of the military force employed as the royal bodyguard in the precincts of the court. And the young captive might have been excused had he trembled a little in passing into the splendid Egyptian home, so different to the simplicity of Jacob's tents. But the Lord was with the young man (2). Better be Joseph in Egypt with God than the brothers with blood on their hands at home. However far from home, the soul is always at home in God (Ps. xci.).

His prosperity (2).—Some old versions say "he was a luckie fellow." All he handled went well. Men might call it luck; but there was another reason—he did all beneath the eye of God, feeling that God had sent him to fill that post. This is the true secret of success (Eph. vi. 5–8; Col. iii. 22). And on all such faithful work God's special blessing rests (Deut. xxviii. 1, 2; Ps. i. 3). The prosperity of some men may be due to the character of some obscure servant.

His temptation (7).—It is in days of prosperity that we are most likely to be tempted. And temptation is always hard when a worldly policy points in one direction and conscience in another. It seemed certain to ruin all his prospects if he did not yield; but had he yielded, he would never have become premier of Egypt. Do right, come what may: stand well with God—promotion cometh from Him. No temptation shall assail which is too great (1 Cor. x. 13). Our true safety is often in flight (12); but where that cannot be, let us trust Jesus to keep us (Ps. cxxi. 5, and 2 Thess. iii. 3). Remember the injunction, "Keep thyself pure" (1 Tim. v. 22).

CHAP. XL. **Joseph in Prison**

Further details of Joseph's imprisonment are given (Ps. cv. 17). He was not only in prison, but there were the clank and hurt of the fetters. He could not move without being reminded, as Paul was, of his bonds (Acts xxvi. 29; xxviii. 20; Eph. vi. 20; Phil. i. 7, 13, 14, 16; Col. iv. 3, 18; 2 Tim. i. 16; ii. 9; Philemon 10, 13). It may be that Joseph's soul would also be perplexed with the mystery of God's ways. Why should he who had done only the right thing suffer, while many who did evil things daily escaped (Jer. xii. 1)? If you reason like that now—wait, and you will see differently, when the Lord's plan has been worked out for you and others in like affliction (Ps. xxxvii.).

Joseph's sufferings wrought beneficially.—Ps. cv. 18, in margin, tells us that his "soul entered into iron." Might we not say also that the iron entered into his soul? It is by suffering rightly borne that our spiritual constitution becomes strengthened. Besides, that imprisonment, though the young captive could not then discern it, was a link in a long chain of events that reached to Pharaoh's throne. "But the Lord was with Joseph" in the prison (xxxix. 21).

Joseph's ministry for others.—The endeavour to lighten the lot of those near to us, who may be in worse case than we are, is the surest way of distracting our minds from the pressure of our own sorrows, and so of ensuring a measure of relief to ourselves. Instead of brooding over your griefs, seek to comfort the sad (**6, 7**).

Joseph's forgiving spirit.—Joseph did not recriminate on any of those who had caused him sorrow. Without entering into details, he stated a simple fact (**15**). He exhibited the true Gospel spirit seventeen centuries before the Gospel times (Luke vi. 35–37; Rom. xii. 19). When we bear a trial patiently, God says, "Thank you!" (1 Pet. ii. 20). And "the word of the Lord" will ultimately clear us, as it did him (Ps. cv. 19). Do not let us wonder at the closing words (**23**): we have often thus treated our best Friend.

Chap. XLI. Pharaoh's Dreams

"Two full years" (**1**). It must have seemed a long and weary time. But though God give patience time to have her perfect work, He comes at length (Ps. xlvi. 5; Matt. xiv. 25). Foolishness and confusion fell upon the wise men; but God showed His secret to the babe (Matt. xi. 25).

Called to the Palace.—"They made him run" (**14,** *marg.*). Even the punctilious etiquette of Egypt must give way when God speaks the word. Hope thou in God; ere long He shall make thee run and dance (Ps. xlii. 5). Notice Joseph's beautiful references to God (**16, 28, 32**). And there was an evident presence of God with him, which impressed those who beheld him, though he wist it not (**38**).

The contrasts.—Jacob rebuked Joseph (xxxvii. 10): Pharaoh welcomes him. His brethren despised him: the proudest nobility in the world opens its ranks to welcome him. His hands are no longer hard with toil: one of them glistens with the signet ring. His feet are free from the fetters; and his neck is girt with gold. What a comment on 1 Sam. ii. 30! And how apt an illustration of the Virgin's song! (Luke i. 51–53).

The parallel.—Joseph in prison: Jesus in the grave. Joseph in fetters preaching a gospel of deliverance to the butler: Jesus declaring liberty to the captives (Isa. lxi. 1). The two prisoners answer to the two malefactors. Like Joseph, Jesus was of Jewish birth, but disowned by Jews; yet exalted to the supreme seat of power, a Prince and a Saviour, and able to work deliverance for myriads of Gentiles. Jerome renders the name given to Joseph by Pharaoh as "Saviour of the world." There is always plenty where the Saviour is enthroned (Ps. lxxii. 1–17).

Chap. XLII. Corn in Egypt

Twenty-five years have passed since the agonizing scene at the pit's mouth; and again Joseph and his brethren meet. And now God takes in hand the work of dealing with their consciences with respect to their terrible crime.

The first step was the pressure of want.—As long as the land was full of plenty Jacob might have mourned alone: but when the famine was sore, his sons were driven out of their nest to get what succour they could; and in all this, though they never suspected it, they were being led to some great discoveries. It is when the mighty famine comes that prodigals repent (Luke xv. 14).

The second step was the rough usage they received.—It was not wonderful that they did not recognize their brother in the man of mature years, clothed in the splendid robes of office. But he knew *them*: perhaps had been on the look-out for them for years. And he at once set himself to repeat the experiences of the pit's mouth. They had, perhaps, accused him of being a spy; and he now says, "Ye are spies" (**9**). And as they had met his protestations to the contrary by violence; so now he met theirs. Perhaps they had thrust him into the pit till his words could be verified; as now he did with Simeon. It was under this strange repetition of the past that conscience awoke; and they said, "We are verily guilty" (**21**). It reminds us of other, but somewhat similar, scenes (2 Sam. xii. 1–14; 1 Kings xvii. 18). We can never be perfectly secure till sin is confessed and put away (Heb. viii. 12; 1 John i. 9).

The third step was in the moments of quiet reflection, when conscience had time to work.—They were all in prison together for three days; then Simeon for a longer period; then came the journey home, and the discovery of the money, before which their heart failed, for it seemed as if God were near (**28**). Are we not all verily guilty concerning Jesus our Brother?—yet how carefully He provides for us and leads us to repentance!

CHAP. XLIII. **Benjamin in Egypt**

In infinite love God hedges up our way with thorns, and shuts up every door, except the one through which we may pass to plenty and happiness. Many a soul would never have thought of its ill-treatment of the great Elder Brother, unless our Father had called for a sore famine, and had broken the whole staff of bread (**1, 2**; Ps. cv. 16). At first we say stubbornly, "I will not yield; I will stand out and have my own way" (xlii. 38). But it is a mistake to wrestle against the love of God. Jacob tried it before at the Jabbok Ford; and he limped for the rest of his life. God will have His way at last, if not at first. It is in vain to try to row the ship to land; the sea will not cease her raging until the runaway is on his way home (Hos. v. 14-15). Well was it when at last the old father yielded (11).

A type of the mercifulness of Jesus.—Though these men had meditated murder; yet does he who might have become their prey here heap kindnesses on them. And thus, though we are inflicting sore wounds on Jesus, He provides us with all kinds of blessings (16).

A type of His unmerited grace (21, 22).—They had vaunted themselves on their good money. That at least could not be challenged; but, lo, it was given back. Is not this the way in which God treats us? The doles with which we thought to purchase His grace count for nothing; but yet the grace is given.

A type of His tender love (30).—Joseph was easily moved. His love started his tears (xlii. 24; xliii. 30; xlv. 2, 14, 15; xlvi. 29; l. 1, 17). But, ah! the great deep of Christ's love to us (Eph. iii. 18).

CHAP. XLIV. **The Cup in the Sack**

God can easily bring down our self-confidence! Little knowing what was in the sack of one of them, Jacob's sons started in high spirits at dawn, Simeon and Benjamin with them; with memories of the governor's handsome treatment; sacks full. Even when accused of thieving, they were so sure of themselves that they courted inquiry (8, 9). But very soon their note altered (13-16). This recalls Job ix. 31. We think ourselves immaculate till God comes and searches us. And it is often with what we counted our choicest quality, our Benjamin, that the fatal cup is found (Prov. xviii. 17).

Anguish is permitted to rend our hearts in order that we may be brought to contrition.—The Elder Brother often seems harsh and rough. But the rude exterior hides a loving heart. It pains Him to see us suffer. But He loves us well enough to hold the bitter cup to our lips, that it may produce the desired result; and we confess the iniquity which we had long sought to conceal (16).

Mark the behaviour which becomes us (14).—Unconsciously they thus fulfilled the dream (xxxvii. 7). Judah had every right to act as spokesman (xxxvii. 26). There is nothing in literature more pathetic than this appeal. How much pathos lies behind the roughest natures, awaiting an occasion! If a frail, sinful man can plead thus, consider what *His* pleadings must be who loves us infinitely (Heb. vii. 25).

Thus Joseph's object was gained: sin was confessed; their feelings to Benjamin were tested; and they clung to him, though his mess had been five times more than theirs, and though he had brought them into trouble (**20–34**).

CHAP. XLV. **Joseph and his Brethren**

This chapter is full of Christ. It is probably a picture of a moment in the future, when the Jews, His brethren after the flesh, will be reconciled to Him whom they rejected and crucified. But it is also a picture of how Jesus treats each of us as we come back to Him.

We meet Him alone (**1**).—As Peter met our Lord alone on the morning of the resurrection (1 Cor. xv. 5), so alone must each man meet Christ.

He names Himself (**3**).—Reminding us of Acts ix. 5. And He is not ashamed to add "your brother" (**4,** and Heb. ii. 11, 12). He adds a beautiful palliation to their grief (**5**), which recalls Acts ii. 23–36.

A loving invitation (**4**).—"Come near!" We are made nigh (Eph. ii. 13). One moment the bare moorland road, with the scene of agony; the next, a promise of ever being near unto Him, nourished and kept with the most tender care (**10, 11,** compared with Eph. v. 29, 30). The distance is not so very great from the far country to the Father's heart, and home, and feast.

The provision for the journey (**19**).—He does not leave us to go on a pilgrimage at our own charges (1 Cor. ix. 7). He makes Himself responsible for the supply of all needs, and contrives that all grace shall abound (2 Cor. ix. 8; Phil. iv. 19). The waggons (**21**) seem to be emblems of the grace of the Holy Spirit, by which we are certified of our Brother's love, and brought on our way. This is the earnest of the Spirit, the first-fruits of our inheritance.

Jacob's spirit revived (**27**).—How cheered must the heart of the old man have been when the assurance that Joseph lived was confirmed by Benjamin, and attested by generous gifts! His note has changed from "All these things are against me" (xlii. 36) to "It is enough: Joseph my son is yet alive!" (**28**).

Chap. XLVI. Jacob goes to Egypt

After the resolve with which the last chapter closes, the patriarch Jacob seems to have been overtaken by sudden qualms as to his duty, especially remembering the disastrous consequences of Abraham's going down into Egypt (xii. 10-20); and therefore he went to Beersheba, to obtain by special sacrifices the distinct guidance of God. How necessary that we should always act on Prov. iii. 5! We cannot wait on God in vain. He will assuredly speak to us and guide us (2). So Acts xvi. 9.

The Divine assurance (3).—How eminently comforting it was! When we know, after patient waiting, that we are on God's plan, we need not fear. The Bible abounds in *Fear nots*! There are *over seventy* of them (Isa. xli. 10). When God goes down with us into Egypt, we have no need for alarm. The promise that Jacob should come up again (4) doubtless refers to the nation of which he was head: it was not to be absorbed into Egypt. And it was sweet to the old man to know that his favourite son would close in death those eyes which had become dim through many tears.

The journey to Egypt.—The number of persons going up out of Canaan is given at seventy (27). Stephen speaks of it as seventy-five (Acts vii. 14), because he adds the children of Ephraim and Manasseh. How slow is the advance of the fulfilment of God's promises! 250 years had passed since xii. 2; and now there is only a handful of souls. But soon the little one was to become a thousand! God keeps a record of His pilgrims.

The meeting (29).—What a contrast to the bitter wail of xlii. 36 (30)! This is somewhat similar to the utterance of Simeon in Luke ii. 29. But Jacob was not to die yet: several happy years still awaited him. What will it not be to see the face of Jesus, and be for ever with Him; as secure under His care, as Jacob under Joseph's! The hatred of the Egyptians to a pastoral people arose from the bitter results of the invasion of the shepherd-kings, whose intrusion on Egypt is a matter of history. But *see* Isa. liv. 17.

Chap. XLVII. Jacob and Pharaoh

Joseph was not ashamed of his kin, though they were shepherds, and his father was old, decrepit, and lame. Would that all young people were equally mindful of those who expended so much care on them in their early years (Eph. vi. 2)! Nor should any of us be ashamed of our Elder Brother, who is not ashamed of us (Heb. ii. 11; Mark viii. 38).

Jacob's presentation to Pharaoh **(7).**—His confession recalls Heb. xi. 13 **(9)**. *Few the days*—Terah, 205; Abraham, 175; Isaac, 180; but Jacob only 130 at this time. *Evil*—what a contrast to Esau's splendid successes! Some might even pronounce Jacob's life a failure. Yet he blessed Pharaoh. "Without any contradiction or controversy, the less is blessed of the better" (Heb. vii. 7). Jacob was greater than the greatest monarch of his time. He was a royal man, with a Divine patent of royalty, "A Prince with God" (xxxii. 28). These things made him royal, as they will make us—prayer, suffering, contact with the Angel.

Joseph's administration of Egypt **(14).**—One-fifth of the entire produce was hoarded in the vast granaries; and when the years of famine came, he sold the stored corn, first for money, and then for lands and cattle; so that by a masterstroke of policy, the Egyptians became tenant-farmers of the crown. He was diligent in business, fervent in spirit, serving the Lord (Rom. xii. 11). His one thought was that God had made him ruler (xlv. 8). Do your daily work, remembering that God has put you just where you are. Therein abide with Him (1 Cor. vii. 24). Our Joseph can not only keep His church, but also feed the dying world.

An old man's faith **(30).**—He had spent seventeen years in Egypt; but his heart was away in the land of promise. He knew that his people should go thither again; and there he longed to lie, that he might be amongst them when the promises were fulfilled (Gen. xv. 16).

CHAP. XLVIII. **Jacob Blesses Joseph's Sons**

The summons of the dying man brought Joseph speedily to his side, and the sound of the loved name revived him. With wonderful accuracy he began to review the past. He dwelt especially on the wondrous vision of the celestial ladder, and on the words of promise **(3, 4)**. Though one hundred years may have passed since he heard those words, they were as fresh as ever. Then he adopted the two lads of Joseph as his own **(5)**. Then his mind wandered to that scene just outside Bethlehem, where he had parted from the beloved Rachel, whom he was soon to meet again (7). But from that reverie the sight of the young faces of Joseph's two sons called him back (8). "And he blessed them."

The names for God (**15, 16**), "the God of Abraham and Isaac."— Let us so live that one bond between our children and God may be that He was our God, before whom we walked. "Which fed me," *i.e.*, shepherded. It was natural to a shepherd to attribute to God the same qualities of shepherdly care that he was wont to exercise (xlix. 24). Here is the first trace of the Shepherd-Psalm. "The Angel which redeemed me" (**16**). He ever accompanies us still (Ps. xxxiv. 7). No evil touches us. What seems evil is good in disguise (Rom. viii. 28, 31).

The distinguishing between the two lads (**14**).—There was nothing arbitrary in this. Certain qualities in Ephraim demanded that he should be in the first place. God is no respecter of persons, and will lift even the youngest to the front rank if in the character there are elements which He approves (1 Sam. xvi.).

Once more the old man's faith flames up (**21**).—Our dearest die; but God is with us for ever (Heb. xiii. 5). And in full assurance Jacob anticipated the apportioning of the land, and appropriated one extra portion to Joseph. There Joseph was afterwards buried (Gen. l. 24–26; Josh. xxiv. 32; John iv. 5).

CHAP. XLIX. Jacob's Dying Bed

A third time did Joseph stand beside his father's dying bed, alongside of his brethren; twelve strong, bearded men. How intense the awe as they heard their names called one by one, and listened to that trembling voice reading their destiny from the pages of the future. And let us always remember that destiny is made of character. This scene is an anticipation of the Judgment-Throne, where all secret things shall be exposed, and the irrevocable doom pronounced.

Reuben sacrificed a proud position and splendid abilities for one act of sin. Instability of character leads to sensual indulgence.

The curse on Simeon and Levi was, in the case of Levi, changed into a great blessing, in consideration of Exod. xxxii. 26. The men of Levi were scattered; but they became the priests of the Lord, and their inheritance was in Him.

Judah became the royal tribe, out of which the Lion was to come (Rev. v. 5, and Heb. vii. 14). Shiloh is Peace-giver, or the Giver of Rest; He who says, "*I will give rest,*" and "*Ye shall find rest*" (Matt. xi. 28, 29). And for the "rest" given, see Heb. iv. 1-11.

The positions of *Zebulun* and the following tribes in the land of promise is accurately foretold. Compare the allotments in Joshua xviii. Notice the exclamation of the dying man in ver. 18. Such waiting cannot be disappointed (Isa. xxvi. 8, 9).

Joseph's blessing is pre-eminently beautiful. *Fruitful.* This is mentioned twice (John xv. 8). But fruitfulness is only possible where there is the *wall* of separation, and the *well* of communion. When these are present, the branches droop over the wall with clusters of blessing to a thirsty world. Let us seek Divine strength, and that the mighty hands of God may be placed upon our own poor, weak hands (Ps. cxliv. 1). When once we are separate, we enjoy blessings beyond count (**26**, and 2 Cor. vi. 17). Then, with another charge about his burial in Machpelah, the weary pilgrim was gathered to his people; went over to the other side, and saw again Rachel, and Leah, and Isaac, and Rebekah; the great host gathering through the ages (Heb. xi. 39, 40).

CHAP. L. **Joseph Dies**

The days of mourning for Jacob were only two less in number than for a king: 300 miles were traversed by that splendid funeral cortège. Not only the family of Israel, but the magnates of Egypt, went also. The words, *beyond Jordan* (**10**), indicate that this book was finished on the further side of Jordan, where afterwards Moses died (Num. xxxii. 32). When God wills to do honour to any servant of His, He can bring it about in the most remarkable way, being quite independent of human methods and reasonings.

Joseph's brethren seem to have felt as if they could not believe that they were really forgiven. Their deep sense of sin made them mistrustful. Have not we all been afflicted thus? "Can such sinners as we are hope for mercy?" At such times let us not look in on ourselves; but at once seek the presence of Jesus, who will graciously reassure us, and speak comfortably to us (**21**). Give God credit for His perfect forgiveness, when once He forgives: it is needless and mistrustful to go to Him again about the same sin.

Joseph's old age came at last. Ninety-three years had passed since lifted from the pit; eighty since he had first stood before Pharaoh; sixty since he had buried his father. He saw the faces of his great-grandchildren (23). There was realized Ps. xci. 16. Again the old promise was referred to (xii. 7; xiii. 15; xv. 7, 14–17; xvii. 8; xxvi. 3, 4). And Joseph commanded that his bones should be unburied, so that at any moment, however hurried, when the trumpet of the Exodus should sound, they might be ready to be lifted up, and borne onward in the glad march for Canaan (Exod. xiii. 19; Heb. xi. 22). This coffin in Egypt (26) to the eye of sense seemed the end of all: to the eye of faith it was the pledge of the Exodus.

A TABLE OF THE PATRIARCHS

Antediluvian and Postdiluvian

Names		Age	Genesis
ADAM	"And God said—'Let us make man (*Heb.* Adam) in our own image, after our likeness.' "—Gen. i. 26	930	v. 5.
SETH	"Another seed, instead of Abel, whom Cain slew."—Gen. iv. 25	912	v. 8.
ENOS	Seth's eldest son	905	v. 11.
CAINAN	Enos' eldest son	910	v. 14.
MAHALALEEL	Grandfather of Enoch	895	v. 17.
JARED	Father of Enoch, and grandfather of Methuselah	962	v. 20.
ENOCH	"The seventh from Adam."—Jude 14. "And Enoch walked with God; and he was not, for God took him."—Gen. v. 24	365	v. 23.
METHUSELAH	His death appears to have taken place in the very year of the Flood, A.M. 1,656; 2,348 B.C.	969	v. 27.
LAMECH	Father of Noah. *See also* Gen. iv. 18–24	777	v. 31.
NOAH	The Flood came in the 600th year of Noah's life—Gen. vii. 6, 11	950	ix. 29.
SHEM	Noah's eldest son	600	xi. 10, 11
ARPHAXAD	Shem's eldest son	438	xi. 12, 13
SALAH	Arphaxad's eldest son	433	xi. 14, 15
EBER	Salah's eldest son. Eber lived 34 years, and begat Peleg (*division*); "for in his days was the earth divided." *Comp.* Gen. x. 25	464	xi. 16, 17
PELEG	Eber's eldest son	239	xi. 18, 19
REU	Peleg's eldest son	239	xi. 20, 21
SERUG	Reu's eldest son	230	xi. 22, 23
NAHOR	Serug's eldest son	148	xi. 24, 25
TERAH	Nahor's eldest son	205	xi. 32.
ABRAHAM	Son of Terah, and father of Isaac	175	xxv. 7
ISAAC	The Child of Promise	180	xxxv. 28
JACOB	The father of the twelve Patriarchs. "Few and evil have the days of the years of my life been; and have not attained unto the days of the years of the life of my fathers."—Gen. xlvii. 9	147	xlvii. 28

From this Table it can be seen that the generations of the antediluvian Fathers overlapped one another: thus—Lamech, the father of Noah, was born while Adam yet lived; and Noah could have received from the lips of his father records which Lamech himself had received direct from Adam.

The Book of Exodus

The word Exodus means a "going out." The main subject is the going forth of Israel from Egypt. The opening word, "Now," closely connects this book with Genesis. The two records were evidently produced by the same pen. And if any further argument were required to prove that Moses was the author, it might easily be gained from the contents, which could only have been written by one who had a thorough knowledge of Egypt and Sinai, and of the internal history of that mighty struggle which preceded the Exodus. In addition to this, Luke xx. 37 is conclusive proof of Mosaic authorship.

Exodus differs from Genesis. Genesis is the book of universal history, and full of minute personal biographies, which gradually taper down to the stories of Israel and Joseph. Exodus, on the contrary, is wholly taken up with the history of Israel; and the only biographical sketch is the life of Moses.

There are three great divisions of this Book:
Israel in Egypt.—1.-xii.
Israel on the March to Sinai.—xiii.-xix.
Israel at Sinai.—xx.-xl.

These stages correspond closely with the history of every saved soul; as well as with the history of redemption.

The great burden of this Book is the object-lesson given in the Passover —of Redemption by Blood. There is throughout a clear division made between Egypt and Israel. Upon the former fall the strokes of judgment; whilst for the other there are light, and deliverance, and salvation. And the only reason adduced for the distinction is—that the one was sheltered from evil by the blood; whilst the other was left unprotected to bear the result of its sins. We, too, enjoy all our emancipation from the curse and darkness of sin, and our admission into the liberty of God's children by reason of the blood (Eph. i. 7; ii. 13; Rom. iii. 25).

After redemption, there is the giving of the Law. We stand beneath Sinai, and learn the inability of the flesh to obey the holy law of God— an experience which drives us more earnestly to the efficacy of the "precious blood" as our only plea. And thus we pass into worship and fellowship, like that which Moses had with God face to face; or that which Aaron had in the Holy Place.

The imagery of this book supplies many of the metaphors in the Book of Revelation. The conflict between Israel and Egypt is that in which the saints of all ages are engaged. And God is ever calling us out of Egypt

(Hos. xi. 1): the Egypt of worldly alliance; the Egypt of the fleshpots of sensual indulgence; the Egypt of mighty forms of human power. But the struggle is ever "unto blood" (Heb. xii. 4); until the victors stand on the sea of glass, having the harps of God, and sing the song of Moses, the servant of God, and the song of the Lamb (Rev. xv. 3).

In order to facilitate the full comprehension of the narratives in Exodus and Numbers, the following table of the stations of Israel in the Wilderness will be found of great service. In many cases the narratives in Exodus and Numbers either overlap or dove-tail into one another.

TABLE OF THE STATIONS OF THE ISRAELITES IN THE WILDERNESS

Y	M	D	Station	Ref.	v.	Num. Ref.	
1	1	15	1. Rameses, near Cairo	Exod. xii	37	Num. xxxiii.	3
			2. Succoth	xii.	37	xxxiii.	5
			3. Etham, or Adsjerud	xiii.	20	xxxiii.	6
			4. Pihahiroth, or Valley of Bedea	xiv.	2	xxxiii.	7
			5. Shur;—Ain Musa } 6. Desert of Shur, or Etham }	xv.	22	xxxiii.	8
			7. Marah—"bitter" waters healed	xv.	23	xxxiii.	8
			8. Elim, Valley of Corondel	xv.	27	xxxiii.	9
			9. Encampment by the Red Sea			xxxiii.	10
1	2	15	10. Desert of Sin, Valley of Baharan	xvi.	1	xxxiii.	11
			Manna, for 40 years	xvi.	35		
			Quails, for a day	xvi.	13		
			Sabbath renewed, or revived	xvi.	23		
			11. Dophkah			xxxiii.	12
			12. Alush			xxxiii.	13
			13. Rephidim			xxxiii.	14
			Water, from the rock Massah	xvii.	1		
			Amalekites defeated	xvii.	13		
			Jethro's visit	xviii.	5		
			Judges appointed	xviii.	25		
1	3	15	14. Mount Sinai, or Horeb	xix.	1	xxxiii.	15
			The Decalogue given	xx.	1		
			The Covenant made	xxiv.	7		
			The Golden Calf	xxxii.	4		
Y	M	D					
1	6		The Covenant renewed (Neh. ix. 18)	xxxiv.	27		
			The first Muster, or Numbering	xxxviii.	26		
2	1	1	The Tabernacle erected	xl.	17		
			Aaron and his sons consecrated	Levit. viii.	6		
2	1	8	Sacrifices of Atonement	ix.	1		
2	1	14	The second Passover	Num. ix.	5		
2	2	1	The second Muster	i.	3		
			Nadab and Abihu destroyed	iii.	4 }		
				Levit. x.	1 }		
2	2	20	15. Desert of Paran	Num. x.	12		
			16. Taberah	x.	33 }		
			Murmuring of the people	xi.	3 }		
			17. Kibroth-hattaavah	xi.	34 }	xxxiii.	16
				Deut. i.	1 }		
			Quails, for a month				
			Plague of the People				
			Council of LXX appointed				
			18. Hazeroth	Num. xi.	35 }	xxxiii.	17
				Deut. i.	1 }		
			Miriam's leprosy	Num. xii.	10		
2	5		19. Kadesh Barnea, in Rithmah; or the "Desert" of Sin, or Paran }	xii.	16 }	xxxiii.	18
				xxxii.	8 }		
			Twelve Spies sent	xiii.	2		

THE BOOK OF EXODUS

Y	M	D					
2	7	6	Their Return	Num. xiii.	26		
			The People Rebel . . .	xiv.	2		
			Sentenced to wander 40 years .	xiv.	33 }		
				xxxii.	13 }		
			Ten of the Spies destroyed .	xiv.	37		
			The People defeated by the Amalekites . . .	xiv.	45		
			Rebellion of Korah, &c. .	xvi.	1		
			Budding of Aaron's Rod .	xvii.	8		
			20. Rimmon Parez . .			Num. xxxiii.	19
			21. Libnah, or Laban . . .	Deut. i.	1	xxxiii.	20
			22. Rissah			xxxiii.	21
			23. Kehelathah . . .			xxxiii.	22
			24. Mount Shapher . . .			xxxiii.	23
			25. Haradah, or . . .			xxxiii.	24
			Hazar-addar, or Adar .	Num. xxxiv.	4 }		
				Josh. xv.	3 }		
			26. Makheloth . . .			xxxiii.	25
			27. Tahath			xxxiii.	26
			28. Tarah			xxxiii.	27
			29. Mithcah			xxxiii.	28
			30. Hashmonah, or . . .			xxxiii.	29
			Azmon, Hezmon, . .	Num. xxxiv.	4, 5 }		
			or Zalmonah . .	Josh. xv.	4 }		
			31. Beeroth	Deut. x.	6		
			32. Moseroth, or Mosera . .			xxxiii.	30
			33. Bene-jaakan, or Banea .			xxxiii.	31
			34. Hor-hagidgad, or . .			xxxiii.	32
			Gudgodah . . .	x.	7		
			35. Jotbatha, or . . .			xxxiii.	33
			Etebatha, or Elath . .	ii.	8 }		
				1 Kings ix.	26 }		
			36. Ebrona			xxxiii.	34
			37. Ezion-gaber, or . .			xxxiii.	35
			Dizahab . . .	Deut. i.	1		
40	1		38. Kadesh Barnea again, after 38 years. (See 19) . .	ii.	14	xxxiii.	36
			Miriam's Death . . .	Num. xx.	1		
			Water from the rock Meribah .	xx.	13		
			Moses and Aaron offend .	xx.	13 }		
				xxvii.	14 }		
			39. Mount Hor, or Seir, on the edge of Edom . . .	xx.	22	xxxiii.	37
			Aaron's Death . . .	xx.	23	xxxiii.	38
40	5		King Arad attacks the Israelites	xxi.	1		
			40. Kibroth-hattaavah again. (See 17) . . .	Deut. i.	1		
			41. Zalmonah, or Hashmonah, again. (See 30) . .			xxxiii.	41
			The People bitten by fiery Serpents . . .				
			The Brazen Serpent erected .	Num. xxi.	8		
			42. Punon			xxxiii.	42
			43. Oboth	xxi.	10	xxxiii.	43
			44. Iim, or Ije-abarim in the border of Moab . . .			xxxiii.	44
			45. The valley and brook Zared .	xxi.	12 }		
				Deut. ii.	13 }		
			46. Arnon	Num. xxi.	12		
			47. Beer, or Beer Elim . .	xxi.	16 }		
				Isaiah xv.	8 }		
			48. Jahaz	Num. xxi.	23		
			49. Heshbon . . .	xxi.	24		
			Sihon defeated . . .				
			50. Jaazer	xxi.	32		
			51. Edrei	xxi.	33		
			Og defeated . . .				
			52. Dibon-gad . . .				
			53. Almon Diblathaim . .	Ezek. vi.	14	xxxiii.	46
			54. Mattanah . . .	Num. xxi.	18		

Y	M	D				
			55. Nahaliel	Num. xxi.	19	
			56. Bamoth	xxi.	19	
			57. Pisgah	xxi.	20	
			58. Abarim			Num. xxxiii. 47
			59. Shittim, or Abel Shittim	xxv.	1	xxxiii. 49
			In the plains of Moab	Josh. iii.	1	xxxiii. 48
			Idolatry of Baal Peor	Num. xxv.	3	
			Midianites punished	xxv.	17	
			The third Muster	xxvi.	2	
40	11	1	Last exhortation of Moses	Deut. i.	3	
40	12	1	Joshua appointed his Successor	Num. xxvii.	18 ⎫	
				Deut. xxxiv.	9 ⎬	
			Death of Moses	xxxiv.	5 ⎭	
			A Month's Mourning	xxxiv.	8	
41	1	1	60. Joshua sends two Spies	Josh. ii.	1	
41	1	10	Passage of the river Jordan	iv.	19	

CHAP. I. **The Oppression**

When Joseph was dead, the people multiplied, and were fiercely persecuted. There is an analogy here to the multiplication and persecution of the early church, after the death of the Lord Jesus (John xii. 24).

The New King (**8**).—More than two centuries had passed. There was probably a new dynasty desiring to prevent the recurrence of shepherd domination. "Let us deal wisely" (**10;** *comp.* Ps. ii. 2). However great are the services rendered to men, they are soon forgotten, as Joseph's were. The only thing which can give lasting satisfaction is the Divine "Well done!"

The First Policy (**12–14**) was to make the lives of the Israelites bitter with bondage (*comp.* Dan. vii. 25). A picture has been discovered on the walls of an Egyptian tomb, in which men, with a Hebrew cast of face, are evidently being compelled to make bricks by Egyptian taskmasters, who stand by armed with sticks. It is possible even that some of the pyramids were built by the enforced toil of the much-suffering Hebrews. But this policy failed (**12**).

The Second Stroke of Policy (**15, 16**) was to begin with the children. Pharaoh and Herod set us an example in turning their attention to young life. Save or destroy the children, and you affect for good or evil the whole destiny of a people. But this policy also failed (**20**). Days of sorrow and anguish have always been growing days for churches and individuals. Let persecution and trouble come, we wax very mighty (Rom. viii. 35–37).

The Heroism of the Two Women (**17**).—On the one hand, was the royal edict; on the other, the Divine fear. It may be that they were

THE BOOK OF EXODUS 59

not Hebrews by birth, but Egyptians who did office for the Hebrew women, and had learnt to fear God. If so, their conduct was more remarkable. But all such action, however obscure and ignorant the doer, is noticed and rewarded by God (**20, 21**). He is never in debt for any kindness done to Himself or His people; and He gave Shiprah and Puah a name and place in Israel.

CHAP. II. **The Deliverer**

When matters have reached their worst in respect to God's people, He is preparing a deliverer. So it was in Egypt. Moses was more than ordinarily beautiful; he was *exceeding fair* (Acts vii. 20). His parents hid him BY FAITH (Heb. xi. 23). Perhaps they had received some special revelation of his great future, on the strength of which they dared to disobey the royal command. And *in faith* they launched him in the ark, not on the Nile only, but on the Providence of God. Miriam stood there to watch. Surely this is the true attitude of faith. There was no fear of consequences, from either crocodiles or royal executioners; but a simple desire to see what God would do. And He inclined the daughter of their greatest foe to preserve the existence of one who was to inflict the direst blow on the national life of Egypt. How little do men realize that they are working out God's plans, when they seem most free to do their worst! (Ps. lxxvi. 10; Acts ii. 23).

We know little of *the Education of Moses*, except what Stephen says (Acts vii. 22). Josephus speaks of him as being a great soldier, and filling important offices in the state. But the memory of what his mother had taught him concerning the hope of his people never deserted him; and he made a choice which decided his whole career (Heb. xi. 24–26).

His First Attempt to Emancipate his People (**11–15**) ended in failure, because it was originated and carried out in the impetuosity of the flesh. "It came into his heart." "He supposed" (Acts vii. 23–25). He thought that a few blows of his might would do it. But this was not God's method (1 Cor. i. 26). And he must be taken to the back side of the desert, in order to be drained of all creature self-sufficiency. So he, who seemed so stalwart and mighty, became as it were a little child in his own sense of helplessness; though even in his long and weary education, God alleviated the hardships of his lot, by finding him a home and love (**21, 22**; Ps. lxviii. 6).

Meanwhile *the Anguish of the People* (**23, 24**) increased. It became almost unbearable, and expressed itself in three different forms. They sighed; and cried; and groaned. And God regarded them. God "heard"; God "remembered"; God "looked"; God knew. O weary sufferers, not one sigh of yours is wasted on the air: all enter into the heart of God; and He will arise to save.

CHAP. III. **The Burning Bush**

God's servants must spend much time alone with him. All the learning of Egypt was not enough to equip Moses for his life-work; but he is taken to the back of the desert. That is God's college. And all who have done anything great in the world have graduated there. Elijah at Horeb; Ezekiel at Chebar; Paul in Arabia; John in Patmos. Whenever we see a man taken into such seclusion and solitude, we may be sure that a great future is in store. God's workers may take their Arts course in the world's universities: but they must take their Divinity course alone with Him.

The Fire which was its own fuel (**2**).—Often in doing daily duty, we come on the grandest revelations of God; and it is always well to be on the look-out for them, and to turn aside to see. The BURNING BUSH has generally been taken as an emblem of the Church existing amid persecution. But there is a deeper meaning. That fire was the evidence of the presence of God. God was there! And the lesson evidently was, that God was in the midst of Israel; and was willing to come into the life of Moses, though it might seem no worthier than the acacia shrub of the desert. And where God is, there is holiness (**5**). We are holy in proportion as God dwells in our hearts. The fire is an emblem of the purity and eternity of God. He is the I AM, needing no sustenance. The sixth verse was quoted by Christ as proving the resurrection of the dead (Matt. xxii. 31, 32; Mark xii. 26, 27; Luke xx. 37, 38).

The "burning bush" constituted a most important point in the history of Moses and of the Jewish nation (Deut. xxxiii. 16; Acts vii. 30-35).

The Promise of Divine Deliverance (**7**).—Note the successive steps. "I have seen," "I have heard," "I know," "I am come down," "I will send thee." There were no merits in Israel, but urgent need. It was enough that they were God's people. All else was secured to them by His own all-sufficient nature. It had seemed long to wait; but God came at length. So will it always be. The sighs and groans of chap. ii. are answered by the coming down of chap. iii. (Luke xviii. 7).

The Hesitancy of the Human Instrument **(11)**.—How unlike the man who, forty years before, had acted with such impulsive haste! (Acts vii. 24.) He had learnt much since then, and most about himself; so that he was diffident of himself, nervous and timid. But there ought to be no such shrinking, when God says, "I will send thee," "I will be with thee" **(10–12)**; and when He further describes Himself as the I AM, Jehovah **(14)**. Demand whatever gift or grace you need, and God will honour the cheque which you may fill in, but which He signs.

CHAP. IV. Moses' Rod

This marvellous chapter describes the manner in which God dealt with the misgivings of His servant Moses.

To his First Misgiving **(1)** God answers by giving him two signs **(2–7)**. Here first we meet with that rod **(4, 17, 20)** which was again and again to be stretched out over the land of Egypt; to make a way through the deep; to bring water from the rock; to help in the fight (xiv. 16; xvii. 9; Num. xx. 11). Moses was but a rod: but what cannot a rod do when handled by the Almighty!

The leprous hand **(6, 7)**.—Leprousy is the type of sin; and the cleansed hand indicates the marvellous power of God to cleanse and sanctify all who will yield themselves to Him, thus qualifying them for service.

To his Second Misgiving **(10)** there was a promise of exceeding beauty, which all who speak for God would do well to ponder **(12)**. It reminds us of Jer. i. 7–9; and of 1 Cor. ii. 4. Strange that we rely so much more on natural gifts than on the Giver. If we truly understood our position, we should glory in our want of eloquence, as affording a better platform on which God may work (2 Cor. xii. 9, 10). God is willing to teach us what to say **(12)**, and what to do **(15)**. (*See* Luke xii. 11, 12; Acts ix. 6.)

To his Third Misgiving **(13)** God gave him his brother as an assistant. But, ah, how great the loss! On the one hand Moses lost half the honour which might have been his: on the other, he was associated with one who was often a great hindrance to him (Exod. xxxii. 35; Num. xii. 1). Humility is a lovely grace; but refusing to take up work which God assigns us is not humility.

There is a mysterious incident at the close of the chapter which shows that we must be willing to put away every act of disobedience to God's law, before we can be used in His service.

CHAP. V. "Let My People go!"

The bondage of Israel in Egypt is an apt type of our bondage to sin. How emphatic are the allusions of Scripture in this sense (John viii. 34-36; Rom. vii. 23-25)! The weary tyranny of besetting sin; the demands of Satan that we should obey him; the absence of all return for our toils—these are striking points of analogy. And, though we weep and struggle, there is no help for us unless it come from without. But this is the glad announcement of the Gospel (Luke iv. 18).

At first the Appeal for Deliverance caused the burden of captivity to be heavier (**6–8, 14**).—No straw! No minishing of the tale of bricks! The charge of idleness! Cruel beatings! Deliverance further off than ever! The darkest hour precedes the dawn. Satan raises the hue and cry over a man who is escaping; whilst he is quiet enough with regard to those who are safe in his power. Conviction of our need necessarily precedes deliverance.

The Conflict with Pharaoh (**15**).—The King of Egypt was not an irreligious man; but he would not admit that Jehovah was supreme over the gods of Egypt. One design of the plagues was to convince him that He was so. And when this had been clearly proved, it became a question of the proud self-will of Pharaoh, which would not yield to God. The plagues left him without excuse. He was conquered, but not converted.

More Speaking to God (**22**).—In all our distresses the Lord is our sure Refuge. Moses was right in carrying his sorrows to the Lord; but he was wrong in doing so in a complaining spirit. But here, as at the burning bush, Moses shows a lack of full confidence in the Lord. Yet, as we shall see in the next chapter, God did not upbraid His servant for lack of faith ("Upbraideth not," James i. 5), but graciously condescends to meet with Moses on his own ground, and to give him an assurance of peace (Ps. lv. 22).

Chap. VI. Jehovah

This chapter should be connected with the close of the former one. Instead of reproving the impatience of His servant, God bade Him wait in patience for what He would do (1).

The statement that God was not known to the patriarchs by His name JEHOVAH (3) is, at first sight, startling; because we remember many passages in Genesis where the name occurs. But this probably arises from the fact that much of Genesis was composed by Moses after the Exodus, and that it was natural for him to apply to God the name which was in daily use among the people at the period of writing. Some affirm that as a name JEHOVAH was known to the patriarchs; but that the full development of the meaning of the name had not been exhibited. The glorious attribute of *immutability* especially had yet to be displayed. To the patriarchs God was the mighty *El*, providing for them; to the Israelites, the unchanging *Jehovah*, fulfilling promises after the lapse of a thousand years (Num. xxiii. 19; Mal. iii. 6; Rom. xi. 29). Jesus loves "unto the end" those on whom He once sets His affection (John xiii. 1).

Notice the "I wills" of God's covenant (6). There are *seven* of them, besides the *two* "I AM'S" with which the list opens and closes. This is like the new covenant of Heb. viii. with its *six* "I wills." We are never secure so long as aught is left to us: but when God alone is concerned, who can stay Him? How often our faith in God is hindered by physical or temporal circumstances (9)!

A fragment of genealogy (14–27).—Only three of the Tribes are here specified. The children of Israel would always look with special reverence and love on their great leaders, and be deeply interested in all that pertained to them. We are here favoured with their line of ancestry, which is also interesting and important, because containing the roots of that great religious tribe, which afterward was to play so great a part in the history of the people. Many of these names are associated with episodes which will demand our later attention. In the meanwhile let us learn how a single human life may light up other lives, and invest the most lowly origin with a halo of undying interest. Who does not turn in thought to that slave hut by the Nile, where Moses and Aaron were born, with profounder interest than to the pyramids where the Pharaohs are buried!

Chap. VII. Hardness of Pharaoh's Heart

The plagues fell on objects that the Egyptians worshipped, and were intended to answer Pharaoh's question, "Who is Jehovah?" also to show God's infinite superiority. It would not have been just to punish Pharaoh with immediate overthrow in the Red Sea. There must first be given evidence enough of the glory and majesty of Him who demanded that His people should go free. The plagues occupied probably a few months, one following on the other. There is a beautiful description of them in Ps. cv. 26-36. The conflict with Pharaoh, probably the great Rameses Sesostris, whose form and face are familiar to us in those colossal representations which stand in our museums, is the emblem of yet greater conflicts with which the Bible closes (Rev. xix. 19, 20; xx. 7-9).

The Magicians (11, 12).—The Apostle Paul gives us their names, and tells us that they shall have their representatives in the last days (2 Tim. iii. 1-9). This mimicry of Moses was probably the result of legerdemain, in which Orientals excel. These magicians were permitted to succeed (11, 22; viii. 7); but they could not go beyond a certain point (viii. 18), that the contrast might become more strikingly manifest. Is not this imitation what we see around us to-day? Satan's most successful resistance to the Gospel is in imitating the form, without the Divine power.

The First Plague (19-25).—This was probably towards the end of June, when the Nile was rising. Its waters were peculiarly sweet; gave fertility to the land; and were worshipped: the blow was therefore the more crushing to sustain. Had the magicians possessed real power, they had better have removed the plague. This they could not do. It therefore suited their policy to produce something which looked like a real miracle, and probably on a very small scale. What a contrast between Egypt's river which failed, and Jehovah Himself! (Isa. xxxiii. 21).

Chap. VIII. The Plagues of Egypt

Pharaoh made four efforts to compromise. The first (25); the second (28); the third (x. 8-11); the fourth (x. 24). Every inch was thus disputed. Satan is willing for us to be religious, so long as we do not separate ourselves from the world. The one thing he dreads most of all is—separation. But nothing can please God which is not clearly separate from evil.

The Second Plague (**2–6**).—The frog was held in honour by the Egyptians. There were a frog-headed god and goddess. Frogs were embalmed and buried in the tombs of Thebes. They now came everywhere, to the consternation of the Egyptians. One frog could not do much; but when they came in myriads they were irresistible. We may accomplish by numbers and unity what would be impossible to individuals. How remarkable is man's inability to trust God. Pharaoh fixed "to-morrow" (**10**); but it would have been quite as easy for the plague to have been removed on that very day. God's time is always TO-DAY; man's TO-MORROW (2 Cor. vi. 2). Under the pressure of sorrow, Pharaoh was willing to yield (**8**; Prov. xxvii. 1; 1 Cor. xv. 32; Jas. iv. 14): but when there was respite, he repented; and in doing so, he hardened his heart. No ice is so hard as that which freezes after a thaw.

The Third Plague (**16–18**).—If these were *lice*, it would be a serious judgment on a nation which made so much of cleanliness; if *gnats*, or sandflies (R.V.), the torture would be intolerable. With what small weapons can God humble the pride of man! What a remarkable confession! (**19**).

The Fourth Plague.—It is thought by some that these were swarms of the sacred beetle, the emblem of the sun. That these venerated insects should become tormentors, to be trodden under foot, or swept from their houses, must have been a severe infliction on the Egyptians. How beautifully Moses used his intimacy with God as an intercessor! (**12, 29**).

CHAP. IX. **Three more Plagues**

This awful conflict between the proud will of Pharaoh and the will of God has its counterpart in the inner history of very many. Even in the case of professing Christians, there is often a terrific struggle in respect to some demand to which they refuse to assent: and many of the sorrows which befall us are sent in order to wean us from our idols; to vindicate the power of God; and to lead us to repentance. So long as we stand out, we bring nothing but anguish and disaster upon ourselves, and all connected with us. Up to this chapter, we are told that Pharaoh hardened his heart: here we learn that God hardened Pharaoh's heart (12). Here there is attributed to God's agency a state of heart which was, in fact, the outcome of the conditions which God set on foot. If Pharaoh had yielded, God would have shown His power in bringing about his repentance and penitent acknowledgment, as in the case of Nebuchadnezzar (Dan. iv. 34); but, alas! since the Egyptian king resisted, he became rather the means of making conspicuous the Divine power in destruction. God always means to bless and save; but, by resistance, we may transform into a curse and bane that which He intends for blessing.

The Fifth Plague (3–7).—"All the cattle of Egypt died" doubtless means (19) that there was death among all the cattle of Egypt—no kind was spared. Probably the mortality was specially among the sacred oxen, which were objects of peculiar veneration. Notice the care of God for the possessions of His own people (6).

The Sixth Plague (8–11).—This touched the persons of the Egyptians, and even of the magicians, in the form of ulcerous eruptions. So the ulcer of sin disqualifies for standing in the presence of God (11). But men think less of their souls than of their skins.

The Seventh Plague (23).—In the middle of February or beginning of March there befell this fearful storm, a phenomenon almost unknown in Egypt; and this extorted the first confession of sin from the proud heart of Pharaoh. How different the tones of confession in 2 Sam. xii. 13; and Luke xv. 18! But Pharaoh's was not a godly sorrow (2 Cor. vii. 10: *Comp.* Rev. xvi. 21 and Matt. xxvi. 75). And how beautiful it is to remark God's care over His own people (26), a severance often repeated afterwards. They were hidden in a pavilion, and in the secret place of His presence, from the pride and wrath of man (Ps. xxvii. 5; xxxi. 20). Is not this an anticipation of the protecting care which shall be exercised over God's people in those perilous times which are coming on in the world? (Isa. xxvi. 20; Matt. xxiv. 22).

CHAP. X. **Two Other Plagues**

There is a crisis in every soul-history, up to which God's methods appear likely to turn the proud will to Himself; but after that crisis is passed, all those methods only seem to harden. Too often the direct result of the most gracious and tender dealings is—hardening;

and it is in this sense that God is said to have hardened Pharaoh's heart. The real conflict lay with his stubborn will, which would not yield (3), although his chosen advisers persuaded him to let the people go (7). The only result of their pleadings was to induce the king to recall Moses and Aaron into his presence, and make another effort at compromise (8–11).

The Eighth Plague (4–15).—The locust is the most terrible plague of Eastern lands. The heat is intense: the air quite still; there is a sound, as of a strong breeze sweeping through a forest; presently the sun is darkened by a cloud, which is composed of myriads of locusts. They cover all surfaces inches deep, and eat up every green thing, so that they leave a perfect wilderness in their rear (15). Notice the confession extorted by deadly fear (16).

The Ninth Plague (21–23).—The Hebrew word for "darkness" is that used of the darkness which covered the deep at the time of creation. The sun was among the chief deities of Egypt; hence there was a horror which might be felt, and which seemed to act as a paralysis (23). But there was light in Goshen. *Comp.* Ps. cxii. 4, and John viii. 12.

The Lord's Claim on His people.—"Not a hoof left behind" (26). Christ has redeemed us all, and claims all; every whit must speak His praise, and do Him service. Nothing must be left to the world. But it is only when we have passed through death and resurrection, and have come clearly out into the new world, that we realize all that His service involves. We go out, not knowing our full sphere; but trusting Him, whose service is blessed and perfect freedom.

CHAP. XI. **Death of the First-born**

"*One Plague More*" (1).—Ominous words were these! And this final act of judgment would smite the fetters from Israel's neck for ever. It is vain for man to enter into conflict with God. God does not crush him at once, as He might; because He is long-suffering and forgiving, and would give opportunity of repentance: but, if man does not yield, the irreparable blow must fall (Ps. vii. 12). The word translated "borrow" is better rendered "ask" (2, R.V.). There is no suggestion in the original of a return being contemplated. It was fit payment for the long, unrewarded toils of the captivity; and the Egyptians understood that they were to part from Israel for ever.

The "Great Cry" (6) reminds us of the piercing wail that rings through an Eastern town when a death takes place; and if every house were thus bereaved, the accumulated anguish would indeed reach a heartrending climax. But there is to be one other such cry (Rev. i. 7; vi. 15–17). God alone can put the difference which divided Israel and Egypt. There was a difference like that which will separate sheep and goats at last. But it was not determined on mere arbitrary grounds. It arose from the difference in the characters of the two peoples. All Egypt inclined to side with Pharaoh against Israel, and Israel's God (Ps. cxxxvi. 10–15).

CHAP. XII. **The First Passover**

Henceforth there was a new order of time, the sacred as well as the civil year (2). We should date our birthdays, not from the cradle, but from the cross, where we received redemption. Our life before conversion is not reckoned in the annals of God.

The Paschal Lamb is a striking type of Jesus (1 Cor. v. 7). "Without blemish" (1 Pet. i. 19). In the prime of life. Set apart before actually required (1 Pet. i. 20). Killed "between the evenings" (**6**, *margin*). The blood speaking to God without; the flesh feeding the host of Israel within. Roasting, and unleavened bread, and bitter herbs, bespeak the intensity of Christ's sufferings, and remind us of that humble and chastened spirit in which we should draw nigh. And does not the pilgrim attitude bespeak the spirit of the Church? (**11**). It would ill become us to sit or lie at our ease: all our life is to be a feast; but at any moment we may be summoned to go forth by the trumpet of the archangel. A separated and pilgrim host.

The foundation of peace.—They not only rested on the blood thus sprinkled, but also on the distinct promise of God (**13**). It did not matter whether the people within doors were aware of the mighty mystery being enacted, or felt as they ought. The one question concerned the BLOOD. All under the blood were safe. If there had been death to the least child, God's word would have been forfeited. And it is just this upon which we rely for our own ultimate salvation. Christ hath said that whosoever believeth shall not perish (John iii. 15, 16). It is not our feelings about the blood, but the blood as seen by God, which secures salvation.

The Exodus (**31–42**).—Plans had been most efficiently made. In orderly arrangement the vast host began to take its way from Egypt —one of the greatest events in history! The efficient men amounted to 600,000, which would indicate the aggregate numbers as being not far short of two and a half millions; to which we must add some thousands more for the mixed multitude, who were destined to be both an inconvenience and a danger. The bulk of them were idolaters, whose spirit was very infectious, and frequently led the people of Israel into sin (Num. xi. 4). They desired the rewards of the pilgrimage, but bitterly found fault with the supplies by the way, and excited the murmurs of discontent.

The law as to partaking of the Passover Supper (**43–49**).—Circumcision has its counterpart in our dispensation (Col. ii. 11). We must have the sentence of death written on our natures, and ever before us, cutting us off and separating us from sin, before we have any right to feed on Christ (Rom. viii. 8). Let a man examine himself also, ere he partakes of the Lord's Supper: and this not to repel him from the Table; but to lead him to put away everything evil, whether in act or thought. It is written, *"And so let him eat"* (1 Cor. xi. 28).

Chap. XIII. The Month Abib

Two customs perpetuated, amongst the children of Israel, that ever-memorable night of Exodus: first—the dedication of the firstborn to God's service (**2**); and, second, the feast of unleavened bread, when the Passover must be killed (**5–10;** Luke xxii. 7). As to the reason for these, it was clearly based on the transactions of this marvellous night in which God's hosts were redeemed by blood, and by a strong hand. How clearly we are reminded of the demand which is made upon all redeemed ones in the direction of personal devotedness and personal holiness. *Comp.* Titus ii. 11–14.

The firstborn sons in after-years were replaced by the Levites (Num. iii. 12), who did for Israel the religious service which would otherwise have been wrought by the eldest sons from every home (*see* xxiv. 5)—a privilege forfeited by sin (xxxii). But still they were only exempted from direct religious service by the offering of a lamb. Every firstborn son lived because blood had been shed (**13;** xxxiv. 20). A forfeited life given back! And, in this act, notice that he was put on the same level as the firstling of an ass, deemed an unclean animal, and demanding also the slain lamb as the only escape from the breaking of the neck (**12–15**). This parable is for us. (*See* Job xi. 12.) Our lives are forfeited as unclean. We are redeemed to serve as God's priests (Rev. i. 5, 6).

The Feast of Passover was often intermitted in the earlier years of the nation. But seven commemorations are of historical importance. This, the first. Then the first one kept in the desert (Num. ix. 1–14); Joshua's (Josh. v. 10, 11); Hezekiah's (2 Chron. xxx. 1–27); Josiah's (2 Kings xxiii. 21–23; 2 Chron. xxxv. 1–18); Ezra's (Ezra vi. 19–22). And finally, the last passover of the life of Jesus, when the substance came in place of the shadow (Luke xxiii.).

The phylacteries (Matt. xxiii. 5) of later times were the outcome of a literal interpretation of the command of ver. **16**.

What tenderness in the choice of route! (**18**).—God had many deep lessons to teach His people, which could only be learnt in the desert (Deut. viii. 2–5). He did not want to show them war until they had first learnt their inexhaustible resources in Himself.

CHAP. XIV. Through the Red Sea

After three days' march Israel reached the head of the Red Sea, and there received the direction, at that time mysterious, to turn southward, and put themselves in such a position between the mountains which border the sea on the west as would completely stay their further progress unless they could pass over the sea in front, or return through the valley behind them, into the heart of Egypt. How strangely does God lead us—apparently into a net of entanglement (3)! But it is only to provide a platform for the putting forth of His might. All is love (Ps. cxxxvi). The tidings were immediately communicated to Pharaoh, who seems to have had a large standing force at hand, with which he started in pursuit (**6, 7**).

Consternation (**10, 11**).—We cannot blame the Israelites. How often have we been panic-stricken, because we have looked upon our perils and our foes, instead of looking up at the stationary cloud, which is the pledge of God's interposition on our behalf. Let us be very wary of ourselves, lest we murmur as they (1 Cor. x. 10).

Stand still! (**13**).—This is impossible to flesh and blood. We must be doing something. We call it the "legitimate use of means." Faith, however, rises above the tumult into the majesty of simple waiting for God, and shelters itself behind Him. If you do not know what

THE BOOK OF EXODUS 71

to do, then calmly wait upon God in earnest believing prayer until you do: it is His business to direct and defend the believing soul. Let God do your fighting (**14**).

Go forward! (**15**).—How? The sea foam lined the beach! There were miles of deep water! But when Israel reached the surf, the billows parted. So will all obstacles yield to us when God leads us on (Ps. lxvi. 6; lxxviii. 13; Isa. lxiii. 12, 13). The very waves we dreaded will be our wall (**22**). The Egyptians owed their safety to the presence of the Israelites; as the ungodly owe their prolonged existence to the presence of the Church (Gen. xix. 22). On which side of God's cloud are you? (**19**). What terror there is in one look from the eyes of God! (**24;** and Heb. iv. 13; Rev. vi. 16).

Our Father is ever choosing the best way. Let us trust Him, and follow the movements of the cloud. The Lord goes before us by day and by night (xiii. 21; John x. 4), He will never fail us, or take away the manifestation of His presence, if only we are willing and obedient (Ps. li. 11, 12; Acts xviii. 9, 10; Heb. xiii. 5).

CHAP. XV. **The Song of Moses**

Israel passed through the Red Sea, as a symbol of death (1 Cor. x. 2). The Red Sea lay between them and Egypt; as the grave of Jesus lies between us and the world which expelled Him from its midst (Rom. vi. 4–6). And on the farther side the ransomed hosts stood as it were on resurrection ground, to sing their song of triumph. That song is the emblem of another (Rev. xv. 2–4). The sea of glass recalls the placid stillness of the Red Sea; the fire recalls the sunrise over the hills of the desert. "They sang His praise" (Ps. cvi. 12).

All praise is ascribed to God.—There is nothing ascribed to *self* (**2**). Circumstances, leaders, all are lost sight of; and God alone fills the whole field of vision. How happy would it be for us if we could enter more fully into this spirit, and praise God thus! (Ps. xcii. 4). Count up the mercies of God, and weave your praises into a crown to cast at His feet.

The range of this song is from Redemption on the one side to settlement in the land on the other. Founding their trust on what God had done, the people were able to boast of what He would do (**14–17**). They sing of guidance as a past and accomplished fact; so sure are they that He who redeemed would lead (**13**). Notice that holy resolution (2). Let us remember that God is willing to inhabit our hearts; and let us make Him room! (Isa. lvii. 15; Rev. xxi. 3, 4).

Marah (23–25).—God leads us to bitterness that we may learn to appreciate the tree which makes all sweet. That tree is the Cross, which turns the bitter things of life into sweetnesses. "Thy will be done!" transforms Gethsemane into Paradise.

Elim (27).—It is not all desert travelling or bitter waters. Full often an oasis shines on our pathway, where we can rest and be satisfied. Green pastures and waters of rest (Ps. xxiii. 2). But Elim is not Canaan; it is only a foretaste.

CHAP. XVI. **Murmuring**

The manna (16) falls. In many points it was a type of Christ (John vi. 32–51). It came down from heaven—angels' food (Ps. lxxviii. 25). Its colour was white; its texture was pure; its taste was sweet. There was enough for all the host: but it must be gathered in the early morning, ere the dew had left the ground; and it must be gathered fresh. The manna of yesterday would not do for to-day. As Jesus fed on His Father day by day, so must we perpetually have fresh glimpses of Himself, or else we shall never be able to sustain the toils of the desert (John vi. 57). And there is urgent need that we get such glimpses, before the busy world has engrossed our thoughts. Those who for some good reason were prevented from gathering their full measure were compensated (18); and those who for certain providential reasons are unable to get as much time as they would like with God, have it made up to them (1 Sam. xxx. 24; Ps. lxviii. 12).

Quails (13) are still known in those lands, flying in vast flocks, so low to the ground as to be easily knocked down. But it was a providence that they came just at this time. All creation serves those who walk with God (1 Cor. iii. 21).

The Sabbath (23).—Evidently, before the law was given from Sinai, the people were accustomed to observe the Sabbath; which, indeed, is of permanent authority, like the rest of the commands of the Decalogue, being made for man, and having come down to Israel from the gates of Eden. We must not hoard God's gifts, lest they breed worms, and stink (19, 20). We may be liberal in using them, for He has unsearchable riches to supply our need.

CHAP. XVII. **Murmuring Again**

How wonderful that the people should chide thus (2), when so recently they had beheld such marvellous interpositions on their behalf. It would be incomprehensible, unless we ourselves had often acted in a similar manner under the pressure of some sudden need, forgetting the goodness of the past (Ps. lxviii. 19, 20). All these trials were permitted to test the hearts of the people, and to afford them opportunities of learning the abundant wealth of the Divine resources (Deut. viii. 2, 3). Trials are the occasions for the putting forth of the Divine power on our behalf.

The smitten rock is the evident type of Christ (1 Cor. x. 4). He is the Rock of Ages, who was cleft and smitten for us on the cross by the nails and spear; and out of Him there have flowed the gracious influences of the Holy Spirit, who could not be given in his fulness until the bitter passion of the cross was over. We may all not only drink of the water, but have it within us, springing up into everlasting life (John iv. 14).

This chiding of the people is referred to more than once in subsequent Scripture (Deut. vi. 16; Heb. iii. 8). We need to be very careful not to allow ourselves to murmur or chide; but to say "Yes" to God's appointments, and to believe that He does all things well.

Amalek is always a type of the flesh. He was the grandson of Esau, who was sensual (Gen. xxxvi. 12). The Amalekites were a treacherous nomad tribe (Deut. xxv. 18). We may be redeemed by blood; but we must expect conflict and perpetual war (16). We are not in the flesh, but the flesh is in us. But victory is sure, if only we will let the Lord fight for us. The attitude which wins the victory is that of the bended knee and the uplifted hand. The Spirit of God lusts against the flesh, so that we may not do as we otherwise would (Gal. v. 17, R.V.).

CHAP. XVIII. **Jethro and Moses**

A joyful meeting.—How humble Moses was in attributing all the glory of the Exodus to Jehovah (**1, 8, 9, 10**). This is the sure cure of pride. When we recount the mighty triumphs with which we may have been associated, let us carefully give all the honour and glory to God. And, indeed, what are we but weapons and instruments, who are no more able to accomplish aught of ourselves than an axe lying at the tree-foot, or the dry jawbone of an ass! (Isa. x. 15; 1 Cor. i. 27).

The names of Moses' sons (**3, 4**) betray the drift of his thoughts when in the wilderness-exile of his shepherd life. May we ever remember that we are strangers here, and that our only help is in God!

The appointment of the elders is described more in detail in Num. xi. 10–25. In addition to what is stated here—not that Jethro instigated Moses—we learn that Moses himself was complaining. He seemed to feel as if he were called on to carry the whole people. But this was not the case (Exod. xix. 4). And he came to see more clearly in after-days that it was not so, but that stronger arms than his were beneath (Deut. xxxiii. 27). How very careful should we be of the advice we give, lest it chime in with the unexpressed mood of some friend, and lead him further than he would have thought of going. In this case no new spirit was bestowed, but some of the spirit which was on Moses was taken from him and placed on these men (Num. xi. 16, 17). If we can trust God utterly, rolling our burdens on Him, there is nothing too heavy for us to bear; for the weight rests not on us, but Him. Let us cultivate the habit of rolling off our burdens on to God as soon as they accrue, and we shall find that there is nothing too heavy for us, or which we cannot perform (**18**; *see* 1 Pet. v. 7).

CHAP. XIX.   **At Sinai**

The plain beneath Sinai, where Israel encamped, has been clearly identified; and the reader should study the books of travellers that will give him a mental conception of the scene. The brilliant colours, in which red sandstone predominates; the shattered, thunder-stricken peaks; the awful silence; the utter absence of vegetation; the level plain on which the vast host encamped, in view of the Mount: all these gave increased solemnity to the scene.

How tender was the Divine address to the people (**4–6**).—Nor are we excluded from these promises if we are the spiritual children of Abraham by faith (Rom. iv. 16). If God could bear three millions of people, He can bear us. *We* may be His peculiar treasure (Tit. ii. 14). We may inherit all things in Him (1 Cor. iii. 21). We may be His priestly kingdom (Rev. i. 6).

The solemn pledge of Israel (**8**) was a great mistake. They knew little of themselves, or they would never have made it. And from that moment God set Himself to show how impossible it is for man to stand before Him on the ground of obedience. It was a long process; and it has to be repeated with each individual man. There is a sense in which we all stand before Sinai, and each protests his ability to do all that is required, and has to learn his impotence.

The holiness of God was taught in object-lessons (**10–13**). The people must wash; the Mount must be fenced; the intruder must be stoned. Moses must be sent down *twice* (**14, 21**) to warn the people; and then he only and Aaron may ascend. All was done to show the people by outward signs the vast distance between themselves and God. Thus did God teach men to understand the meaning of holiness. What a contrast exists between that dispensation and ours (Heb. xii. 18–24)!

CHAP. XX. **The Ten Commandments**

The law was given by Moses, by the disposition of Angels (John i. 17; Acts vii. 53). It tells us not what God is—that is only to be seen in Jesus; but what man ought to be. It is held up in the face of sinful men, as God's standard of perfect manhood, that they may learn to know themselves, and to see how infinitely short they come of it, and that they may be so emptied of all self-confidence as to be driven to the only hope of sinners in the unmerited grace of God (Rom. v. 20; vii. 9, &c.). So utterly unable is man to fulfil the law of God, by the weakness and evil of his nature, that the best man living must be under its curse (Gal. iii. 10). The law knows no mercy; one flaw in keeping its requirements is fatal.

The ten commandments are the embodiment, in a concise form, of Divine requirements which were in existence from the creation; and were written on the consciences of man (Rom. ii. 15). It is probable that the fourth is no exception to this. We should judge ourselves by these "ten words," that we be not judged. They are useful to us for purposes of self-examination. We may read their deeper meaning in Matt. v. The first table sets forth duties to God; and the second, duties to man, and are capable of being gathered into two all-comprehending precepts (Mark xii. 29–31). And in a sense they focus into a single word—LOVE (Matt. xxii. 37; Mark xii. 30, 31; Luke x. 27; Rom. xiii. 10; Gal. v. 14). Christ has fulfilled for us the requirements of the law, and borne for us the penalty of the broken law.

The law is not our ground or rule of life (Rom. vi. 14).—But we are under the law of love to Christ; and that law, being wrought in us by the grace of the Holy Spirit, produces in us the same results as would have been secured, if we had been perfectly able to obey the original requirements (Rom. x. 4).

The dread of the people (**19**).—This is graphically described in Deut. v. 22–27. And yet God requires our worship (**24**), and purposes to meet us at the altar, and to bless us, if we approach in all humility, offering sacrifices of blood (Eph. ii. 13; Heb. x. 19–22).

CHAP. XXI. **Laws of Conduct**

Here is the beginning of a code of laws, civil, political, ceremonial, which were afterwards given in detail in the Books of Leviticus and Deuteronomy. There is a great difference between the moral law, which is eternal as God, and is written on all hearts—and the ceremonial and political law, which had a more limited range as pertaining to the history of Israel. It was in great advance of all similar codes of that age; but it was far inferior to that of Christ. It did not impose the highest Christian demands on these untutored people, but sought to lead them by gentle ascents from the grossness of Egypt and surrounding nations (Mark x. 4, 5).

The law of the Hebrew slave (**2–6**) is a beautiful lesson. He served at first, because there was no other way of wiping out his debt; but afterwards he served because he loved. He elected to remain in slavery for ever, and learnt perfect freedom. Love is the true source of service.

The other laws: those concerning the female slave (**8–11**); those on the punishment of acts of rude violence (**12–27**); those of disputes as to animals (**28–36**)—are all very instructive, and rest upon principles which a little thought will enable the reader to appreciate. But it is necessary to add that these laws of Exod. xxi. are not rules for the present dispensation. The Mosaic enactments are abrogated. In examining the laws themselves, we have to read in the light of Matt. v. 3–46; xix. 8; Mark x. 5–9; Heb. viii. 13.

But the main conception of the Mosaic code is retaliation **(23–25)**.—Our Lord Jesus Christ alluded to this (Matt. v. 38), and insisted that His own followers should adopt a higher code—that of merciful love, after the example of their Father. How well it is for us that He has not dealt with us on the principle of absolute justice, serving us as we have served Him and others (Ps. cxxx. 3, 4). But what a picture do these laws give of the depravity of man's heart, which demanded them!

CHAP. XXII. **Further Laws**

Restitution is one of the prime thoughts in this chapter **(1–14)**. Alas that this is far from being recognized by us Christians as it should be! But it is the first sign of a genuine work of grace (Luke xix. 8). It is not enough to confess to God: we must also confess and make restitution to man. Men are very often kept from peace and trust, by their memory of some wrong, which they have not made right. But no amount of religious observance will compensate for the failure to adjust, so far as possible, the wrong-doing of the past.

Mercy also shines in many of these enactments **(21–30)**. God says, "For I am gracious" **(27)**: that was a reason and a motive why they should be tender and gentle in their dealings with strangers; the defenceless; and the poor. Infraction of these commands was severely alluded to in after-days (Amos ii. 6–8). We must not forget that God now demands of us that similar mercy be shown towards the weak and poor; as is enjoined in this chapter: and in this matter faithfulness greatly commends His children to Him (Ps. xli. 1; Luke vi. 31; James i. 27).

God's nearness is taught. He hears any cry that is raised **(23–27)**, and He comes nigh to avenge the cause of the poor. He was the invisible King of Israel **(28,** R.V.**),** who beheld each of His subjects with searching and minute inspection, judging the evil and the good, and interposing on the behalf of those who could not help themselves. This is the meaning of a Theocracy.

Holiness was God's prime requirement. Here first is the demand, "Ye shall be holy men" **(31)**, which was destined to ring throughout

78   THE FIVE BOOKS OF MOSES

the remaining books of Moses, and is the appeal of all Scripture (1 Pet i. 15, 16). Holiness means separation *from* and *to*. When we yield ourselves only to God, we are weaned from, and lose our taste for, the things which once fascinated us (31).

CHAP. XXIII.   Laws and Promises

This chapter is full of sweet and profitable reading. Many of the laws breathe the spirit of the New Testament. Do we not sometimes raise and receive (**1,** *marg.*) false reports, and circulate them? Are we not all influenced by the opinions and actions of the multitude (**2**)? Do we exert ourselves to help those whom we hate, in their conflict with difficulties (**4, 5**)? Are we always careful to keep our hands free of anything false, or bribes (**7, 8**)? Do we never take advantage of those who may not be as well acquainted with our methods or language (**9**)? Sometimes professing Christians take undue advantage of foreigners. Do we think enough of the poor, and of the rest required by our servants and animals (**11, 12**)? Alas, too, how often we mention "chance," and "fate," and the names of heathen gods, as "Jupiter," "Jove"! (**13**).

The three feasts are elsewhere mentioned at greater length (Lev. xxiii.), and are significant of certain great events in the story of redemption. The feast of PASSOVER speaks of the Cross; the offering of the FIRSTFRUITS, of the Resurrection; and the final feast, of a completed HARVEST of Pentecost.

A precious promise closes these injunctions (**20**). That Angel, with the attributes of God (**21**), still goes before us, to set us in the way of His steps, and to lead us to the "many mansions" prepared. Happy are they who keep behind Him, allowing Him to face all their spiritual foes (**23**), and who obey Him utterly! How tender is that thought of us which deals with us by "little and little" (**30**). It is so that all noble character is built up. Obey in little things; and God will lead you into the very fulness of blessing (John xiv. 21, 23).

CHAP. XXIV.   Mount Sinai

In xx. 21 we learn that Moses remained in communion with God whilst receiving the regulations detailed in xxi., xxii., xxiii. On the following day, this covenant between God and the people was solemnly ratified. The altar built under the hill (4) probably represented God; and the twelve pillars the tribes of Israel. The young men (5) did the work of the priests according to xiii. 2, until the tribe of Levi was set definitely apart for this work. It must have been a very solemn scene, when Israel and their King thus entered into the holy compact; and the copious sprinkling of blood intimated that the people could not have stood as parties to that covenant with God, unless by virtue of shed life. This scene is specially referred to in Heb. ix. 18–20. There were three ascents of Sinai.

I. *Moses went up with the elders* (9).—Of course they did not really see God (1 Tim. vi. 16, and Deut. iv. 15). But, doubtless, there was some symbol or emblem of the Divine Presence, like the Shekinah of after-days. The azure blue tessellated pavement (10) is very suggestive of the purity and beauty of the outward surroundings of this Theophany. But the glory did not smite them dead: they were even able to eat and drink with equanimity (11), because they stood on the basis of shed life. This feasting on the flesh of slain victims was the precursor of the peace-offerings, and has its counterpart in the Lord's Supper.

II. *Moses went up with Joshua* (13–16).—These tables of stone were evidently of Divine workmanship (xxxi. 18). At an elevated spot, within the circle of the illuminated cloud, Moses waited for six days (16); and this must have greatly tested his patience and faith. How often God keeps us waiting thus! Some cannot endure it (1 Sam. xiii. 12).

III. *Moses went up alone* (18).—On the day of rest, he went into the heart of the "devouring" glory. But where God bids us come, we need not fear to go.

CHAP. XXV. **The Ark of the Covenant**

We now begin a distinct section of this book, which tells of the construction of the Tabernacle, beginning with the Ark of the Covenant of the manifested presence of God, and working outwards to the brazen altar at which He met man. This is the pathway trodden once by Christ, from the throne to the cross. The Tabernacle signifies two things: first, it is a pattern of things in the heavens, and gives material representations of the spiritual realities of our worship and service (Heb. ix.); secondly, it is a type of the body of Christ (Heb. x.).

The materials were drawn from the presents made on leaving Egypt, and the spoils of the Egyptian host washed on shore: or were derived from barter with commercial caravans passing through the peninsula. There were mines for metals in the neighbourhood; and the Israelites themselves must have acquired many arts during their sojourn in Egypt.

The plan was given by God.—This was repeatedly insisted on (xxv. 9, 40; xxvi. 30; xxvii. 8; Heb. viii. 5). Well would it be for us did we obey this heavenly injunction, and construct the fabric of our lives only on God's plan as revealed to us by His Word and providence.

The Ark was the throne of God (**22**): it contained the law (1 Kings viii. 9), covered by the mercy-seat or propitiatory (Rom. iii. 25), which was sprinkled with blood once each year (Lev. xvi. 14, 15). It was meant to travel (**12–15;** Num. iii. 31; iv. 5, 15), until 1 Kings viii. 6–8, and Ps. cxxxii. 8. As to *the cherubim* (**18–22**), *see* 1 Pet. i. 12.

The Shewbread table (**23–30**) held the bread of the priests (Lev. xxiv. 5–9); which was called *presence bread*, because it was constantly exhibited before the Lord. It consisted of twelve loaves, made of fine flour, setting forth the provision made in Jesus for our nourishment.

The Candlestick, or lamp-stand (**31**), had seven branches, three on each side, and one in the centre. Each bowl or cup was like the *calix* of a flower; the knops were round balls or bosses; the flowers were lilies. The light was of pure olive oil, probably always burning (Lev. xxiv. 2, 3). The value of the material of the candlestick and its tongs and snuffers would be about £5,500 (**39**). Is not this *candlestick* a type of Christ, our Light; and of the Church's work in the world?

These and all the articles in the Holy of Holies were either constructed of, or overlaid with, "pure gold." Oh for more of that spirit of willing offering! (*See* Rom. xii. 1).

Chap. XXVI. The Tabernacle Curtains

The Tabernacle consisted of upright boards, over which were thrown curtains, here described: these probably prefigure certain aspects of Christ's character and work; because, in a mystical sense, the Tabernacle and Temple prefigured His nature (John ii. 21; Heb. ix. 11). Each curtain was sixteen yards long and over two yards broad; and they were coupled together lengthways, making a vast awning.

The first set of curtains (**1–6**) was a splendid piece of tapestry, embroidered with cherubim, in various colours of blue, scarlet, and purple—the cunning work of a damask weaver. The texture set forth Christ's matchless manhood; His heavenly nature; His royalty; and His death.

The second set of curtains (**7–13**) flung over the first, was made of goats' hair; but these were longer and broader, so as to protect those beneath. How few saw the inner beauty of Jesus! (Isa. liii. 2, 3).

The third and fourth sets (**14**) were of rams' and badgers' skins, respectively. How splendid even these were; the one dyed red, recalling the precious blood-shedding; the other dyed blue (probably) pointing heavenwards.

The boards of shittim wood (**18**) were the walls of the Tabernacle. Twenty on the north side, twenty on the south, six on the west; knit by five cross bars. The boards stood in silver sockets, buried in the sand.

The vail (**31**) was of the same materials as the inner curtains, and divided the holy from the most holy place. Alone did the high priest pass through the vail, thus entering the most holy place once every year, not without blood (*see* Lev. xvi. 2–34; Heb. ix. 7, 8, 25). How minute are God's directions in all these matters! Surely it becomes us to study them minutely; and to remember how microscopic God's interest is in all the details of our lives.

CHAP. XXVII. **The Brazen Altar**

The Brazen Altar here claims our attention. It was about three yards square, and over one yard and a half high, made of shittim wood, like the golden altar of incense; but overlaid, not with gold, but with brass, because there sin was to be dealt with by fire. The shittim wood in each case represents Christ's humanity; but, while in the golden altar He is the medium of our praise, in the brazen altar He bears our sins in His own body on the tree, and endures the penalty of sin. "The horns of the altar" were angular projections, in the form of horns. Animals to be sacrificed were bound to these (Ps. cxviii. 27), and part of the blood was applied to them (xxix. 12; Lev. iv. 25).

The court of the Tabernacle (9–19) was about sixty yards long by about thirty broad, and was formed by a connected series of curtains, made of fine twined linen yarn: the curtains were suspended on sixty brazen pillars, standing on brazen sockets, with silver fillets and hooks. Brazen pins were used to fix the curtains in the sand, so that they might not be swayed about by the wind.

The oil for the light.—This was specially prepared. It was "pure" and "beaten" (20; Lev. xxiv. 2–4). None shine so well in this dark world as those who are pure in heart and poor in spirit. McCheyne used to say, "Beaten oil for the sanctuary," referring to the care with which ministers and others should prepare for their work. The lamp was never to go out, but was to burn "continually." We too shall shine under the care of Him who tends His candlesticks still: sometimes using snuffers, which, however, are of gold (Rev. i. 20; *see also* Zech. iv. 2–12). *A statute for ever* (xxviii. 43; xxix. 9, 28; xxx. 21; 21; *see also* Lev. iii. 17; xvi. 34; xxiv. 9, &c.).

CHAP. XXVIII. **The High Priest's Robes**

We have here a description of the Robes of the High Priest, "for glory and beauty."

The ephod (6) was very gorgeous; it was short, reaching from the breast to below the loins; and was kept in position by straps, called shoulder-pieces, which were united on the shoulders by two onyx stones (9), set in gold (11), and engraven with names. "The government shall be upon his shoulder" (Isa. ix. 6). *The girdle* (8) was wrought with threads of gold, blue, purple, and scarlet: this girdle wound twice round the upper part of the waist (*see* Dan. x. 5; Rev. i. 13).

The breastplate (15–30) bore twelve precious stones, each containing the name of a tribe, and arranged in four rows of three in each. Stones corresponding to these lie at the foundation of the New Jerusalem (Rev. xxi. 19). Thus are our names written on the heart of Jesus; and none can tear us thence. In the breastplate were the Urim and Thummim (30), which were probably large and lustrous stones, which flashed with the Divine "Yes," or dimmed with the Divine "No" (*see* Deut. xxxiii. 8), and are possibly referred to in the white stone of Rev. ii. 17.

The robe of the ephod (**31**) was worn under it. It was of blue, and had a hole through which the head was thrust (**32**); so that it was carefully formed of one piece (*comp.* John xix. 23, 24). It ended in a fringe, in which bells and pomegranates of gold were alternated.

The headplate (**36**) bore an inscription such as each of us should wear always on our fore-front, and should write on our commonest duties (Zech. xiv. 20, 21).

The clothing for the ordinary priests (**40–43**) was very simple— pure white linen. This is the garb in which we should all be attired (Ecc. ix. 8; Rev. iii. 18; xix. 8). And if there should be any stain or spot, go at once to the laver of the blood of Christ (Eph. v. 26, 27; James i. 27; 1 John i. 9).

CHAP. XXIX. **Consecration of Priests**

The Consecration of Priests was an elaborate and impressive ceremony. They were first washed in water (**4**), intimating the necessity of personal purity on the part of God's priests (Heb. x. 22). Then they were attired in their official robes (**5**). All God's priests should be clad in the beauty of holiness (Ps. cx. 3; cxxxii. 9, 16). The anointing oil (**7**) is the emblem of the Holy Spirit, whose unction is essential to the right performance of all priestly service (2 Cor. i. 21; 1 John ii. 20, 27). It is not enough to have the Holy Spirit within for character: He must be *upon us* for ministry.

The sacrifices appointed for the occasion were significant. The bullock for sin (**10–14**; Lev. viii. 2; xvi. 6, 11; Heb. vii. 27). One ram as a burnt-offering (**15–18**; Lev. viii. 18), indicating the willingness to be only God's (Rom. xii. 1). A second ram, yielding blood for sprinkled ear, and hand, and foot, in token of the necessity of dedicating all the powers to God (**19, 20**). Part of the flesh was waved up and down in token of its being offered to God: it was then burnt. The rest was eaten by the priests: and thus it seemed as if God and man met together, and feasted on the same flesh, in token of peace and fellowship. The breast of the ram of consecration was the portion of Moses (**26**; Lev. viii. 29).

The very altar must be cleansed and sanctified (**36**); for it was made of materials which were under the contagion of sin (Heb. ix. 21, 22).

Daily sacrifices were instituted (**38**). These were to last throughout all the history of the chosen people, till the Lamb of God was given. They were presented in the name of the whole people (Num. xxviii. 2–8).

The assurance with which this chapter closes (**45, 46**) is precious indeed: and there is a sense in which each one of us may share in it (John xiv. 23; 2 Cor. vi. 16; Gal. ii. 20; 1 John iv. 13).

CHAP. XXX. **Altar of Incense**

Here at last is the *Altar of Incense*, 3 ft. 6 in. high, by 21 in. broad. It was overlaid with gold, and stood immediately before the vail. It was covered with pure gold, as were the Ark of the Covenant and the Mercy-seat in the Holiest of all; and as was the Table of Shewbread, which, with the Golden Candlestick and the Altar of Incense stood in the Sanctuary. Gold and white ever symbolized the presence of God—preciousness and purity. It symbolizes our life of prayer, accepted for Christ's sake (Rev. viii. 3). The priest who officiated there was, therefore, like Christ in a very special sense (Luke i. 10, 11). This incense altar needed blood (**10**); and all our prayers need to be cleansed in the blood of Jesus ere they can be acceptable.

The Atonement Money (**11–16**) was paid by all alike. In the matter of atonement there can be no distinctions. This is referred to in Matt. xvii. 24–27. The money-changers gathered about the Temple in after-days to give the holy shekel in exchange for common or heathen coins (Matt. xxi. 12; Mark xi. 15; John ii. 14, 15).

The Laver (**18**) reminds us of our need of constant daily washing. We need the putting away of sin, not only once when we come to the cross, but always (John xiii. 3–12). It is very necessary to keep constantly in the cleansing efficacy of the grace of Christ (1 John i. 6, 7). The laver was made out of the brazen looking-glasses of the women (xxxviii. 8). It was a good use for them. Is there not some allusion to the Word of God, which is as a mirror and as water? (2 Cor. iii. 18; Eph. v. 26).

The composition of the Oil is a matter of very careful direction. A "holy anointing oil." Surely here is a type of the varied graces of the Holy Ghost, which were found in Jesus Christ (Ps. xlv. 8); and will reveal themselves also in us (Gal. v. 22). There must be no imitation of those graces (**32, 38**). And they must be put to no common use; because all that is fair and lovely in character is for God alone (**37**).

Chap. XXXI. Skilled Workmen

The Equipment of the two skilled artificers, Bezaleel and Aholiab, for their Work stands first in this chapter (**1–11**). When we follow God's pattern, we may always count on the requisite workers and gifts being provided. It was the same Holy Spirit that rested on Moses which wrought in these men. The Spirit which filled the Apostles, and made them such powerful witnesses of the Resurrection (Acts iv. 31) filled these two, and made them able to devise and to execute (1 Cor. xii. 4–6). It was in each case the same Holy Spirit of God. Why should we not seek His aid to fit us for doing our daily work? And why should we not view as sacred all toils, in connection with which we may claim and count upon His presence.

The Observance of the Sabbath was again Appointed (**12–17**).— The law as to this had been given more than once (xvi. 23; xx. 8–11; xxiii. 12). However great might be the pressure of preparing the Tabernacle, it was not to interfere with the Sabbath rest. Our work for God must not break our rest in God. The Sabbath was a sign (**13, 17**; Ezek. xx. 12, 20). The equivalent of the Sabbath in our time is not only the Lord's Day, but more especially the rest of faith. And there is no such sign of a soul being right with God, as when it is able to cast all its sins and sorrows, its cares and troubles, on the Lord. We should keep a perpetual Sabbath in the heart (Neh. xiii. 19).

The Tables of the Law (**18**) were written on stone, to denote their lasting obligation. God wrote them once on stone; but in our case He gives a heart of flesh, before He writes there with His own finger His holy will (2 Cor. iii. 3). The Tables were entrusted to Moses, a fact referred to afterwards in contrast to the work of our Lord (John i. 17).

Chap. XXXII. The Golden Calf

A notable chapter! We are taught *the nature of idolatry*, which craves some outward symbol of the Unseen (**1–6**). This episode was not a violation of the *first*, but of the *second* commandment. It is always dangerous to associate our worship of God with a material emblem, for in time men invest the emblem with the properties of God Himself. People are willing enough to part with ornaments in the service of an idol (3). Why are we so slow in giving up all for the love of Christ, grudging no expenditure, and counting no cost too great? The people's worship was, no doubt, associated with some of the obscene practices to which they had become accustomed during their stay in Egypt.

Moses' intercession (11-13).—God announced the people's sin to Moses in such a manner as to establish two things—first, the noble character of Moses, which stood out very conspicuously in great relief; secondly, that there were grave grounds of alarm that Israel might yet miss the privileges that seemed so sure. God is not changeable (Num. xxiii. 19; James i. 17); but He treats men differently, according to the measure in which they alter their attitude to Him. The change is not in Him, but in them; and He acts as one might do who had literally changed his mind. This intercession (*see also* 32) reminds us of the Saviour and the Apostle (Luke xxiii. 34; Rom. ix. 3).

The result was terrible (19). The broken tables betokened the inability of man to keep the law of God. The excuse of Aaron— "There came out this calf"—was childish (24); and put him in great danger (Deut. ix. 20). Many fell by the sword, and the plague (28, 35). The rallying of the Levites at this critical moment (26-28) was never forgotten, and laid the foundation of their selection for the priesthood (Deut. xxxiii. 9; Mal. ii. 4, 5). The presence of Jehovah was to be exchanged for that of an angel (34; xxxiii. 2); but Moses appears to have obtained an alteration as to this (xxxiii. 14-17).

CHAP. XXXIII. "Without the Camp"

When the tidings that God's personal Presence was to be taken from the camp reached them, the people were filled with dismay; and they divested themselves of their ornaments (4). It was needful that God should deal with them in this way, that they might, through symbols, learn to understand what sin was, and how it grieved Him, and how certainly it would ruin all their prospects. The pitching of the Tabernacle without the camp was a significant sign of the inability of God to remain amid so much evil (7). It was in all likelihood a temporary structure, which had served for purposes of worship since the exodus.

Moses' intimacy with God.—"Face to face" (11) expresses vividly the intimacy of that converse which in some sense is still possible (2 Cor. iii. 18). What a noble prayer for us all is this of Moses! (13). Surely the great end of life is to serve God in *His* way. He asked two things, one for the people, that the Divine Presence should go with them; the other for himself, that he might see the Divine glory. The first of these received a complete and immediate answer (14). Wherever God's Presence goes there is rest; and if He is with thee ever, thou shalt drink of waters of rest (Matt. xi. 28). It is when the holy heart is in abiding fellowship with God that it can have its way (John xv. 7).

The Rock (21) is a type of Christ, the Rock of Ages cleft for us (*comp.* Isa. xxvi. 4, *marg.*). It is in the clefts of that rock where His saints hide (Sol. Song ii. 14). We can only know and enjoy God when we are standing in the very shadow of God's Rock. Yet when we know the most of God, it is only, so to speak, His back parts. How little we know of Him at the best! (Job xi. 7-11).

CHAP. XXXIV. The Two Tables Renewed

God had been reconciled to Israel, stripped of their jewels (xxxiii. 5, 6), through the mediation of Moses; and the broken covenant must be restored. The material in this case was to be provided by Moses himself; but God wrote the holy words (1, 28). Would that He would do as much for us! (Heb. viii. 10).

Moses' Vision of God.—The name of God is His character. In olden days names betrayed some prominent feature in the natures of the bearers. To know the name was to know the person (Gen. xxxii. 29). What a list of attractive titles (6, 7). "Will by no means clear" is rendered by some, "I will not utterly destroy" (Jer. xxv. 29). Iniquity was not visited on the children beyond the third and fourth generation—*i.e.*, the great law of heredity was curtailed in its action. Amid all the rapture of that moment Moses was true to the people, and with rare self-oblivion began to plead again for Israel (9).

The Renewed Covenant (**10–27**).—It was a marriage covenant (Jer. iii. 14; xxxi. 32): idolatry was therefore adultery. The Israelites were, consequently, bidden to destroy all traces of idolatry; to reject all treaties of alliance in marriage; and to refuse all invitations to idolatrous feasts (**12–16**). How jealous is God of His people's love; and how careful should we be to give Him all our love! (James iv. 4). The three Feasts were recapitulated: Passover; Feast of Weeks, *i.e.*, Pentecost, seven weeks after Passover; Feast of Ingathering, or of Tabernacles. God will always take care of our interests, if we do not flinch from obedience to Him (**24**; Matt. vi. 33).

Thou shalt not seethe a kid in his mother's milk (**26**).—The excessive tenderness and delicacy of this injunction is most noteworthy. Some would sneer at the prohibition as mere "sentimentalism"; but injunctions such as these helped to form the character of the nation.

Moses' Vail (**33**).—Communion with God did literally for him what it does spiritually for us. The light was different to Christ's, in being from without, while Christ's was from within (Matt. xvii. 1, 2). True holiness is unconscious of its beauty (**29**). The vail taught the obscurity of that dispensation, which is now done away (2 Cor. iii. 13). "But we all with open face," &c. (2 Cor. iii. 18).

Chap. XXXV. **The Sabbath**

The Sabbath was again enjoined with peculiar solemnity. We are obviously not bound by these strict injunctions (**3**); but there are spiritual obligations quite as searching and minute.

Israel's free-will gifts teach us a great lesson. The willingness is repeatedly noticed (**5, 21, 22, 29**). Different gifts all found specific and sufficient scope. The rich gave of their wealth (**5–9**); the skilful of their handicraft (**10**); and the women found appropriate spheres (**25, 26, 29**). So in the building-up of God's Church, in which He is to make His abode, it becomes every child of His to contribute something—either wealth, or service, or skill (1 Cor. vii. 7; 1 Pet. iv. 10). And that which beautified and elevated the whole of this willinghood was the repeated thought that the giving was *to the Lord*. One powerful motive for this outburst of liberality was the memory of recent forgiveness. There is nothing that so constrains generosity as gratitude (Matt. x. 8; 2 Cor. v. 14). We do not hear

THE BOOK OF EXODUS 89

of any murmuring during this busy time: one of the best preservatives against this sin is to be all at work, and always at work.

The two artists were now specially called to their work (30–35).—When God summons His servants to special work, He endows them with special gifts. The wisdom to devise and the power to work are alike from Him; and of the faithful use of all such precious talents we must give account. Even the power to teach is here expressly ascribed to the Spirit of God (34). We do not depend enough on the Spirit of God to find and prepare labourers for God's great work in the world. But all is of Him; and He is the Great Worker in the Church (1 Cor. iii. 7–9). How much better it is to construct than to destroy! To build up is God-like; to pull down is the devil's work. Let each find the sphere in which he can do the best service, and keep to it, envying none, interfering with none (Mark xiii. 34; 2 Cor. x. 16).

CHAP. XXXVI. Israel's Liberal Gifts

"Then."—There was no needless delay. From the moment that the Divine will and pattern were made known, till the final completion of the sacred edifice, the workers laboured with untiring energy and devotion. The heart-stirring and the liberal gifts seem to have come together (2, 3). We are reminded of the zeal and speed with which the people laboured in after-years in the erection of the Temple (Neh. iv. 6).

The morning gifts.—Like other Oriental magistrates, Moses sat on the seat of justice every morning; and it was then that the people came to him with their gifts. And surely it was much better for them to come thither on such errands than for purposes of litigation. It might be that during the night some of them finished self-imposed tasks; other gifts were prompted by meditation during the night-watches. Piety, penitence, and gratitude would contribute the impulses that led them to the place where Moses sat. Would it not be well if we came each morning to God, not only to receive from Him, but also to give to Him the offerings of our love, and praise, and service (Phil. iv. 18; 2 Cor. ix. 12; 1 Cor. vi. 20).

The restraint put on the people's gifts was very unusual (6, 7), and has rarely needed repetition. In general, men need to be pressed to give rather than requested to withhold. May we not be rebuked by this outburst from a nation of emancipated slaves? The men who did the work were evidently men of strict integrity; or they might have kept the overplus as payment or perquisites: they set an example to many professing Christians.

The scrupulous care with which each of God's commands about the Tabernacle was carried into effect is very instructive; and this elaborate enumeration (8-38), when so many things are left unmentioned, shows how important was the religious education of the people.

CHAP. XXXVII. **The Cherubim and the Mercy-Seat**

The description here given of *the furniture within the sacred edifice* is almost identical with chap. xxv. It is not, however, useless; it emphasizes the minute and scrupulous care with which God's commands were carried into effect, and with which He expects to be obeyed. In His code there is nothing too trifling or insignificant for our obedience.

The skill shown in this work was admirable (7, 17). It was not a small matter to beat out with the hammer from a solid piece of gold figures measuring from two to three feet in their outstretched wings. It would be a triumph in the art of the present day. How much more so then! Why do such work with the hammer, when it would have been so much easier to cast it—a process with which Israel was familiar? Doubtless there was a sufficient reason, and one perhaps connected with the sufferings and patience of our Lord; from whose nature, as from gold molten in a furnace, there has been beaten out, by the ponderous hammer of suffering, those marvellous qualifications to help and save us.

Let us remind ourselves of our sacred duties and relationships. The MERCY-SEAT bids us hold fellowship with God on the ground of the sprinkled blood. The ALTAR OF INCENSE prompts us to praise and prayer. The CANDLESTICK demands of us to shine as lights in the world. The table of SHEW-BREAD signifies our urgent need to feed daily on Christ, eating His flesh, and drinking His blood. The many preparations for moving the Tabernacle remind us that here we have no continuing city, but are pilgrims and strangers seeking one to come (Heb. xi. 13; 1 Pet. ii. 11).

Chap. XXXVIII. Altar of Burnt-Offering

In every age *Women* (8) have been among the most steadfast and generous contributors to the work of God. Women were last at the cross, and women brought sweet and costly embalmments to the grave. In the early days of Christianity women readily received the Gospel (Acts xvi. 13; xvii. 4). In Israel the devout women seem to have often gathered at the entrance of the tent of meeting. It must have cost some self-denial to part with their adornments; but love makes such sacrifices light.

The Court (9) was made of very light materials, conformably with the pilgrim state of the people, and because the whole structure was but temporary. The time would come when the place of the tent would be enlarged, and its cords strengthened to make room for the Gentile world (Isa. liv. 2, 3). The courts were, especially in after-days, the home of the Levites: "Blessed are they that dwell in Thy house; they will be still praising Thee" (Ps. lxxxiv. 4). The area of the court was about 180 ft. long by 90 ft. wide, enclosed by hangings of linen suspended from pillars nearly 9 ft. high, and standing the same distance apart. The pillars were kept firm by cords, and by tent-pins of bronze. If we may not be pillars, let us be thankful to be tent-pins strengthening them.

The cost of the Tabernacle (21) was reckoned up by the Levites, under the direction of Ithamar. All the *gold* was a freewill offering (24; *see also* xxxv. 22). Every man brought what he could. It amounted in all to £175,000 of our present money: of this were made all the golden furniture and vessels. The *silver* was levied as a kind of poll tax (xxx. 11, 15), and amounted to nearly £38,000: of this were made the sockets into which the boards of the tabernacle were let, and on which they rested. A *bekah* is half-a-shekel. Every man in Israel was therefore compelled to give the same amount towards these foundations of their Tabernacle; and this was perhaps intended to teach that, however we may differ in other matters, we must all take an equal interest in—as, indeed, we all have an equal need of—the foundation truths of Christ's atonement and work. All this amount of money was accumulated in the last days of their stay in Egypt (xii. 35, 36). But surely the readiness with which they parted with their hoarded treasures is a lesson and example to the Church.

CHAP. XXXIX. **The Priestly Garments**

The Priests' Garments **(1–31)** were very rich. We have already described them in Notes on chap. xxviii. These garments have a spiritual meaning as setting forth those gifts, graces, and offices, which the Lord Jesus assumed when He undertook the work of our salvation, as our High Priest. All the spiritual Israel were borne on His shoulders and carried on His heart, and presented in the breastplate of judgment to the Father; whilst the holy crown of pure gold, engraven with "Holiness to the Lord," stood manifestly on His brow. True believers are spiritual priests (1 Pet. ii. 5); clothed in fine linen (**27**; Rev. xix. 8), which we must ever keep white in the precious blood (Eccles. ix. 8; Rev. vii. 14).

The completed Tabernacle was the type and emblem of Jesus Christ. "The Word was made flesh, and *tabernacled* among us" (John i. 14). As the Shekinah dwelt in the sanctuary, filling it with a light and glory which sometimes flowed over into the outer courts, so did God dwell in the person of Jesus, sometimes irradiating His whole being, as at the transfiguration, "We beheld His glory" (John i. 14: *see also* Col. ii. 9; 2 Pet. i. 16, 17; Rev. i. 16). The Tabernacle is also a symbol of every true child of God; for God still dwells in human spirits, and shines out through them, so that there is no part of them left dark. "Know ye not that your body is the temple of the Holy Ghost which is in you?" (1 Cor. vi. 19). The Tabernacle is also a type of the collective Church, in whom God dwells (2 Cor. vi. 16; Eph. ii. 22). It must have been a very affecting and triumphant moment when Moses looked on the completed Tabernacle, not yet set up, but awaiting the next step of erection.

"*And Moses looked upon all the work*" (**43**).—So does God look on all our work, even before it is evident to the world, and blesses us in proportion to the entireness of our obedience.

The exact obedience of the people is expressly and repeatedly emphasized. Underline in this chapter and the next the repetition of "as the Lord commanded Moses." We are too inexact in our obedience. We content ourselves with general principles, to the frequent neglect of minor points. But how much depends on absolute obedience! (John xiv. 21; Acts v. 32).

Chap. XL. The Tabernacle Erected

The time for setting up the Tabernacle (**1-17**) was fixed on the anniversary of the Exodus. How much had been done in that short time! When there is unanimity among His people and good direction, God's work goes on apace. Moses took the same pleasure and care in erecting the Tabernacle as the workmen took in making it. There was no rivalry or emulation, except as to who should do his part most expeditiously and efficiently; and thus without friction or ill-feeling the whole of this great work was brought quickly and successfully to a close.

The frequent use of oil (**9-11; 13; 15**) should be noticed as teaching our incessant need of the grace of the Holy Ghost, without whom the fairest work is unacceptable to God. How greatly do we need to receive the daily unction of the Holy Spirit on ourselves as priests (**13-15;** 1 Pet. ii. 5, 9), and on all our work! (**10**). And how necessary also that we should make constant use of the laver, washing whenever we undertake any service in the name of God (Ps. xxvi. 6).

The solemn consecration (**34**) was made by the descent of the cloud of the Shekinah, filling the tabernacle with light so insufferable that even Moses could not enter (*see* Zech. ii. 5). That cloud was the symbol or manifestation of God, and, like the royal standard flying from the battlements of a palace, it intimated that the King of Israel was literally dwelling among His people; was "in residence." We have not now the outward symbol; but we have the essential reality (Matt. xxviii. 20). That cloud became the guide of Israel's march (**36-38;** Num. ix. 15-23; Neh. ix. 19; Ps. lxxviii. 14). Sometimes it demanded long patience as it tarried; and the people had no other alternative than to wait. And when we are not sure of our way, we must wait till we can see what God's will may be (Ps. xii. 1). But we ought never to go in front of Him (John x. 4), nor should we lag behind. And we must ever remember that the presence of our God with us is not only a guide and a glory, but a defence. When God is in the midst of us we cannot be moved (Ps. xlvi. 5). Oh, happy is the people whose God is the Lord, and who obey His commandments!

THE TEN PLAGUES OF EGYPT

Exodus vii.	17–25	1. All the waters that were in the river were **turned into blood.** *The magicians also worked this miracle.*
viii.	1–15	2. **Frogs** came up and covered the land. *The magicians also worked this miracle.*
	16–19	3. All the dust of the land became **lice.**
	20–32	4. A grievous swarm of **flies.**
ix.	3–7	5. A very grievous **murrain.** And all the cattle of Egypt died.
	8–12	6. A **boil** breaking forth, **with blains** upon all the Egyptians.
	13–35	7. There was **hail, and fire** mingled with the hail, throughout the land of Egypt.
x.	1–20	8. The **locusts** went up over all the land of Egypt, and they covered the face of the whole earth.
	21–29	9. A **thick darkness** over all the land . . . which might be felt.
xi.	4–10	10. **The Death of the First-born.**—The Lord smote all the first-born in the land of Egypt. And there was a great cry in Egypt, for there was not a house where there was not one dead.

The Book of Leviticus

The word "Leviticus" is used by the LXX. and the Vulgate as a comprehensive designation of the subject of this book, meaning the rites and ceremonies for whose celebration the tribe of Levi was set apart. The word, however, does not occur in the Hebrew Bible: there the book is designated, as in other instances, by its opening word, "Vayikra," the first part of the sentence, "And the Lord called unto Moses," &c.

It may be called the book of Israel's ritual, or the priests' directory, as it is chiefly occupied with the laws of sacrifices and of purifications, and other priestly functions. It is very lacking as to formal arrangement; but the following general divisions of the book may be found useful:—

LAWS OF THE OFFERINGS (i.–vii.).
CONSECRATION OF THE PRIESTS; WITH HISTORY OF THAT OF AARON AND HIS SONS (viii.–x.).
LAWS OF PURIFICATION (xi.–xv.).
DAY OF ATONEMENT; AND EXPLANATION OF THE USE OF THE BLOOD (xvi., xvii.).
PROHIBITED MARRIAGES AND EVIL PRACTICES (xviii.–xx.).
PRECEPTS AS TO PRIESTLY DUTIES (xxi., xxii.).
FEASTS (xxiii.).
THE OIL FOR THE LIGHT; THE SHEWBREAD; BLASPHEMING (xxiv.).
THE SABBATH YEAR AND THE YEAR OF JUBILEE (xxv.).
PROMISES AND THREATENINGS; VOWS (xxvi., xxvii.).

To the Christian the book is of deep interest, as being far more than a record of bygone and now discarded observances. For, as the Epistle to the Hebrews teaches us, Israel's "worldly sanctuary" was intended to prefigure the great things of Christ's salvation. All pointed to Him. He was the Sanctuary or Temple (*see* John ii. 21). He was the Altar (Heb. xiii. 10) as well as the Sacrifice (Heb. x.), and also the Priest (Heb. vii.). Thus also the laws of the offerings present us with so many different aspects of His offering and sacrifice; and the distinctions of meats (clean and unclean), and the various purifications and festal celebrations, set forth the purification from sin effected by His great sacrifice, and its application to the walk and ways of His people. In no book of the Bible do we more need His presence to expound to us "the things concerning Himself" (Luke xxiv. 27).

Of all the books of the Bible LEVITICUS is the text-book on holiness. All creation has been so constructed as to be the exponent of moral and spiritual truth; and beneath the sacred and sanitary legislation which God gave to Israel lie hidden treasures of wisdom and knowledge—deep things of God—all things that pertain to life and godliness.

Chaps. i.–vii. contain the Law of the Offerings, showing how the redeemed sinner may, under whatever spiritual condition, draw nigh to God, and have communion with Him through the blood of the cross.

Chaps. viii.–x. contain the consecration of the priests, and show that our God is a consuming fire, not only to the offering on the altar, but to those who offer strange fire before the Lord.

In chap. xi. we are taught, by means of the lower creatures, to discriminate between clean and unclean, that we may partake of the one and avoid the other. The habits of the insect and animal world teach us to discern between good and evil; and everything that walks or flies, that swims or crawls, thus becomes a teacher instructing us how to please God in our daily life.

From chap. xii. we learn that the effects of the Fall are such that we cannot bear fruit without needing the atoning blood; and Luke ii. 22–24 shows that there is no exception to this rule, even though the fruit borne be absolutely holy.

While hitherto SIN has been spoken of as transgression, and as an inherent defilement, chaps. xiii. and xiv. reveal it as a deeply-seated and virulent disease, to be dealt with by the priest, and to be cleansed by the blood of the atonement.

The following chapter (xv.) shows that all the issues of the flesh are unclean, a truth which is further emphasised by Ezek. xliv. 17, 18, which forbids the priests to enter the inner court girded with anything that causeth sweat, because every exudation of the flesh is unclean, and unfit for the presence of the Holy One.

Chap. xvi., which prescribes the ordinances of the Great Day of Atonement, foreshows how all our iniquities and all our transgressions in all our sins, as soon as they are confessed, are atoned for and for ever put away; while comparison with Heb. x. shows that no provision of the law could really purge the conscience, which could in those days only be relieved as faith saw the promises from afar, and was persuaded of them, and embraced them. Thus Abraham saw the day of Christ, and was glad; and Moses esteemed the reproach of Christ greater riches than the treasures in Egypt.

That the life of all flesh is in the blood, and that the shed blood of the appointed sacrifice is that which maketh an atonement for the soul, constitute the teaching of chap. xvii.; and the prohibition to eat the blood, under the Law, which made nothing perfect, prepares the way for the precious truth, "My flesh is the true food, and My blood is the true drink," the life-giving food and drink of the soul (John vi. 55, R.V., marg.).

The relationships of life are used in chap. xviii. to teach us that respect for ourselves and for others which becomes those who have been redeemed by the precious blood of Christ to be the people of the Lord God.

The four chapters, xix.–xxii., contain statutes and precepts which are an amplification of the Ten Commandments and an anticipation of the Sermon on the Mount. Compare the last verse, so often repeated in Moses, and the Prophets, and the Psalms: "I am Jehovah that brought you out of the land of Egypt to be your God," with the confidence of Paul (Phil. i. 6), that He which hath begun the good work in us will perfect it until the day of Jesus Christ.

Then follow in chap. xxiii. the Feasts of the Lord: of which the Passover and the Pentecost, with their marvellous blessings, have fully come; while we wait yet a little while for the fulfilment of the Feast of Tabernacles.

The pure oil-olive beaten for the light, and the flour ground fine for the holy bread, prefigure the suffering Christ as the Light and Life. The stoning of the blasphemer proves that the Lord will not hold him guiltless that taketh His name in vain (xxiv.).

The great truths—that the land throughout the whole earth belongs to God, and that we are leaseholders under Him; that we rebel against Him if we oppress our weaker brother; that there is a fiftieth year, of which the shorter cycle of the fifty weeks was the precursor and the promise—a jubilee year of redemption and of everlasting joy—all this and much more is unfolded in chap. xxv. Then chap. xxvi. tells of judgment without mercy, and of mercy rejoicing against judgment, and foreshows how both shall be fulfilled. And the last chapter contains laws concerning vows and relating to things which men have sanctified to God.

Here is a divinely-inspired course of instruction and training as to our worship of God, our conduct to one another, and our use and treatment of the inferior creation; a scheme of education in religion and moral science, in history and prophecy, in personal and social purity.

We have named this last, because it is often said that it is better that children should grow up in ignorance of those things which make for purity or the reverse in our personal and relative habits of life. We ask, Would there be anything incompatible with the sacred relationship of parent and child, in making the Book of Leviticus a study? And if this were done, would not the children necessarily become, in the holiest way, acquainted with all that is necessary to be known in order to promote personal and social purity in our relation to God, our fellow-creatures, and the inferior creation?

Chap. I. Burnt-Offerings

In the last chapter of Exodus we read of how, on the Tabernacle being reared up, "the glory of the Lord filled the Tabernacle."

LEVITICUS begins by the Lord speaking unto Moses, "out of the tent of meeting" (R.V., *i.e.*, of meeting with God—and so always where A.V. has "tabernacle of the congregation"), for He is not now speaking "from heaven," as in Exod. xx. 22, but from the sanctuary which He has now condescended to make His dwelling-place (Exod. xxv. 8). As God is now dwelling in the midst of His people, it may well be said, "Bring an offering and come into His courts." Hence the early chapters of Leviticus contain the law of the OFFERINGS; for no will-worship is here permitted: as every earthly court has its own laws of ceremonial for approaching the sovereign, so must it be with the King of Israel. He who is to be worshipped must alone prescribe the mode and manner in which He is to be approached; the more so as these offerings and sacrifices are all intended to typify the great Offering and Sacrifice who is to appear "when the fulness of the time is come."

This chapter contains the law of the Burnt-offering, which presents the most general aspect of the work of Christ, that in which "through the Eternal Spirit He offered Himself without spot to God." Hence it was the leading characteristic of this burnt-offering that (as contrasted with others in which only the fat was placed upon the altar) the whole animal, the skin alone excepted, ascended up in fire and smoke, as it were, to God. The Hebrew word for burnt-offering comes from a root which means to ascend (*Alah*).

Mark five points which were prescribed as essential to a valid Offering. It must be: (1) *A perfect offering*, "a male without blemish"; (2) *at God's chosen place*, "the door of the tent of meeting," R.V. (*see* xvii. 3–6, for the penalty of infringing the law); (3) *with a definite object*, "that he may be accepted before the Lord," R.V. ("of his own voluntary will," A.V., is now rejected as a wrong translation); (4) *with a ceremony of identification*, "the laying-on of hands," typifying faith (*see* Heb. vi. 2); (5) *with priestly ministration* for sprinkling of the blood and burning the offering by fire unto the Lord.

Three grades of offering suited to the varying means of the worshipper (herd, flock, fowl) typify varying degrees of the believer's apprehension of the value of Christ's giving "Himself for us an offering and a sacrifice to God for a sweet-smelling savour."

Chap. II. Meal-Offerings

The subject of this chapter is the Meat-offering or (better in R.V.) Meal-offering, of fine flour, the type of the perfect character, the sinless nature of the Lord Jesus. Mark two accompaniments of this Offering: (1) "He shall pour oil upon it"; (2) "and shall put frankincense thereon": typifying how God anointed Jesus with the Holy Ghost, and how fragrant His perfect obedience ever was to God. "This is My beloved Son, in whom I am well-pleased" (Matt. iii. 17; xii. 18; xvii. 5).

As in the former chapter, so here and afterwards, no offering could be offered except through a priest, and that one of God's appointment. "He shall bring it to Aaron's sons, the priests" (2). So Jesus, after fulfilling in His own person and work all that was needed for offering and sacrifice, went up into the heavenly sanctuary as the true Priest, to carry out all needed priestly service for those "that come unto God by Him" (Heb. vii. 25).

Rome's self-appointed priests carry on their mummeries in a worldly sanctuary, which is an offence against God's dispensational arrangements ("he shall think to change times and laws," Dan. vii. 25), and a deliberate rejection of the priesthood of the Lord Jesus, "which passeth not from one to another" (Heb. vii. 24, *marg.*).

No leaven was permitted in the meal-offering (11); and of the Lord Jesus it is said (1 John iii. 5), "in Him is no sin." An exceptional case seems referred to (12), that of the firstfruits, in which, as in the thank-offering (vii. 13), as well as the Pentecostal loaves (xxiii. 17), typifying the Church, leaven was tolerated. "If we say that we have no sin, we deceive ourselves, and the truth is not in us" (1 John i. 8).

No meal-offering is permitted without salt (13); and no exception to this rule (as in the case of leaven) is recognized. Salt typifies grace (*see* Matt. v. 13; Col. iv. 6), and salt must never be absent: when leaven is present salt is specially requisite, for "it is the contrary of leaven"—*Speaker's Commentary*. (*See* Gal. v. 17: "These are contrary the one to the other.") A sinless Christian is a self-deception; but a graceless Christian is a self-contradiction.

Chap. III. Peace-Offerings

The Lord Jesus has been set forth in chap. i. as the burnt-offering in relation to God, and in chap. ii. as the meal-offering in relation to man. We are now to regard Him as the Peace-offering, to rectify the disturbed relations between God and man. The supplemental details as to the peace-offering in chap. vii. 11, &c., need to be combined with what we read here, in order to get a comprehensive view of the whole subject.

The leading characteristic of the peace-offering is—that, in addition to its strictly sacrificial nature, it supplied food to God in the fat burnt upon the altar (**16**); to the priests in those parts specially reserved for them (vii. 33, 34); and to the worshipper in the part which he might appropriate (vii. 15). Thus it was a feast upon a sacrifice which had effected reconciliation, and in which both parties reconciled took part, and with them the priest who officiated in effecting the reconciliation. A beautiful typical picture of the truth set forth in 1 John i. 3, 4: "Our fellowship is with the Father and with His Son Jesus Christ; and these things write we unto you, that your joy may be full."

Mark a solemn warning as to the need of holiness in maintaining communion with God, conveyed by the words (vii. 20), "The soul that eateth of the flesh of the sacrifice of peace-offerings that pertain unto the Lord, having his uncleanness upon him, even that soul shall be cut off from his people."

Chap. IV. Sin-Offerings

The subject of this chapter is the Sin-offering, and that in a fourfold adaptation to the case of: (1) the Priest; (2) the whole Congregation; (3) the Ruler; and (4) any one of the People. The distinction between 2 and 4 is that expressed by the words *collectively* and *individually*, hence the importance of the person and of the occasion calls for a "bullock" in the first two cases; whilst a "goat" suffices for the two latter. An able German writer on the offerings (Kurtz) notes this distinction between the burnt-offering, the peace-offering, and the Sin-offering. "*The act of burning*" was the culminating point of the burnt-offering. *The sacrificial meal* was the culminating point of the peace-offering. While that of the sin-offering was *the sprinkling of the blood*. Hence the special object of the sin-offering was expiation; all the rest fell into the background beside this sharply defined purpose."

Whilst the blood of the sin-offering for the priest or for the whole congregation (a bullock) was brought into the holy place and sprinkled "seven times before the Lord, before the vail of the sanctuary," the blood of the two inferior sin-offerings for the ruler or the individual (a goat) was only sprinkled on the horns of the brazen altar: in the former case Christ and His Church being more distinctly typified.

The character of the sin for which the sin-offering was permitted is expressed by the words, "through ignorance," A.V.; or "unwittingly," R.V.; and in *margin*, "through error." It is the word used of the unintentional man-slayer (Num. xxxv.), who "without enmity" or premeditation may kill a man. It distinguishes deliberate, wilful sin from that of which it may be said, "they know not what they do" (Luke xxiii. 34); of which sin the Apostle Peter could say, "I wot that through ignorance ye did it" (Acts iii. 17).

Chap. V. Trespass-Offerings

The subject of this chapter is the Trespass-offering, which bears the same relation to the sin-offering as the meat-offering or meal-offering of chap. ii. does to the burnt-offering of chap. i. As the meal-offering presented Christ's perfect manhood meeting all claims of human requirement, as a supplement to the burnt-offering which showed His satisfaction of God's claim—so the trespass-offering following the sin-offering, wherein God's estimate and judgment of sin in its relation to Himself are set forth, presents another aspect of sin in its injury to man; and so the trespass-offering carries with it as its leading idea the thought of compensation for injury inflicted.

The first five verses set forth different kinds of sins that came under the designation of trespass, such as a witness not divulging what he has seen or heard, when adjured to do so, &c., all of which more or less illustrate what Gesenius considers the root idea of the Hebrew word for trespass—viz., "Failure of duty, negligence." In addition to the sin itself against God which calls for a sin-offering on the altar, the injury which such negligence inflicts upon one's neighbour must be met by a compensation or payment of the sum which the neighbour may have lost by the injury inflicted, with a fifth part added as a fine.

The great lesson which the trespass-offering teaches us has been well put by the late Rev. William Howels: "I cannot offend any of my fellow-creatures without offending God. Every offence committed against man is primarily to be considered an offence against God. Our soliciting and conferring forgiveness of and upon each other is oft-times little more than collusion amongst thieves. God is forgotten altogether; and there is often a vast deal of hypocrisy and deceit, malice, and envy inhabiting the bosom, while we are lying with our tongues to God and to each other. We sometimes hear of two individuals who cannot agree: at length we hear of their being reconciled. It requires but half an eye to see that they hate each other profoundly, notwithstanding their professed reconciliation. Do any of you know what this is? Let me advise you to lose sight of each other immediately, and consider yourselves but as dust and ashes; and whatever offences you may have committed against each other, consider them primarily as offences against God."

CHAP. VI. **The Offerings**—*Continued*

The first seven verses continue the subject of the Trespass-offering, and properly belong to chap. v., as in the Hebrew Bible. The view of the trespass-offering, just presented in the extract above, is confirmed by the words, "If a soul sin, and *commit a trespass against the Lord*, and lie unto his neighbour," &c., followed by various injuries to man. The restoration of the principal, with a fifth part added, might be compensation to the injured neighbour; but the trespass, viewed in its relation to God, requires that "he shall bring his trespass-offering unto the Lord" (6).

Then follow (8-13) some laws bearing upon the burnt-offering, with special reference to the perpetual fire to be kept upon the altar. "The fire shall ever be burning upon the altar; it shall never go out." As the fire originally came down from God (ix. 24), so was it to be kept up as a symbol of His never-ceasing satisfaction with that great offering and sacrifice of which these Levitical offerings were but types and shadows. The word used for burning upon the altar is a different word from that used for the fierce devouring flame that consumed the sin-offering outside the camp (iv. 12): *that* symbolized the wrath of God against sin; while *this* symbolizes God's satisfaction with the offering, on which His justice could, as it were, feed. See iii. 11: "It is the food of the offering made by fire unto the Lord."

The peculiar sanctity of the flesh of the sin-offering is pointed out in the last verses of the chapter (**24–30**). This seems to have been intended to emphasize the fact that when the real Sin-offering should be offered, who should "once at the end of the world appear to put away sin by the sacrifice of Himself" (Heb. ix. 26), there should be sin on Him, but no sin in Him. "Him *who knew no sin* He made to be sin on our behalf" (2 Cor. v. 21, R.V.). Hence the peculiar holiness of the flesh of the sin-offering. The Lord Jesus never appears in such absolute perfection of holiness as on Calvary. He was always "the Holy One of God." On Calvary He appears as "the Most Holy," for it was the climax of His obedience (Phil. ii. 8).

CHAP. VII. **The Offerings**—*Continued*

This chapter continues the instructions to the priests, as to the laws of the respective offerings. The trespass-offering, as being an extension of the sin-offering, shares with it the characteristic noticed above, of the flesh thereof being "most holy" (*see* **6** and **7**). Our Lord seems to speak as the trespass-offering when He says (in spirit, through David), "Then I restored that which I took not away" (Ps. lxix. 4), immediately afterwards appropriating the language of the sin-offering: "My sins are not hid from Thee"; though He who thus speaks is personally "most holy"—"the holy of God." When imputed sin is contemplated, it is the more necessary to emphasize the absolute holiness and sinlessness of the Sin-bearer, lest it should be thought that the sin spoken of is His in any other sense than imputatively.

At verse **11** commences the subject of the law of the peace-offerings, containing additional and supplemental directions to those given in chap. iii. They are classified as (1) Thank-offerings; (2) Vow-offerings; and (3) Voluntary offerings. The recognition of "leavened bread" (**13**), along with and supplemental to "unleavened bread," in the thank-offering, seems to point to the presence of sin in the worshipper, though "not imputed" by virtue of the sinlessness of Him whom the sacrifice with its unleavened bread prefigured.

The prohibition as to the flesh of the thank-offerings, or vow, or voluntary offerings remaining beyond the morrow of the day of the sacrifice, has been explained by some as denoting that the sacrificial food was "not to be polluted by any approach to putrefaction." Others think that it was to enforce a "liberal distribution of the food, particularly amongst the poor." Perhaps an allusion to the great Antitype is the most satisfactory explanation, viewed in the light of Ps. xvi. 10.

Chap. VIII. Consecration of Priests

This and the two following chapters (ix. and x.) contain an account of the inauguration of the Tabernacle service by the consecration of Aaron and his sons to the priest's office; and their commencement of sacrifice, which was at once owned of God by the descent of the sacred fire (ix. 24). It is "the only historical portion of the Book of Leviticus, with the exception of the short narrative of the death of the blasphemer."

As the consecration of Aaron and his sons to the priesthood was a ceremony in which "all the congregation" were directly interested, as the priesthood was to represent them in all sacrificial action before God—so all were summoned to (or towards) the door of the Tabernacle. As the ceremony lasted for a week (33), there would be time for all in turn to see something of what was going on. It was of the utmost importance that the divinely-appointed distinction between the priesthood and the people should be clearly seen. It is a common mistake to suppose, from Exod. xix. 5, 6, that Israel had been set apart as a "royal priesthood." What was then offered was conditional upon their obeying God's voice indeed and keeping His covenant. But this they failed to do. And so the house of Aaron was taken out of the nation, and set apart to discharge the priestly office on behalf of the people, as types and shadows of a better priesthood, which should be in due time brought in in the person and work of God's anointed One.

Aaron's descendants are the only sacrificial priests whom God has ever recognized on earth. Christians, in virtue of their union to

Christ and their anointing in Him, are spiritually priests; but their sphere of service is heavenly, not earthly. The sacerdotalism which prevails in the professing Church is a grievous sin before God, and as presumptuous a rebellion against God's appointment as was the rebellion of Korah. Its coming doom is clearly pointed out (Jude 11) as similar to that of Korah.

Mark the identification of Aaron's sons with him in their consecration. "Ye are an holy priesthood, to offer up spiritual sacrifices, acceptable to God by Jesus Christ" (1 Pet. ii. 5).

CHAP. IX. **Priestly Sacrifices**

The consecration of Aaron and his sons lasted seven days. On the eighth day (symbolizing the resurrection, when the priesthood of Christ first came into operation) Aaron offered sacrifices first for himself, then for the people: this, with his blessing the people which followed (23), and fire coming "out from before the Lord" (24) to consume the sacrifice, form the subject of this chapter.

"It was" (the *Speaker's Commentary* says) "a striking acknowledgment of the true character of the Levitical priesthood, that the very first official act of the anointed priest should be to offer a sacrifice for his own sinful nature. 'The law maketh men high priests which have infirmity; but the word of the oath, which was since the law, maketh the Son, who is consecrated (*marg.* perfected) for evermore' (Heb. vii. 28)."

In the offerings for the people (15-21), we have *the order* in which any combination of different offerings should be presented to God: (1) Sin-offering; (2) Burnt-offering; (3) Meat-offering; (4) Peace-offering. The double blessing of verses 22 and 23 is worthy of note. First, that of Aaron alone, who, when he offered the offerings, "lifted up his hand toward the people and blessed them." Then he and Moses retire for a short time into the Tabernacle, and together come out and unitedly bless the people; and then, and not till then, does the glory of the Lord appear. So Christ as Priest, after offering His offering and sacrifice, pronounced His first blessing: "He lifted up His hands, and blessed them" (Luke xxiv. 50). He then entered into the holy place not made with hands, whence we look for Him to come again as King and Priest united in one person, when He will pronounce the final blessing, and then shall the glory of the Lord appear (*comp.* Heb. ix. 24 and 28).

For fire coming down from the Lord to consume the sacrifice as indicating His acceptance of it, *see* Judges vi. 21, xiii. 20; 1 Kings xviii. 38; 1 Chron. xxi. 26; 2 Chron. vii. 1. The fire which thus "came out from before the Lord" was maintained as a perpetual fire, as directed in vi. 13.

CHAP. X. "Strange Fire"

The great majority of commentators, Jewish as well as Christian, regard the sin of Nadab and Abihu (1) as consisting in not using the sacred fire which "came out from before the Lord," as that with which alone incense should be burned. It is probable from xvi. 12 that injunctions had been given that from the time the sacred fire came forth from God, none other should be used for incense. Thus we are taught the striking lesson that the very fire of God which had come forth to testify His acceptance of the sacrifice became a fire of judgment to those who slighted its value by offering other fire with their incense. So the Spirit of God which came down at Pentecost to testify to the acceptance of Christ's offering and sacrifice became a spirit of judgment to Ananias and Sapphira, who worshipped God with the strange fire of their own corrupt hearts, which Satan had filled with deceit, rather than with the fire of the Holy Spirit (Acts v.). Natural piety or ecclesiastical will-worship cannot be accepted of God. "They that worship Him must worship Him in spirit and in truth" (John iv. 24). How much of the religion of Christendom is but strange fire calling for judgment from Him who says!—"I will be sanctified in them that come nigh Me, and before all the people I will be glorified" (3).

The prohibition following, as to the priests drinking wine or strong drink when going into the Tabernacle (9), makes it probable that these two sons of Aaron were under the influence of strong drink when they committed this sin.

The other two sons of Aaron, probably under a sense of their unworthiness (19), as their father explains it, neglected to carry out the law of vi. 26 as to eating the flesh of the sin-offering in the holy place. They are excused on account of the circumstances which Aaron pleads in mitigation of their offence. As two of his sons had been cut off by Divine judgment, so two are spared by Divine forbearance.

Chap. XI. **Clean and Unclean**

As creation has fallen under the bondage of corruption owing to the sin of man (Rom. viii. 20, 21), the animal kingdom, in many of its forms and creatures, bears the image of sin, so that man instinctively loathes and rejects certain animals as food, and especially those creeping things that come near in appearance to the serpent, on whom was pronounced the curse (Gen. iii. 14). Hence the Lord, to inculcate lessons of holiness upon His people, uses as outward signs (or object-lessons) abstinence from certain animals which typified moral and spiritual evil, and gives permission to use as food those which typified holiness and spiritual life. As a rule, all creeping things were forbidden (**41**) as typifying the grovelling instincts of sinful, fallen man, under the influence of the old serpent, the devil. Two things, when combined, marked animals that might be eaten (**3**), "Whatsoever parteth the hoof and cheweth the cud." These point to the two distinguishing characteristics of the people of God. One of these is Faith, which grasps the promises and mounts up on high, as animals with parted hoofs grasp the rocks and mount up by this means (*see* Hab. iii. 19; Ps. xviii. 33, "He maketh my feet like hinds' feet, and setteth me upon my high places"). And the other is meditation on the Word of God, as the ruminating animal "chews the cud" (*see* Joshua i. 8, and Ps. i. 2: "In His law doth he meditate day and night").

It is a remarkable thing that it is in connection with these prohibitions to eat creeping things, which typify the grovelling character of the natural mind, that God reveals His "holy commandment" (2 Pet. ii. 21), "Be ye holy; for I am holy" (**44**; 1 Pet. i. 15, 16). The holiness inculcated is therefore heavenly. Where there is no faith to mount to high places, nor feeding on the Word and meditation therein, there cannot be the holiness which God commands, though there may be strict morality.

Chap. XII. Purification

Short as is this chapter, the lesson it teaches is far-reaching and important. It points back to the Fall (Gen. iii.), and emphasizes the connection there established between birth and sin. "Behold, I was shapen in iniquity, and in sin did my mother conceive me" (Ps. li. 5). In these days, when the consequences of the Fall are so often either denied or ignored, it is well to be reminded that what is taught in Gen. iii. 16 is recognized in God's law to Israel, and should be recognized by each one of us in our own case, as by David in his.

It is worthy of note that the ceremonial uncleanness which thus called for purification did not attach to the child, but to the mother, perhaps as showing that until the age of responsibility sin is not imputed (*see* Rom. v. 13). Nevertheless, the irresponsibility of the age of infancy does not alter the fact of the inherent sinfulness of infancy ("by nature the children of wrath," Eph. ii. 3). It only postpones personal responsibility till the age of consciousness.

Israel, therefore, was taught that not death alone, but even birth should be regarded as involving uncleanness needing purification. Bähr explains it thus: "Birth and death are the two poles within which the sinful and curse-stricken life of humanity moves. By birth the sinful life of man is brought into existence; by death it is brought to an end: hence birth comes under the same aspect of uncleanness as death itself." Job's lamentation over the day of his birth as the commencement of his life of sorrow may illustrate this (Job. iii.).

There is one birth, however, that has brought in an antidote to all this evil and a remedy for all this distress. *See* 1 Tim. ii. 15, R.V., "the child-bearing": which Bishop Ellicott explains to mean that "the peculiar function of her sex, from its relation to her Saviour, shall be the medium of salvation" to woman as well as to man. Let us observe that to Mary the mother of our Lord was granted no exception with regard to the law of purification (Luke ii. 22). In face of this fact, the Romish fiction of the immaculate conception falls to the ground.

Chap. XIII. On Leprosy

Leprosy was a sort of living death, involving, not only exclusion from the fellowship of the sanctuary, but exclusion from the fellowship of the living. "Consequently the process of restoration consisted of two stages."

First (1–59) re-admission to the fellowship of the living, depending on the cure of the disease, which God alone could effect. Secondly (xiv. 1–32) re-admission to the camp and to the sanctuary, depending on the due performance of the prescribed rites of purification.

This chapter is wholly occupied with the former of these, and consists of a very detailed enumeration of the signs and tokens by which the various stages of the disease might be discerned. Viewed as a type of sin, there are some striking coincidences between the signs of an approaching cure as discernible in leprosy, and in that terrible evil, sin, which it typifies. *See* especially **12, 13:** "If a leprosy break out abroad in the skin, and the leprosy cover all the skin of him that hath the plague from his head even to his foot (*comp.* Isa. i. 5, 6) wheresoever the priest looketh; then the priest shall consider: and, behold, if the leprosy have covered all his flesh, he shall pronounce him clean that hath the plague: it is all turned white: he is clean."

Isaiah was commissioned to act as a priest to Israel as a nation in detecting that there was "no soundness in it; but wounds, and bruises, and putrefying sores" (Isa. i. 6–17); but he was also empowered to proclaim an approaching cleansing for all who would avail themselves of the proffered mercy: "Come now, and let us reason together, saith the Lord: though your sins be as scarlet, they shall be as white as snow; though they be red like crimson, they shall be as wool" (Isa. i. 18).

God's priests of this dispensation, those who "have an anointing from the Holy One, and know all things" (1 John ii. 20, R.V.), ought to be quick to discern that deep conviction of sin which enables them to pronounce by anticipation that the sin-convinced sinner is clean.

CHAP. XIV. **Cleansing the Leper**

When the disease was pronounced cured, or so far on its way to a cure that it might anticipatively be pronounced clean, then commenced the rite of the leper's purification: firstly, in relation to his restoration to the fellowship of the living, or his return to the camp **(1–9)**; secondly, in relation to the fellowship of the Sanctuary **(10–20)**, or his re-admission to the Tabernacle. In the type of the two birds (**4**) we see foreshadowed the death and resurrection of Christ as the only real delivering and restoring power for the sinner. Two birds were necessary to carry on the type of resurrection after death. This was done by the living bird dipped in the blood of the other being let loose into the open field; as John Newton explains it:—

> "Dipped in his fellow's blood,
>   The living bird went free:
> The type well understood
>   Expressed the sinner's plea;
> Described a guilty soul enlarged
> And by a Saviour's death discharged."

The sprinkling of the cleansed leper seven times took place outside the camp; and its effect was to restore him to the camp, but not as yet to his tent (**8**): that was only effected after seven days, and as the result of further personal purification. Finally, restoration to the Sanctuary (**10, 11**) was effected on the eighth day, when he was anointed on the tip of the right ear, right hand, and right foot, with the blood of the trespass-offering, and then with oil (a sort of priestly consecration; *see* viii. 24). This twofold purification, thus separated in the type by seven days, is typical of the twofold privilege which the Christian enjoys by virtue of faith in Christ—justification, and sanctification. Not only "washed (or freed) from our sins in His own blood," but "made kings and priests unto God" (Rev. i. 5, 6).

The remarkable case of leprosy in a house (**34-48**) and its appointed cleansing (**52**), may have been intended, as supposed by some, to teach important lessons as to church discipline, and putting away of evil from the congregation; but it is prefaced by a confession of evil which churches of the present day are slow to make: "It seemeth to me there is as it were a plague in the house" (**35**). If there were more of such confession of evil, our ecclesiastical houses would be the sooner cleansed.

CHAP. XV. **On Cleansing**

The ceremonial defilements here calling for purification were of a far less serious character than leprosy, and were for the most part little more than natural infirmities. Nevertheless, they were treated as involving uncleanness, on account of the especial holiness required of Israel, as "God's Tabernacle was among them." Hence provision was made in the rites of purification here prescribed, to "separate the children of Israel from their uncleanness, that they die not in their uncleanness when they defile My Tabernacle that is among them" **(31)**. As the means of purification consisted in divers washings and sometimes sacrifices **(14–29)**, they typified the cleansing of sin effected by that "precious blood of Christ" (1 Pet. i. 19), to which all these Levitical purifications pointed.

The less serious character of the defilement arising from sins of infirmity often tempts the Christian to regard them as in less need of cleansing by means of Christ's blood than the more serious outbreaks of sin, the defilement from which is undeniable. The teaching of this chapter should therefore lead us to value the more, and by faith to sprinkle our consciences the more, with the blood of the Lord Jesus Christ, which "cleanseth us from all sin" (1 John i. 7).

Let us be warned by the teaching of this chapter to palliate no sin by regarding it as mere natural infirmity. Let us seek more of the teaching of God's Holy Spirit to see sin as He sees it, and to own it as He would have us do.

Chap. XVI. The Holy Place

One of the most important chapters in the whole Bible. It describes the ceremonies of the Day of Atonement, the most solemn day of the whole year; the only day on which the Holy of Holies—type of "heaven itself" (Heb. ix. 24)—was entered by the high priest, "not without blood, which he offered for himself and for the errors of the people" (Heb. ix. 7).

Mark the contrast between the high priest of Israel, "after the flesh," and our "great High Priest." The former, being a sinner, must first offer sacrifice for himself, before he could offer for the people **(11–14)**; and this double offering must be repeated every year: whereas, our High Priest, having no sin of His own, offers but Himself, once for all; an offering never to be repeated. Hence the abiding results of His once-offered sacrifice, which admits of no repetition, and secures "eternal inheritance" (Heb. ix. 15). Those, therefore, who are truly trusting in Him as their Priest not only need no further repetition in any form of the once-offered sacrifice, but dare not insult the majesty of His eternal Priesthood by recognizing any earthly sacerdotal priesthood that pretends to obtrude itself into the sphere of His sacrificial service. These words (17) should be noted, "There shall be no man in the Tabernacle of the congregation when he (the high priest) goeth in to make an atonement in the holy place, until he come out, and have made an atonement for himself, and for his household, and for all the congregation of Israel." All priestly function of every kind was to be suspended, the Tabernacle itself (the sphere of sacrificial service) was to be deserted, *until he came out* (Heb. ix. 28).

Observe too that the scapegoat was not offered as a sacrifice, but was a second goat (like the second bird, xiv. 4–7) added to complete the type by showing the efficacy of the sacrifice of the first goat. It bearing away into a "land of separation" (*marg.*) the sins confessed over its head finds its correspondence in "their sins and their iniquities will I remember no more" (Heb. viii. 12).

CHAP. XVII. **At the Tabernacle Door**

An important chapter, viewed as a supplement to the last. If the blood even of bulls and goats was to prefigure such a wonderful result as that expressed in the words of xvi. 30, "That ye may be clean from all your sins before the Lord," how carefully must its sanctity be guarded from common use, so that its sacrificial efficacy may be duly recognized! The typical significance of the blood is expressed thus (11): "For the life (Heb. 'soul') is in the blood: and I have given it to you upon the altar to make atonement for your souls: for it is the blood that maketh atonement *by reason of the life* (Heb. 'soul')," R.V. The italics mark the improved rendering of the Revised Version, which throws light on the whole passage, as showing that the atoning efficacy of the blood lay in the life it contained.

But mark carefully that it was in the life *poured out*, not in the veins, wherein the atoning efficacy lay. This is an important point, and refutes the notion that the blood of Christ means the life of Christ. The word for "life" when used of Christ's life is a different word, both in Hebrew and Greek, from that here used. The word here is "soul." The same word is found in Isa. liii. 12, where its meaning cannot be mistaken: "He hath poured out His soul unto death."

THE BOOK OF LEVITICUS 113

It is, then, the death of Christ, not the life of Christ, which is meant when His blood is spoken of, and no better parallel can be found to explain the meaning of "The blood of Jesus Christ His Son cleanseth us from all sin," than that of Lev. xvi. 30, of which (in the Greek version) the Rev. H. C. G. Moule remarks, "This is a close and impressive verbal parallel to 1 John i. 7."

CHAP. XVIII. **Admonitions**

The subject of this chapter is an expansion of its opening words, in which, after assigning as a motive, "I am the Lord your God," the Lord says, "After the doings of the land of Egypt, wherein ye dwelt, shall ye not do: and after the doings of the land of Canaan, whither I bring you, shall ye not do" **(2, 3)**.

Had Israel been faithful to the orders received to drive out the nations of Canaan, there would have been less necessity for the latter part of the above command; but He who could foresee their failure in this respect warns them of the danger which the Canaanites whom they had failed to drive out would prove. "They shall be snares and traps unto you" (Joshua xxiii. 13). So it is with the professing Church. She has become mingled with the world to such an extent that Christians need to be warned, not only not to do after the doings of the ungodly world, out of which they have come, but also not to do after the doings of the professing Church into which they have come.

The various unlawful marriages and offences against purity which are here forbidden, exhibit both the low state of morality of the heathen world, and the uncompromising opposition thereto of God's holiness. The sanction on which the whole code rests is—"I am the Lord your God" **(2, 30)**. With this the chapter begins, and with this it ends.

Let us in all our efforts to "follow holiness, without which no man shall see the Lord" (Heb. xii. 14), remember that in these words, "I am the Lord your God," we have not only a motive, but also a power. Hence we read (xx. 7, 8) not only "sanctify yourselves," but also "I am the Lord which sanctify you." This power of sanctification which the Lord is to His people is spoken of in 1 Thess. iv. 7, 8, in a passage which may well be quoted as a New Testament commentary on this chapter: "God hath not called us unto uncleanness, but unto holiness. He therefore that despiseth, despiseth not man, but God, *who hath also given unto us His Holy Spirit.*"

CHAP. XIX. Further Admonitions

The many detached prohibitions and commands which this chapter contains have no perceptible connection beyond being all of them practical directions as to holiness of walk in matters of everyday life. They are introduced with the reason, urged in chapter xi. 44, "Ye shall be holy, for I the Lord your God am holy." Could there be a stronger motive than this as an incentive to holiness? Let us observe that the eighth commandment is expanded in verse **11,** so as virtually to forbid cheating and lying. In cheating we rob a neighbour of truthful dealing, to which he has a right at our hands; and in lying we rob him of truthful speaking, to which he is rightly entitled from us.

The prohibition in verse **16,** "Neither shalt thou stand against the blood of thy neighbour," has been variously explained—probably, Keil's explanation is the best. He treats it as a prohibition against conspiracy against a neighbour's life: "Thou shalt not set thyself against the blood of a neighbour"—*i.e.*, to seek his life. Thus it would appropriately follow the prohibition against talebearing, which is the prelude to strife, variance, and enmity. The spiritual meaning of the prohibitions in verse **19,** "not to mix things which are separated in God's creation," is clear from 2 Cor. vi. 14-18.

CHAP. XX. Against Idolatry and Vice

Various forms of wickedness are forbidden in this chapter, the ground of such prohibition being—the holiness expected of Israel as a people of whom Jehovah could say, "I have severed you from, other peoples, that ye should be Mine" **(26)**. When this new relationship to Him was clearly seen, the argument arising from God's own character was irresistible: "Ye shall be holy unto Me, for I the Lord am holy." For the *third time* we have the injunction to holiness in this form: (7: *comp.* xi. 44; xix. 2). Observe the twice repeated "I have separated you from other peoples" **(24, 26)**. Mark also the type (creeping things) in **25,** where the carnal-minded heathen from whom Israel has been separated correspond to unclean things creeping on the ground. To eat such unclean food was typically to associate with or find pleasure in the morally unclean people and ways of heathendom.

New Testament exhortations to holiness are likewise grounded on the separation which redemption effects between a world that "lieth in the wicked one" and those of whom the Apostle John can say, "We know that we are of God" (1 John v. 19): and if this separation is not admitted, much of the teaching of Scripture as to holiness loses its point and power. The universalism of the day, which ignores the distinction between the Church and the world, loses thereby the chief Scriptural motive to holiness. We hear much of "humanity" and of what it is capable; but little of separation from it as a fallen and corrupt race, out of whose guilt and coming doom believers have been delivered, to be "a chosen generation, a royal priesthood, an holy nation"—"a people for God's own possession, that ye may show forth the excellences of Him who called you out of darkness into His marvellous light" (1 Pet. ii. 9, R.V.). Compare with this, as parallel to the subject of our chapter, 1 Pet. i. 15, 16, R.V.: "As He which called you is holy, be ye yourselves also holy in all manner of living; because it is written, Ye shall be holy; for I am holy."

CHAP. XXI. **Laws for the Priests**

This chapter contains laws of Holiness for the Priests. "The priest's family was to be the model of purity." Priests were forbidden (1–4) to contract defilement by contact with the dead, except in the case of their own immediate family—the exceptions being father, mother, son, daughter, brother, and unmarried sister. It will be observed that celibacy was no law for God's priesthood, though it is for that of Rome.

The reason for the holiness of the priesthood, as given in verses **6** and **8**, is their being appointed to offer the bread (or "food": it includes whatever was offered on the altar by fire) of their God. Those who were appointed to convey to God that whereon He (typically) fed, must be themselves holy. "The offerings of the Lord made by fire, the bread of their God, they do offer: therefore they shall be holy" (**6**, R.V.).

Any physical blemish disqualified a priest from offering the food of God to Him, though he might partake of such food himself (21)—*i.e.*, such parts as were reserved for priests. How often are Christians debarred by their spiritual blemishes from offering to God those sacrifices with which He is well pleased (Heb. xiii. 15, 16), though mercifully not debarred from feeding on the portion which He assigns them. They may receive; but they must not offer. All such disqualifying blemishes should be avoided by the royal priesthood; and where they exist—healing, which happily is not beyond reach—should be sought. The first two disqualifying blemishes are blindness and lameness. Compare, as to the remedy for these, Rev. iii. 18: "Anoint thine eyes with eyesalve that thou mayest see"; and Heb. xii. 13; "That which is lame . . . let it rather be healed."

CHAP. XXII. **Holiness**

Another aspect of the holiness which God requires in those who draw nigh to Him is presented to us in this chapter. Not only were priests to abstain from things that would defile them, but when they themselves happened to be defiled by infirmity (4), or contact with "uncleanness" (5) they were to abstain from contact with holy things, lest they should defile that which is holy.

A practical application of this principle would make Christians—members of the royal priesthood—careful lest they themselves happen to be in an unspiritual state, and so contract defilement of conscience, thus communicating their defilement to others. Let them rather "cleanse themselves from all filthiness of the flesh and spirit, perfecting holiness in the fear of God" (2 Cor. vii. 1); and then they will be fit companions for the "sons and daughters of the Lord Almighty," of whom God has said: "I will dwell in them, and walk in them; and I will be their God, and they shall be My people" (2 Cor. vi. 16–18).

The priest who happened to be defiled was not, however, cut off from contact with that which was to be his food, holy though it was, if only he first "wash his flesh in water; and when the sun is down he shall be clean, and shall afterward eat of the holy things; *because it is his food*" (7). So let not any sense of defilement hinder the believer from repentance and faith in the "precious blood of Christ," which is the New Testament fulfilment of the injunction: "Wash you; make you clean; put away the evil of your doings from before Mine eyes" (Isa. i. 16). Then let him appropriate all the soul-sustaining virtue of Christ as the bread of life, *"because it is his food."*

CHAP. XXIII. **The Feasts**

We have in this chapter a detailed account of the "feasts (or appointed times) of the Lord"—set feasts, R.V. These are seven: (1) The weekly Sabbath; (2) Passover; (3) Feast of Unleavened Bread; (4) Pentecost; (5) Feast of Trumpets; (6) Day of Atonement; (7) Feast of Tabernacles. Of these the three latter occurred all of them in the seventh month of the year, and the one before them, Pentecost, was connected, as a supplement, with the feasts of the first month, Passover and Unleavened Bread. So that virtually the Jewish year was divided into nearly two equal parts by the feasts of the first and of the seventh months, at each of which times the feasts clustered round a sacrifice of the highest importance: the first group round the Passover, the second round the Day of Atonement, each striking types of the sacrificial death of the Lord Jesus.

But each of these, the Passover and the Day of Atonement, presented a different aspect of the work of Christ. The Passover, which commemorated Israel's deliverance from Egypt, presented a type of Christ's death viewed as deliverance from the power of Satan, the prince of this world. The Day of Atonement sacrifice, which gave the high priest admittance within the vail into God's presence, typified the death of Christ as opening up heaven itself, and bringing His people near to God. We have both aspects combined in 1 Pet. iii. 18. Mark the ordinance of the sheaf of firstfruits connected with the Passover, to be waved before the Lord "on the morrow after the Sabbath" (**11**): this represents "Christ risen from the dead, the firstfruits of them that slept." The two wave loaves for firstfruits offered unto the Lord fifty days after represent the Church on the day of Pentecost—"a kind of firstfruits of His creatures" (Jas i. 18).

CHAP. XXIV. **The Lamps and Shewbread**

The first nine verses of this chapter describe Aaron's duties and responsibilities with regard to providing and tending the oil used for the lamps in the holy place, as well as the shewbread there to be set forth upon the table. Though the children of Israel were to bring "pure oil olive," the responsibility for seeing that it was provided, and for "ordering" it when provided, was laid upon Aaron. "It appears that the responsibility of keeping up the lights rested on the high priest."

Would that we who are called to "shine as lights in the world, holding forth the word of life" (Phil. ii. 15, 16), could bear this more in mind; and so, instead of trying ourselves to shine by our own efforts, go more frequently to our great High Priest, who is responsible, and draw upon His resources: then should we find that "the excellency of the power" (for *shining*, see 2 Cor. iv. 6, 7) is "of God and not of us."

From the 10th verse to the end, there is narrated the death of the blasphemer—the result of a mixed marriage thus implicitly condemned—and in the mode of his public execution by stoning we learn a valuable lesson as to the meaning of "the laying-on of hands" (*see* 14), "let all that heard him lay their hands upon his head." The sin was thus put back upon him who committed it by those who, having heard him, were responsible. So he is made to "bear his sin" (15), which involved its immediate judicial punishment.

The condemnation of murder and injury which follows (7–22) seems intended to discriminate between the judicial punishment, by the death penalty, of sin deserving it, and that killing which, if without judicial sanction, is but murder.

Chap. XXV. The Jubilee

The Sabbatic year was appointed for a rest to the land, and also in order that its spontaneous produce that year should be a gift to servants, strangers, and cattle (Exod. xxiii. 10), the rights of the owners being apparently suspended for that time, and their wants being supplied by a special blessing from God upon the sixth year, which (21) was to produce enough for three years.

The year of Jubilee (8–17), at the end of seven times seven years, or every fiftieth year, was to be a universal release to all debtors and dispossessed owners: thus once in the average life of every Israelite he would see around him a shadow of good things to come.

"Ye who have sold for nought
　Your heritage above,
Shall have it back unbought,
　The gift of Jesus' love:
The year of jubilee is come;
Return, ye ransomed sinners, home!"

It is apparently to the sounding of the Jubilee trumpet (9) that Ps. lxxxix. 15 refers: "Blessed is the people that know the joyful sound"; for the word for "joyful sound" is that used of the Jubilee "trumpet."

The Jubilee Year not only brought restoration of the land to those who, through debt or poverty, had sold it away; but the expectation of the Jubilee Year was to diminish the value of the land as the time drew nigh (16).

So should the expectation of the Lord's Second Coming, the true redemption Jubilee, which so many signs attest to be nigh, diminish the value we are apt to attach to the world, and the things that are in the world (1 John ii. 15–17).

A principle of the greatest importance to Israel is contained in verse 23, "The land shall not be sold for ever; for the land is Mine: for ye are strangers and sojourners with Me."

When the Lord returns to claim His own, then, and not till then, will Israel be put in possession of the land by an indefeasible title, and that by One who can say, "The land is Mine."

The Jubilee Year

The Jubilee Year! the Jubilee Year!
The bondman rejoices to hail thee near;
Sevenfold Sabbath, and Year of Grace,
The burdened, and weary, and poor, to bless.

'Tis the Day of Atonement! The utmost bound
Of Israel's land hears "the joyful sound"
Of the silver trumpet, so loud and clear,
Proclaim the gladsome Jubilee Year.

Fifty years' burdens of sorrow and wrong
Fall from their shoulders; and homeward they throng
To their fathers' possession, their childhood's home:
Like doves to their windows, they come, they come.

The fraud and the folly, the struggle and strife,
Of half-a-century's human life,
The usurer's riches, the poor man's cares,
Are all dissolved by this Year of years.

To Moses Jehovah rehearsed the tale
Of the glories hidden within the vail;
In Jeshurun's ears did their king recount
The things he had seen in the Holy Mount:

Shadows on earth of the things above,
The Father's grace, and the Brother's love;
Promise of glorious things to come,
The enduring substance, the Heavenly Home.

Deliverer, Jesus, my Friend, in Thee
Jubilee, Sabbath, and Home, I see:
Thou hast wearily laboured that I might rest;
Thy soul was afflicted—and I am blest.

The atonement is made, and the trumpet's voice
Bids every sinner, "Rejoice! Rejoice!"
The Gospel proclaims an eternal release,
And bids the debtor go home in peace.

O God, for grace not to set our love
On the earthly things, but the things above!
For while the Jubilee Year draws nigh,
They lessen in value, they fade and die.

In a little while shall the firmament ring
With the trumpet that heralds earth's patient King,
Who has sat so long at His Father's side,
That the world may know how He loved and died.

What then shall profit the stores of wealth,
Whether justly gotten or gained by stealth?
When every object of man's desire,
In the flaming flood rising ever higher,
Proclaims our God a consuming fire!

CHAP. XXVI. **Warnings**

This chapter contains an epitome of Israel's future history. *First,* we are reminded of their failure to obtain the blessings promised to obedience (**1-13**); but the fulfilment of this part of the chapter may be looked for hereafter, when the nation is restored and converted. *Secondly,* of their successive downward steps of sin and rebellion, culminating in the horrors of the siege (**29**), and consequent desolation (**32**), and dispersion among the nations (**33**).

Mark five successive warnings ("if ye will not") in verses **14, 18, 21, 23, 27,** each followed by a threat of increased punishments. These are: (1) Deliverance into the hands of their enemies; (2) Scarcity; (3) Wild Beasts; (4) Pestilence and Famine; (5) Horrors of Siege and Desolation: followed by sharp distress in their dispersion. The Book of Judges illustrates the first—and the destruction of Jerusalem by Titus the last—of these judgments.

There is a remarkable expression used in **41**, and again in **43**— "Accept of the punishment of their iniquity": as though God's controversy with Israel was as to their not owning and accepting their true position as guilty in His sight. We see them thus in Zech. xii. 10, accepting their guilt, especially as to having "with wicked hands crucified and slain" the Son of God. This will be the prelude to their blessing.

The last words of the chapter seem intended to close the book, the next chapter being afterwards added as supplemental. The concluding verse sums up all the previous "statutes, judgments, and laws" which the Lord made between Him and the children of Israel in Mount Sinai "*by the hand of Moses.*" Is it not to this that St. Paul refers (Gal. iii. 19), when he uses the very phrase "in (or, 'by,' R.V.) the hand of a mediator"? If so (and as we think), the assertion here of there being two parties to the covenant "between Him and the children of Israel" suggested St. Paul's comment: a "mediator is not a mediator of one; but God is one": *i.e.,* the Abrahamic covenant was unconditional, a covenant of gift involving but one party—the Giver. The law, on the other hand, is a covenant of works; and the failure of one party to the covenant is the failure of the whole. Thank God, believers in Jesus are "not under law, but under grace."

Chap. XXVII. Redemption

The redemption by money-payment of persons, or things, which had been consecrated by vow to the Lord, forms the subject of this chapter. As to vows in general, *see* Deut. xxiii. 21.

"The vow of a person was perhaps most frequently made in cases of illness or danger. A man might dedicate himself, his wife, his child, or his bond-servant, on condition of recovery or deliverance."

In viewing the valuation of a person according to age (3–7), one cannot but think of Him "whom they of the children of Israel did value" (Matt. xxvii. 9); and whose value, viewed only as a man according to his age (3), would have been fifty shekels: but He says, "they weighed for My price thirty pieces of silver," adding: "A goodly price that I was priced at of them" (Zech. xi. 13).

Things that belonged to the Lord were not to be dedicated to Him by vows; for they were His already (26). We should not as Christians dedicate by vow ourselves or our services to the Lord, for we are His already: "Ye are not your own, for ye are bought with a price; therefore glorify God in your body, and in your spirit, which are God's" (1 Cor. vi. 20).

The word rendered "devoted thing" (28) is mostly applied to persons doomed to death, as the inhabitants of Canaan—God's judgment for their wickedness; or to property devoted to destruction as under a ban or curse: such could not be redeemed. A practical application of this principle might, perhaps, lead Christians to destroy things that have been a snare to them rather than "sell them for charity." The Word of God records with approbation the destruction rather than the sale of books of the value of 50,000 pieces of silver (Acts xix. 20).

THE JEWISH FESTIVALS

Dates	Festivals	Exod.	Exod. xxxiv.	Lev. xxiii.	Num. xxviii.	Deut. xvi.
Abib 14	The Passover	xii. 3–28		v. 5 Passover	v. 16 Passover	v. 1 Passover
15–21	Unleavened Bread	xxiii. v. 15 Unleavened Bread	v. 18 Unleavened Bread	v. 6 Unleavened Bread	v. 17 Unleavened Bread	v. 3 Unleavened Bread
16	First-Fruits	v. 16 Feast of Harvest or First-Fruits		v. 10 Wave Sheaf		
Sivan 6	Feast of Weeks (or Pentecost: Acts ii.)		v. 22 Feast of Weeks or First-Fruits	v. 17 Wave Loaves or First-Fruits	v. 26 Day of First-Fruits or Feast of Weeks	v. 10 Feast of Weeks
Ethanim 1	Feast of Trumpets			v. 24 A Blowing of Trumpets	xxix. v. 1 A Blowing of Trumpets	
10	Day of Atonement			v. 27 Day of Atonement	vv. 7–11 "Ye shall afflict your souls."	
15–21	Feast of Tabernacles	v. 16 Feast of Ingathering	v. 22 Feast of Ingathering	v. 34 Feast of Tabernacles v. 39 Of Ingathering v. 40 Of Booths	v. 12 "Ye shall keep a Feast"	v. 13 Feast of Tabernacles
Adar 14, 15	Feast of Purim	Esther ix. 18, 21, 28.				
The Seventh Day	The Sabbath of Rest (or Holy Convocation)	Gen. ii. 2; Exod. xvi. 23; xx. 8; Lev. xix. 30; xxiii. 3; Isa. lviii. 13; Matt. xii. 10; xxviii. 1. There were seven other days in the year known as "days of Holy Convocation."				

At the Feast of Unleavened Bread, the Feast of Weeks, and the Feast of Tabernacles, all the males were to present themselves before the Lord "in the place where He should choose" (Exod. xxiii. 14, 17; xxxiv. 23; Deut. xvi. 16). In contrast to this, there is in Zechariah an intimation that hereafter the Gentiles—or certain nations of the Gentiles—are to go up to Jerusalem *once a year* to observe—*not the Passover* but—the Feast of Tabernacles (Zech. xiv. 16).

THE BOOK OF NUMBERS

THIS Book is so called, because it records the numberings of the people of Israel—of which the first was made at Sinai, in the beginning of the second year after their departure from Egypt; and the second, thirty-eight years afterwards, just before their entrance into Canaan (i.-vi. and xxvi.). The Book is therefore the divinely-inspired history of the wanderings of the Israelites in the wilderness for the interval between these two episodes, a period of some thirty-eight years and ten months. It is the Book of the Wilderness, full of the story of journeyings, service, and all the vicissitudes of wilderness life. It is therefore a most valuable *vade mecum* for the Church in her journey through the wilderness world to the true home and rest of God (1 Cor. x. 1–11).

The divisions of the Book are as follows:—

(1) THE FIRST NUMBERING OF THE ISRAELITES (i.–iv.).
(2) THE RIGHT ORDERING OF THE CAMP AND MARCH (v.–x. 10).
(3) THE JOURNEY FROM SINAI TO THE BORDERS OF CANAAN (x. 11–xiv.)
(4) THE OUTLINES OF THE HISTORY BETWEEN THE TURNING BACK AT THE BORDERS OF CANAAN, AND ISRAEL'S RETURN TO THE SAME SPOT AFTER THIRTY-SEVEN YEARS (xv.–xix.).
(5) THE FIRST VICTORIES OVER THE PEOPLE OF CANAAN (xx.–xxxvi.).

CHAP. 1. Numbering the Tribes

Thirteen months had elapsed since the Exodus. About one month had been occupied with the journey, and the rest of the period spent over the events recorded in the two previous books. Before starting on the march, their Divine Leader commissioned Moses and Aaron to take a census of the people. This census had already been incidentally mentioned (Exod. xxxviii. 25, 26); but it is now described in detail, to show the relative strength of the tribes.

The figures are given in *fifties*; it is probable, therefore, that all less numbers are omitted. And the men of twenty years old and upwards, who were able to go forth to war, were alone counted; whilst the Levites were excluded (**47–49**). But notwithstanding these deductions, the total number amounted to 603,550 (**46**). Including, therefore, the Levites, the women and children, the whole population, according to the usual average, must have amounted to 2,400,000—a prodigious host, living always on the bounty of God, who dwelt in the midst of them as Father and King, sustaining and controlling them.

Every child of God should be able to go forth to war against the evil that assails the inner life, and the evil that is in the world (Eph. vi. 10–17, and 2 Tim. iv. 7). But before doing so we should be able to tell our pedigree (**18**). We must be able to appropriate the repeated *"we know"* of the first Epistle of John. The witness of the Spirit will ever accompany simple faith in Jesus Christ (Rom. viii. 16).

The Levites were not included, because in a very special manner they were God's, having taken the place of the firstborn of Israel. They were, therefore, typically, a dead and risen people, not available for the purposes of war, but for holy Tabernacle service.

Chap. II. The Standards of the Tribes

It was not enough for every man to be able to declare his pedigree: he must also know and pitch beside his standard. Hebrew writers say that the standards of the tribes were symbols borrowed from the prophetic blessing of Jacob, Judah's being a lion, Benjamin's a wolf, &c.; and that the ensigns or banners were distinguished by the same colours respectively as shone in the breastplate. We are not informed certainly on these points. It is enough that God was the promoter of order in the camp, and that every tribe, family, and individual, knew exactly where to pitch around the central Tabernacle, where God dwelt as King. It must have been a fair spectacle; and we cannot wonder at Balaam's exclamation (Num. xxiv. 5, 6). The camp must have extended over an area of twelve square miles.

Judah, with two other tribes, Issachar and Zebulun, lay on the east of the Tabernacle, and took the lead in the march (**3–9**). Reuben, with Simeon and Gad, occupied the south, and followed (**10–16**). Then came the Levites, who encamped immediately before the Tabernacle, and who bore the most sacred possessions of the host (**17**). Ephraim, with Manasseh and Benjamin, occupied the west, and came next (**18–24**). Whilst Dan, with Asher and Naphtali, occupied the north, and brought up the rear (**25–31**).

What a fit emblem is all this of the unity of the Church of Christ in different positions, with varying emblems, but all part of the same great host circling around the invisible Lord and King! Let us not fret about our position therein, whether it be in the van or rear; but let us be only careful to be where God would have us be, doing every man his work (Mark xiii. 34).

CHAP. III. **The Levites**

In this chapter the Levites are the theme. Aaron's family constituted the order of priesthood; the rest of the tribe performed the more laborious duties of ministering in and transporting the Tabernacle. The term *bring near* (**6**) is a sacrificial one, denoting the presentation of an offering to God (Lev. xvi. 9). The Levites were subordinate to the priests, who alone possessed the privilege of entering the holy place (**9, 10**).

The consecration of this tribe to the service of God was due to the special appointment of God. In memory of the last judgment on Egypt, from which the firstborn were redeemed through blood-shedding, the eldest son in every Jewish family was regarded as specially God's (*see* Exod. xxiv. 5; Num. viii. 13–18). But after the making of the golden calf a change was made, and Levi was taken instead (**12, 13**). Is not this the position of every child of God? May not God rightfully employ about each of us the term *Mine* (1 Cor. vi. 20)? and may we not look up and say, "I am Thine; save me"? We have been redeemed by the blood of the Lamb, that we might be God's, and minister to Him, caring for His own holy work in the world.

The Gershonites, as oldest, pitched westward of the Tabernacle, and had charge of all the hangings and curtains. The Kohathites, because Aaron belonged to that division of the tribe, pitched southward, and had charge of the sacred vessels. The Merarites pitched northward, and had charge of the boards and sockets, &c. It was enough for each to know that God had appointed their place and charge. Even the carrying of pins became honourable work when the bearer remembered that God had appointed it as His work.

Those of the firstborn of the eleven tribes who were over and above the number of males of the tribe of Levi had to be redeemed with *money* (**39–51**). These amounted to 273 (**46**). *All* had to be redeemed. None of us would have had any right to live unless the blood of Jesus had redeemed us to God (1 Pet. i. 18, 19).

CHAP. IV. **The Tabernacle and its Vessels**

Thirty is the age of full maturity (3): hence it was the period of life at which John the Baptist and our Lord entered on their respective ministries (Luke iii. 3, 23).

The sacred vessels were hidden from the gaze of the people, whilst being carried on the march, by the rough covering of badgers' skins. Aaron and his sons covered them in the first instance; and then the Kohathites came to bear them. Badgers' skins were the universal covering, except in the case of the ark, which had a cloth wholly of blue over the coarser material, setting forth, doubtless, the heavenly character of the Lord Jesus. The table of shew-bread had cloths of blue and scarlet, under the badger skins, whilst the golden candlestick and altar had only blue. The brazen altar was covered with "purple" instead of "blue" or "scarlet," because it prefigured the blood-shedding of the cross, which led to the royal enthronement of the Redeemer. There is a meaning in every word of God's appointments, hidden from the wise and prudent, but revealed to babes (Matt. xi. 25). The greatest care was to be exercised in the removal of the sacred vessels and holy things. Neglect might lead to death (17–20); and an inventory must be carefully kept (32). How careful should we be who bear the vessels of the Lord—(Isa. lii. 11).

What a marvellous exchange all this was for Levi! Remember what old Jacob said of him (Gen. xlix. 5–7). But now, in consequence of one noble act (Exod. xxxii. 25–29), it seemed as if the whole destiny of the tribe were altered, and the curse was transformed into blessing (Deut. xxxiii. 8–11; Mal. ii. 4–7). Ah! how much depends on the response to the challenge, "Who is on the Lord's side?"

CHAP. V. **Law of Restitution, &c.**

Three topics occupy this chapter. *The removal of the unclean from the camp.*—The reason is given in the announcement of God's indwelling (3). We may not judge each other's innermost thoughts;

but directly there is anything manifestly evil in the life, we are called upon to exclude the evil-doer from our fellowship. This is the clear teaching of 1 Cor. v. 11-13. But should we not also put away all evil things from our own hearts and lives? The exclusion of lepers has been acted on from the time of the Exodus to the present day.

The law of restitution (**5–8**).—God looked not for confession to Himself only; but for confession to the injured party, and restitution with the addition of the fifth part. This principle of restitution holds also for us (Matt. v. 24; Luke xix. 8). We should carefully cultivate a tender conscience, exercising ourselves thereto (Acts xxiv. 16). There is a species of introspection, which is very harmful; but there is a self-judgment, a mercilessness to self, a habit of confession and restitution, which we do well to practise.

The trial of jealousy (**11–31**).—This law strongly discouraged conjugal infidelity on the part of the wife, and protected her from hasty and groundless suspicion on the part of the husband. "Holy water" was water from the laver. "Dust" was an emblem of vileness and misery and contrition (Ps. xxii. 15). The fragile earthen vessel was afterwards destroyed. The whole of this awful ceremony—her position, her uncovered head, the bitter potion, the adjuration of the priest (**19**)—all was calculated to make a deep impression. This, too, bears on us. God loves us unutterably, and is jealous of our love. If there has been an unfaithfulness on our part, it must be thoroughly judged: we must be true in the inward parts to the great and faithful Lover of souls (Ps. cxxxix. 1–6).

CHAP. VI. **The Nazarites**

The law of the Nazarite, which is the subject of this chapter, is full of instruction, because we learn that for special purposes of holy service, we may be called upon to sever ourselves from things which, though not absolutely sinful in themselves, are calculated to interfere with that intense consecration of heart which is set forth in the true Nazariteship. The term signifies "separated to the Lord." Three rules are given here:—

Not to touch any product of the vine (**3**).—This was also forbidden to the priests (Lev. x. 9–11). Wine is the symbol of ordinary social festivity; and it is very difficult to go into such scenes of revelry and mirth without losing something of that holy separation to God which we should cultivate. If we must have some special exhilaration, let us seek it elsewhere (Eph. v. 18–20).

Not to cut the hair (5).—Hair is regarded as the sign of natural vigour and strength. The unshorn locks therefore signified the dedication of all natural powers to the service of God. How many razors Satan has by which to rob us of our full devotion to God! Let us see to it that we do not rest our heads upon Delilah's lap (Judges xvi. 19).

Not to touch the dead, however dear (7).—How careful should we be in our contact with those who are dead in sins, lest we become defiled by the association! Though, if we be involved, almost unknowingly (9), we must instantly seek forgiveness and cleansing (10), and begin again (12). We must get back to where we were at the beginning (Gen. xiii. 3, 4). But ah, those lost days!

The ceremonies at the completion of the term of the Nazarite vow (13–21).—Sin-offering for the sin that mingles with our holiest service; burnt-offering as an expression of entire devotion to God; peace-offerings as thanksgiving for grace to complete the vow.

The benediction which comes in here is very beautiful (24–26). It evidently refers to the sacred Trinity, and has its counterpart in 2 Cor. xiii. 14. God promised to give effect to the priest's words (27).

Chap. VII. The Gifts of the Tribes

This and the two following chapters wind up the story of the stay at Sinai, ere the host started on their pilgrimage. This is one of the longest chapters in the Bible, and gives a detailed statement of a stately ceremonial which was repeated once a day for twelve days; each of the princes of Israel, the respective heads of the tribes, making a presentation in turn. It is very beautiful to find the careful minuteness with which the sacred historian details the successive gifts. We might have bulked them all together, saving the precious space; but the inspiring Spirit dwells lovingly on each special name and gift, so that every one stands out in its own distinct beauty and grandeur to man's eye as to God's thought. Is not this a page out of God's book of remembrance, in which each alabaster box stands noted by itself? (*Comp.* Matt. xxvi. 13; Mark xiv. 9).

To the Gershonites, who had to transport the hangings and drapery of the Tabernacle, two waggons were assigned; to the Merarites, who had charge of the solid parts, four waggons (7–9). The Kohathites bore the sacred vessels on their shoulders.

The aggregate worth by weight of the whole of the offerings would be £438 (**84–88**). But the real worth, when measured by the relative values of that time, especially just after the erection of the Tabernacle, must have been much greater. How munificent were these Jews to the house of God! Do they not shame us? We are carried forward to 1 Chron. xxix. Let us begin to imitate them by setting apart a fixed proportion of all we receive and have (1 Cor. xvi. 2).

What a precious glimpse of heart-to-heart fellowship is that with which this chapter closes! (**89**). Liberality is a poor substitute for fellowship. The two must be combined. Christ is the mercy-seat (Rom. iii. 25); and to the purged ear God speaks to us through the Holy Word day by day.

CHAP. VIII.   **Ordination of the Levites**

In the midst of the wilderness journeyings we come to a paragraph about the *Candlestick* (**2**). All through her earthly journey the Church must be the light of the world. Beaten out of one lump of gold, we see a type of its essential unity. The various parts indicate variety of function (1 Cor. xii. 4–6). The oil is the grace of the Holy Ghost, by which alone, daily received, can our testimony be maintained (Zech. iv. 3, 12).

The ordination of the Levites follows (**5–22**).—They were *first* symbolically cleansed: by the sprinkling of the water of purification; the washing of their garments; and the shaving off of their hair, *i.e.*, the application of the razor of death to all natural growth and strength. This was all required ere these men, naturally so fierce and cruel (Gen. xlix. 7), could be employed in holy service. *Next*, they were symbolically presented to God in the stead of the people, to do on their behalf the duties which otherwise had been incumbent on the entire host through their first-born sons (Exod. xxiv. 5). A special tribe was devoted to do the work of ministry to which the first-born were designated by their deliverance from death through the blood of the Passover Lamb (**5–9**; iii. 11–13). This saved them from plague which had otherwise visited them in the least neglect of duty (**10**). The offering of sacrifice was intended to atone for the sin of the holiest service, and to typify the entireness of consecration (**12**).

The age at which the Levites commenced their work had been fixed at thirty years (iv. 3, 23). But for permanent service, in the land of rest, when a great number of Levites were required, not only for the Tabernacle service, but for teaching the people throughout their tribes, the Levites began their work at an earlier age. David arranged that the age should be lowered to twenty (1 Chron. xxiii. 27), so that there might be a larger supply.

Oh for the covenant of Levi! (Mal. ii. 4–6).

Chap. IX. The Passover in the Wilderness

The Passover was celebrated in Egypt (Exod. xii.); in the wilderness **(2–5)**; and in the land of Canaan (Joshua v.). Redemption by the blood of Jesus thus lies at the root of all the great events in the history of God's children. There was a special circumstance that made this one memorable, because of the institution of "the little Passover" **(6–12)**. It is thought that these men were Mishael and Elzaphan, who buried their cousins Nadab and Abihu within a week of the Passover (Lev. x. 4, 5). Moses had no answer to give to the inquirers, and he did not try to invent one; but adopted the better course of waiting upon God **(8)**. How blessed is it to learn that God allows for the disabilities over which we have no control; and is willing to receive us in some other way, if unavoidable difficulties prevent us from obeying in the ordained fashion (2 Chron. xxx. 13–20).

The cloud in its movements guided the march of the host **(15–22)**. It first appeared Exod. xiii. 21, and it led them amid all their wanderings. How could they have threaded their way through that great and terrible wilderness without its guidance? Our blessed Lord obeyed the movements of the cloud of His Father's will throughout His life; and so should we. We may not know our place from one day to another; but we need not be anxious, if only we are absolutely following the indications of His will (John viii. 12). If you do not know exactly what to do, wait still where you are. You may be very stupid; but God will make His meaning as plain as the movement of the cloud, if you will let Him. And when once you know His will, then strike your tents and follow! He will lead you out to work. He will lead you into rest. "My soul, wait thou only upon God; for my expectation is from Him" (Ps. lxii. 5).

Chap. X. The Silver Trumpets

The silver trumpets spoke God's message to every circumcised ear. Hence they were blown only by the priests **(8)**. Each trumpet was made of one piece, and fulfilled several purposes. They were used for the summoning of an assembly; the movement of the camp; and the gathering to war. Would that the Church in these days were as careful in giving God's messages to the people on the silver trumpet of testimony!

At the eleventh verse we enter upon the third main division of this book. All had been divinely ordered "according to the commandment of the Lord." Each man knew his pedigree and standard; every tribe knew its appointed place, whether in march or rest. The command given generally that the Tabernacle should occupy the central place in the line of march, after the camps of Judah and Reuben (ii. 9, 16, 17), was slightly modified; or at least more specific directions were given **(17, 21)**.

Hobab seems rather to have been the brother-in-law of Moses: the Hebrew word will bear either rendering **(29)**. Jethro had returned (Exod. xviii. 27); but Hobab seems to have accompanied Israel (Judges i. 16; iv. 11). It has been suggested that there was here some failure in Moses' faith, which led him to rely more on Hobab's general sagacity and knowledge of the desert than on God. But probably he had learnt God's will on the matter before asking Hobab to stay **(31, 32)**.

The ark went first in the march **(33)**. So does Jesus ever precede His people. He goes first to make crooked places straight, and rough places plain (Isa. xl. 4). When He puts forth His own sheep, He goes before them and leads them into rest (John x. 3, 4). How good it is to see His goings in the van of our life-march meeting our foes before they can touch us! (Isa. lii. 12).

Chap. XI. The Murmuring

We cannot wonder at the people murmuring, as they were unaccustomed to the fatigues of the desert, and it seemed so far to the land of rest; but, perhaps, we have never realized how great a sin is querulous complaining in the sight of God. Let us beware of it!

(1 Cor. x. 10). Let us also guard against mingling ourselves with those who are not like-minded with ourselves: "the mixed multitude" was largely composed of Egyptians (Exod. xii. 38), from whom the evil example spread to Israel (**4**). When our religious life is low, we tire of angels' food, and our hearts turn back to the world we had left.

Moses' complaint (**10–15**).—How marvellously accurate is the Bible in its delineation of the character and failure of its noblest men! What an evidence of its truthfulness! The eye of Moses had turned from God to self; or he would not have spoken as if the duty of providing flesh were his. God never imposes a burden for which He does not give sufficient strength; but we must not look at the burden apart from Him. As the day so the strength. He can make all grace abound.

Divine relief came in the appointment temporarily of seventy men to help him. But what a pity it was that he did not claim strength enough for his needs! And yet how tender was God's considerateness of His overwearied servant! (*See* 1 Kings xix. 4, 5). The Jews say this body of elders afterwards constituted the Sanhedrim. Note the unselfish exclamation of this generous spirit in which jealousy found no foothold (**29**). The answer to verse 23 is Isa. lix. 1.

The quails even now fly in vast quantities. Exhausted by their long flight these flew about three feet above the earth, and so were easily felled. But the passionate haste in eating brought about a woeful plague, which left its story in the name of their halting place (**34**; *see* Ps. cvi. 15).

CHAP. XII. **Speaking against Moses**

It is a very serious matter to speak against any servant of the Lord, especially when he has been specially honoured and used. But even against the meanest we cannot speak without serious risk. The Lord overhears; and He takes such words as an insult to Himself. Let us seek to discover the good and lovely traits in men, and dwell on them.

Moses' behaviour was very beautiful. The verse about his meekness (**3**) was probably inserted by some later hand; but meekness was a notable trait in his character. How different to the fiery spirit of earlier days! What cannot the grace of God effect! When we are spoken against, it is much wiser not to answer back again, or to rush into self-defence; but to follow the example of our Lord, and to hand over the battle to God (1 Pet. ii. 20–25: *see* Rom. xii. 19–21).

This Ethiopian wife may have been Zipporah; or more probably some other woman whom he had married after Zipporah's death: but is it not an illustration of the way in which Christ's love to the Gentile Church has aroused the hostility of the Jewish people? Yet how high a commendation was passed on Moses by God Himself (**7,** quoted Heb. iii. 2, 3). We are appointed servants in God's household; and His one demand is for faithfulness (Mark xiii. 34, 35; 1 Cor. iv. 1, 2).

Miriam's punishment and restoration are very significant. The outer leprosy symbolizing the state of heart, cleansed as the result of intercession (**13, 14**), but leaving behind certain disabilities and entailing privation and shame, not on herself alone, but on others (**15**). Let us watch and pray, lest we enter into temptation.

CHAP. XIII. **The Spies**

The mission of the twelve spies, which is the subject of this chapter, was evidently demanded by the moral state of the people, as we learn from Deut. i. 19–22. Had there been a living faith in God, there would have been no talk about spies. What need is there to spy out the land which we know is ours by the gift of God? The thought of sending spies, which God assented to, was one of the first stages in Israel's unbelief.

The time (**20**) was about August; and the spies traversed the land to the extreme north. They seem to have gone up by the Valley of Jordan, and returned by the western borders of the land. Eschol is a little S.E. of Hebron, and its sloping hills are still covered with the choicest vines; one cluster sometimes weighs 10 or 12 lbs. The muscular and tall frames of the warriors of Canaan must have been even more impressive when contrasted with the almost puny and diminutive Egyptians.

The evil report (**26**).—They looked at circumstances, as Peter looked at the winds and waves: and directly we begin to count up the numbers of giants and walled cities, and other difficulties, we shall not only be depressed ourselves, but shall depress others. "We be not able" (31) is the language of unbelief and despondency; but if it is followed by "Our God whom we serve is able" (Dan. iii. 17), then it is the glad shout of faith and assured victory.

Faith as represented in Caleb does not ignore difficulties; it is quite aware of them: but it does not concentrate its gaze on them, but on the living God (xiv. 8). In every life there are Amelekites, sins of the flesh; and the Hittites, Jebusites, and Amorites of besetting sin. None must dare to suppose that we must always be overcome by them. But trusting in God we may confidently expect that they will be put under our feet (Rom. vi. 14).

CHAP. XIV. **Murmuring Again**

Amid the *murmurings of the people,* of which this chapter is a melancholy monument, Joshua and Caleb stood firm as rocks, though at the risk of their lives (10). How important it is to bear, at all costs, an unwavering witness against the evil around us! But we can only do so when we are living in the light of God ourselves, and are following Him fully (24). Are we doing this? If so, we shall not fail of the Land of Promise. Difficulties are the bread by which the soul grows strong (9).

The Land of Promise, in our own lives, is the type of that life of rest and victory which is within reach of all God's children. It is a mistake to consider it only or principally as relating to heaven. Heb. iii. and iv. clearly show that it is a matter for to-day. Its New Testament equivalent is the heavenly places of the Epistle to the Ephesians. We are to live by faith, as heavenly citizens, who are still exposed to the wiles of the devil, but who have learnt the secret of the overcoming life. Let us see to it that we do not miss it through want of faith, and have to turn back to the wilderness of restlessness and failure.

Moses' intercession was very noble (13-19). He had no unholy or selfish ambition. His one thought was God's glory and his people's good. We must not think that God was less merciful than His servant; but that these intercessions were the expression through human lips of the tender mercies which were in the heart of God.

The fruit of unbelief (28).—As unbelief shut them out of Canaan, so will it shut us out of the blessings of the New Covenant. It would seem as if God Himself stood paralysed before unbelief (Matt. xiii.

58). The antidote is found in the concentration of the heart on promise. "The breach of promise" is rather change of purpose. God never alters in His dealings with men; hence He must change, when they change from faith and obedience to their opposites. It is useless to attempt to carry things with a high hand, when God is against us (**44**).

Chap. XV. **The Meal-Offering**

What *a marvellous contrast* between the closing verses of the previous chapter and the opening ones of this! In the one we read man's failure and the punishment of unbelief; in the next the faithfulness of God, whose purpose should be ultimately realized. Israel had forfeited all; yet they should still come into the land (**2**). The wine and oil could not be freely offered till they came into the land of vineyards and oliveyards; and, therefore, this was prospective (**4-10**). Joy and gladness are the accompaniments of life in the Land of Promise, which is inherited by faith.

The stranger was carefully remembered (**14-16**), an anticipation in those days of the time when the Gentiles should share in the privileges of Israelites (Eph. ii. 13-22). "Ye shall offer up a cake": it is said that the Jewish housewife still fulfils this custom in her bread-making (**20**).

The distinction between sins of ignorance and of presumption (**22-31**).—For the former ample provision was made: sacrifices were prescribed, which forcibly typify the various aspects of our Saviour's death. How clear is it then that sins of ignorance are equally sins in God's sight, needing to be acknowledged and forgiven. For these, if for no other reason, we require daily to seek cleansing. Sins of presumption were treated rigorously; and a solemn instance is given of one who violated the Sabbath, and who, after careful consideration, was stoned (**34, 35**). What need for David's prayer! (Ps. xix. 13).

The ribband of blue (**38**) was a heavenly memorial attached to the borders of the garments, so that the Israelite might be kept in mind. We have something better in the ministry of the Holy Spirit, whose special office this is (John xiv. 26). Beware of turning God's appointments into occasions for self-display (Matt. xxiii. 5).

Chap. XVI. The Rebellion of Korah

Here the *wilderness story* is resumed, teaching us what man is and what God is—man's failure; God's grace. Jude calls it the gainsaying of Core (Jude 11). It was a very formidable conspiracy (2), and originated in a dissatisfaction at the transference of the priesthood to a family so closely identified with the great leader (3).

The conduct of Moses was most praiseworthy: he committed his cause to the Lord, and left on Him the responsibility of dealing with the malcontents. He soon received the test which was to decide the case (5, quoted 2 Tim. ii. 19). Would that we might be caused to draw near! (Ps. lxv. 4). It is always sweet to leave our questions and difficulties with God, saying, "The Lord will show," and "The Lord will choose." After all, it is not our matter, but God's; and it is for Him to say what position He would have any of us occupy in the body of Christ. There seems to have been *some further cause for this conspiracy*; because in the case of Dathan and Abiram, Moses sought for a special interview (12). Whilst Korah sought the priesthood (10), they seem to have chafed against the civil supremacy of Moses (13). Though the meekest of men, he could not restrain his indignation at the unjust and groundless charges.

The doom of these families was very terrible (27); and yet it is needful in such circumstances to act with promptitude and decision (27-33). If this spirit had spread, the whole camp would have become a mob. "Quick" is the old English word for "alive" (30).

What a remarkable type of Christ was Aaron, when he stood between the living and the dead, and the plague stayed! (48). "I will consume them" (45), is the language of justice; but God's mercy prevailed (Rom. v. 21).

Chap. XVII. Aaron's Rod

The controversy about the PRIESTHOOD demanded a final and authoritative settlement. For the removal of all doubts and the silencing of all objections, a notable miracle was wrought in the budding of Aaron's rod. There was no room left for man: he was put out of the way, and only God appeared (10).

The rod of Aaron was probably that which had been used by

Moses, in working so many miracles. Such rods were dry staves, or wands of office, usually transmitted from father to son. And surely, besides serving their immediate purpose, they were apt figures of Israel's condition, and indeed of the condition of everyone of us by nature—without sap, or life, or power.

The miracle was very remarkable (8), and a beautiful illustration of what grace can effect in each of us. And after all there is no test of true discipleship, or of a call to the ministry, which can be compared to fruitfulness. This is God's seal of acceptance and designation to His work. We need to be grafted into Christ; so only can we bear fruit (John xv. 4, 5; Hos. xiv. 8).

The complaint of Israel (12, 13) was indicative of a sad want of simple trust and love. It seemed to be entirely forgotten that they had brought all their sufferings on themselves. How many of our own sorrows are self-originated!

CHAP. XVIII. **The Priests' Portion**

It was not all honour conferred on Aaron and his house; there was also considerable responsibility. It was God's answer to the complaint of the people in xvii. 12. "That there be no wrath any more" (5). The brethren of the house of Levi were to be joined to Aaron—they worked with the high priest; and it will be well indeed for us when we learn to work with Christ for holy service: joined unto the Lord in one spirit (1 Cor. iii. 9).

The priests' portion (8-20).—We too are priests by reason of the anointing of the Holy Ghost (8; *see also* 1 John ii. 27); and we too must learn to feed our souls in the tabernacle (1 Cor. ix. 13). An enumeration is made of the various offerings on which they were to feed, by a perpetual covenant, as endurable as salt (19). How pleasant is it when the Lord says to a soul, "I am thy part, and thine inheritance" (20; Joshua xiii. 14; Ps. xvi. 5; 1 Cor. iii. 21). But we must be clean to enjoy what God provides (11); and we must give God our best.

The Levites' portion (21).—As the people assigned a tenth to the Levites, so *they* were to assign a tenth to the priests (28); and when this was done they (the Levites) might use the remainder for themselves. Even the very ministers of God are not exonerated from giving Him a certain proportion of all they have.

How well did God provide for them all! And He will provide also for us. There is nothing that He will withhold from us if we walk uprightly (Ps. lxxxiv. 11). Alas for us, when we depend for our support on the world which knows Him not! There would be no sin in the priests and Levites thus feeding on hallowed things (31, 32); because God, whose they were, had freely given them. The labourer is worthy of his hire (Luke x. 7).

Chap. XIX. **The Red Heifer**

The red heifer was a beautiful type of Christ. No spot, no blemish, no yoke of sin ever came on Him (2). Led forth without the camp (3; Heb. xiii. 12, 13). That outside place becomes not Him only, but us also. Let us go forth unto Him! The blood was sprinkled, when the heifer was slain: a figure of the perfect presentation of Christ's blood to God, as the meeting-place between God and the conscience (Heb. ix. 13, 14). Seven is the number of perfection. Christ's sacrifice is once for all, entirely and for ever satisfactory. The precious blood of Jesus for ever pleads and claims our peace with God. Our acceptance with God is not determined by our feelings, but by the blood of Christ (Eph. ii. 13–15). The body of the heifer was burnt to ashes (5, 6), which were carefully collected and brought into the camp, and used to purify those who were ceremonially defiled (18).

Death is the type of sin; and it is impossible for us to go through the world without being almost unconsciously defiled. Our hearts ought to be as closed vessels; but too often they are open. Hence we need daily cleansing, and to come to the precious blood of purification; or we must not stand in the presence of the holy God.

This daily cleansing from sin is beautifully taught in John xiii., where Jesus washed the feet only, which had been contaminated by the dust of the highway. We need daily to resort to Him; and, though we go to Him seventy times seven, we may unhesitatingly count on His complete forgiveness (Matt. xviii. 22). And such forgiveness will make sin increasingly abhorrent.

Chap. XX. Deaths of Miriam and Aaron

This was the second time the Israelites had come to Kadesh. The first encampment is recorded in xiii. 26. Between the two there is a long interval of thirty-eight years. Nothing is known of that interval but the bare record of encampment (xxxiii.); but Ps. xcv. would lead us to conclude that it was one long series of provocations. How much time we lose out of our lives through disobedience! We have to come back to the place where we dropped the thread of obedience; and all the interval counts for nothing.

Miriam was associated with Moses' earliest years (Exod. ii. 7); with his greatest triumph (Exod. xv. 20); and it must have been a sorrow to the brothers to lose her. Fellow-pilgrims must part company; but God hath pledged Himself to be with us to the end (Isa. xlvi. 4). On one occasion only does it appear that there was a difference between Miriam and Moses: and then Divine judgment fell heavily upon Miriam (xii. 10). At the time of her death she had probably attained an age of nearly 130 years.

The murmurings of the people broke out again. The wilderness of Zin (**1**) is spoken of as "great and terrible" (Deut. viii. 15). It was very sad to see this fresh ebullition of the untamed spirit of the people, who threw the blame entirely on Moses for bringing them into that sterile and arid region. The leaders fled to the Tabernacle, as an asylum of refuge, and for the purpose of seeking Divine direction. It is into the presence of God that we should always go with our burdens.

Moses' sin consisted in disobedience. He failed in meekness and obedience, which had always been his strongest points. He struck the rock; but the smiting of the true Rock cannot be repeated (Rom. vi. 9, 10). A word would have sufficed, though he could hardly believe or realize it (**12**). His address to the people was hasty and passionate, and cost him Canaan.

The refusal of Edom was very churlish (**20, 21**). Israel's proposal was right and generous (Deut. ii. 2–6). Those whom God blesses can afford to be generous. In after-years the penalty for this refusal was heavily exacted, though now Moses quietly turned away (1 Sam. xiv. 47; 2 Sam. viii. 14; Obad. 1–19).

Aaron's death (**24–29**) was lovingly arranged to do him honour, with one last view of the camp, and a glimpse of the Promised Land

THE BOOK OF NUMBERS 141

(xxxiii. 38, 39). This death is a striking evidence of the imperfection of the Aaronic priesthood, and a contrast to the unchangeableness of the priesthood of Christ (Heb. vii. 23-25).

CHAP. XXI. **Kings Arad and Sihon**

Arad was an ancient town, situated in the south of Palestine. Its king came out to fight. The first failure came to teach the Israelites to expect the conquest of the land solely from the favour and help of God.

The fiery serpents still infest that part of the desert, but this was a miraculous judgment. How significant the lesson! When we yield to murmuring, we put ourselves at the mercy of the serpent. It was by the serpent affixed to the pole that the serpent bite was healed. Like cures like. So the look of faith to the Lord Jesus, crucified for us, saves (John iii. 14, 15). *Compare* Gen. iii. 14 and Gal. iii. 13. This brazen serpent became a kind of *fetish* (2 Kings xviii. 4). Then Hezekiah broke it in pieces, and called it Nehushtan—a piece of brass.

Oboth (10) is of interest, because we do not read of the children of Israel murmuring after this halting-place.

A fragment (14) is here quoted from some historical document, which has long ago been destroyed. What a volume must that be which is being written, through the ages, of the wars of the Lord!

A beautiful little song is given next (17). The princes were able to use their official rods in putting aside the brushwood which hid the well, and its discovery was greeted by songs. How often does God open springs for us which we do not acknowledge! Let us be more prone to give thanks.

Sihon challenged the people to battle (23). They had done nothing to provoke his attack. He himself had been an invader; and as a proof of this a passage is quoted (27-30) from a poet of that country, describing the invasion of the land; the burning of the Moabite cities of Heshbon and Ar; and the erection of new Amorite cities in their place. This was recapitulated by Jephthah (Jud. xi. 13-27). Chemosh was the idol-god (Jer. xlviii. 45, 46).

Chap. XXII. Balaam

This and the two following chapters present a marvellous contrast between the covetous prophet and his sublime prophecies (2 Peter ii. 14–16). And it is evidently possible still for us to speak God's truth, and yet to have neither part nor lot in the matter (Jude 11).

The plains of Moab had been wrested from Moab by Sihon, but still bore the name of their original owner: they had been just possessed by Israel, and lay between the Jordan and the frontier-hills of Moab. *Balak*, as had been predicted, was sore afraid (**3**; Exod. xv. 15; Deut. ii. 25). The elders of Midian were his neighbours and allies. How little did Israel know what was on foot! But God was on their side, against those who hated and plotted against them (Rom. viii. 31).

Balaam came from Aram (xxiii. 7), *i.e.* Mesopotamia. He was acquainted with God, who was known in those regions from before the time of Abraham. And it was in the name of God that he uttered those incantations which were supposed to carry with them blessing or bane. In the Burmese war magicians were employed to curse the British troops. But no such power can injure those who are under the care of God (Deut. xxiii. 5; Josh. xxiv. 10; Neh. xiii. 2; Micah vi. 5).

His refusal (**13**) was good, but it hinted that he would come if he could; and the very fact of asking again (**19**), when the first answer had been so plain, proves how bent he was on following his own will. Thus the permission accorded by Divine Providence was in accordance with an invariable rule (John xiii. 27; Rom. i. 24). How mercifully God stands in the pathway of sinners; rebuking them, staying their progress, and raising up unexpected voices! We have New Testament confirmation as to the ass speaking (2 Peter ii. 16).

Chap. XXIII. Balak and Balaam

It was a strange medley to build altars to God on the high places of Baal (**1**). And there was no need to erect seven. The false prophet, in ordering so many, designed to mislead and delude the king. And yet we learn that God met him; and we infer that God will meet and speak to those who desire to harm His people, frustrating their designs, and compelling them to work out His plan (Acts iv. 28). It is an awful fact that men may be the spokesmen of Divine truth, of which they personally know nothing (Matt. vii. 22; John xi. 49–51).

Separation is the key-note of the first prediction (9). And this has been remarkably fulfilled in the history of the chosen people. Found in all lands, but at home in none. Dwelling amid all peoples, but absorbed with none. Such should God's children be always (2 Cor. vi. 17, 18; Titus ii. 14).

Balaam's pious wish was not fulfilled (10; xxxi. 8). Like many more, he wished for the blessedness of God's people in death and hereafter, but was not prepared to lead a corresponding life.

Balak was surprised and disappointed, and thought that he could reverse the adverse words, by limiting the seer's vision (**11–13**); and so took him to a point of view where the view of the entire camp was intercepted by intervening heights. It is not possible to reverse God's decisions.

The positive beauty and strength of Israel are the subject of the next burst of prophecy (**19–24**). They are regarded, not as they were in themselves, but as they were in the thought and purpose of God. Oh, children of God, let us deeply ponder verse 21, in spite of our sinfulness; verse 23, in spite of our enemies; verse 24, in spite of our evident weakness and helplessness. Such are we in Christ!

CHAP. XXIV. **Balaam's Prophecies**

What a remarkable statement of openness to receive Divine communications is given us here! (**3, 4**). The Divine afflatus was so strong as to fill his whole soul with the overpowering light of its revelations. May we not pray for moments of insight into truth, if not of vision into the future, the eyes of the heart being opened? (Eph. i. 17, 18). And let us yield to the Divine teaching, and speak out what we see.

The sight of Israel must have been very beautiful; and if the second line of the parallelism (5) refers to the settled habitation of Canaan, then there must indeed have been enough to stir the prophet's soul. Why should not we too be as watered gardens, and as planted trees? (Isa. lviii. 11; Ps. civ. 16).

The kingdom of Israel (7) attained its predicted eminence in the reigns of David and Solomon, and still more in the exalted kingdom of the Messiah.

This time-serving effort to please two masters ended in failure to please either (**11**; Matt. vi. 24). Oh for the single eye and the devoted heart! (1 Sam. ii. 30; John xii. 26). Balaam at least gave the monarch one good piece of advice. When the terror-stricken king asked whether Jehovah would be propitiated by hecatombs of victims and the immolation of his eldest son, the prophet answered truly (*see* Micah vi. 5–8).

Israel's future supremacy was next described. The star would be a symbol of dignity and power: the sceptre—of a victorious king (**17**). This was fulfilled in David (2 Sam. viii. 2–14); and also in the supremacy of Christ over the nations of the world. Amalek's fate had been previously predicted, and was awfully fulfilled (*comp.* Exod. xvii. 16 and 1 Sam. xv.). The mention of Assyria here is most remarkable (**22**); and the transportation of the Kenites is related in the Ninevite inscriptions. The ships of Chittim refer, undoubtedly, to the troops of Greece and Rome, which were brought across the sea; and which destroyed not only Assyria, but the other gigantic despotisms of the East (covered by the word "Eber," which signifies "those across the river").

Balaam started towards his home; but he did not reach it, but turned aside into the plains of Midian (xxxi. 8). He is a terrible warning of one who allowed noble talents and great light to be obscured by a desire to obtain the rewards of the world, without losing his spiritual position or favour in God's sight. A divided heart leads to ruin, equally with the heart that chooses evil.

Chap. XXV. Phinehas

The wickedness here referred to was the result of a deeply laid plot. Unable to curse Israel directly, Balaam suggested to Balak that he should draw the people away from their allegiance to Jehovah by the fascinations of the daughters of Moab (Rev. ii. 14), as the surest way of bringing down on them the judgment of their God. The Midianites, among whom the prophet had retired, were also active participators in this guilty plot (**6, 14, 17**; xxxi. 2, 3).

The women of the country invited the men of Israel to visit at their houses at some festal season; and after partaking of meats, some portion of which had been offered in sacrifice to idols (1-3), they were the more ready to join in the sensual revelry and rites which characterized the worship of the heathen.

All the people did not fall into this sin (Deut. iv. 3, 4; 1 Cor. x. 8). But it brought severe punishment on the wrong-doers. And it was indeed sorrowful that after all their opportunities they should so suddenly and dreadfully fall. God is a very jealous God, and He must chastize His disobedient children (Col. iii. 6): 23,000 perished by the plague (1 Cor. x. 8), and another 1,000 beneath the hand of the judges. Like the amputation of a diseased limb, it was needful to cut out these licentious idolaters.

Phinehas attained a notable distinction (10-13): and his posterity was to hold the priestly office as long as Israel existed (Mal. ii. 4-7; iii. 1; Ps. cvi. 30, 31; *see also* Ezra vii. 1-6; viii. 2, 33). Determined acts like this in dealing with sin are strong, but necessary; and are manifestations of character which are precious in God's regard.

Chap. XXVI. A Second Numbering

The terrible visitation of the preceding chapter swept away the remainder of the old generation (Ps. xcv. 11). This new census (2) was very important: first, as showing the immense numbers to which Israel had grown, notwithstanding the severe judgments they had suffered; and, secondly, as being an arrangement of the people in their families and clans preparatory to their entrance into the land.

It is interesting to read these catalogues through (5-51), because of the real historical interest attaching to some of the names. Remark especially verse 11: Korah's descendants became great musicians, having their names affixed to fourteen Psalms. Reuben and Simeon had diminished: the latter considerably (7, **14**; *comp.* ii. 9, 13).

The division of the land by lot (55) would make the Divine appointment indisputable (Prov. xvi. 33). It is said that provision was thus made for upwards of 600,000 yeomanry, with from ten to twenty acres of land each.

The census of the Levites was taken separately, and conducted on different principles. There was an increase of 1,000 from the last numbering of this tribe (62: iii. 39). Its slow increase may be accounted for by the fact of its having been deeply implicated in Korah's rebellion.

On comparing chapter i. and chapter xxvi., it appears that decrease had taken place in Reuben, Simeon, Gad, Ephraim, and Naphtali, to the total amount of 61,020. All the rest had increased to the total amount of 59,200. Thus, as a judgment on their sins, there was a total decrease of 1,820. Let us see that we too be not excluded from God's rest (Heb. iv. 1, 2).

CHAP. XXVII. **Joshua Appointed**

In the census given in the previous chapter males only are mentioned; and these five young women, noticing that, in consequence of there being none in their household, their family was omitted, represented their hard case to Moses. They would have no share in the land; and their father's name would cease in Israel (4). Theirs was a noble request. They felt sure that there was a portion for them; and they claimed it. What a mistake it is for any of God's children to allow themselves to be deprived of their inheritance in the risen heavenly life, the rest of God, the heritage of promise!

Moses constantly fell back for direction on the teaching of God (5; xv. 34; Exod. xviii. 15, 19). How wise it is not to lean to our own understanding! (Prov. iii. 5, 6).

The sisters' request was abundantly vindicated (7); and they also established a precedent for all future time. God always delights to own a faith which simply and fearlessly appropriates all that He has given; and which refuses, even in the face of nature's weakness and death, to surrender a single jot or tittle of the promised inheritance (Matt. xv. 28).

The closing paragraph is sad and solemn (12). Moses personally suffered for his disobedience: but dispensationally it is true that the law cannot take us into the Promised Land, and therefore the great Lawgiver could not go over Jordan. But how meekly he yielded to the Divine decision! How solicitous he was that the people should be well cared for! (16, 17). Mark how God retained for Himself the right to lead the congregation; so that their appointed head had always to take his directions through the priest. We, too, need to consult the Divine Oracle within our hearts (21; Josh. i. 8, 9; Ps. i. 2; xxxvii. 31; cxix. 11).

Chap. XXVIII. The Offerings

A repetition is here made of several laws previously enacted. This was rendered necessary, because a new generation had sprung up since their first institution. It may even be that during the weary wandering of forty years the religious rites had remained in disuse, and were only revived now that they were approaching the settled land of their inheritance.

Notice the remarkable expressions, *My* offering, *My* bread, *My* sacrifices, a sweet savour unto *Me* (2). Evidently these offerings typified certain characteristics in God's people, and above all in Christ, which are precious to the heart of God. Do we daily offer such sacrifices? (Heb. xiii. 15, 16).

The divisions are marked. The daily offering (**3-8**), the Sabbath offering (**9, 10**), the monthly offerings (**11-15**), which were accompanied by the blowing of trumpets, by the suspension of all labour, by the celebration of public worship (2 Kings iv. 23), and by social and family feasts (1 Sam. xx. 5). The passover offerings (**16-25**). The day of the first fruits (**26-31**).

The remarkable thing in all these sacrifices was the prevalence of the burnt-offering (**3, 6, 10, 13, 19, 23, 27, 31**), which signifies the devotion of the whole being to God (Rom. xii. 1). But this can never be acceptable to God, apart from the sin-offering, by which alone we are rendered able to stand for a moment in God's holy sight. We must remember that these abundant sacrifices were partly intended for the maintenance of the great body of priests and attendant Levites employed in the house of God. What sunny, holy days must have been those of convocation (**18, 26**), when the land rested, and the hymns of worship mingled with the shouts of festal crowds!

Chap. XXIX. The Seventh Month

The solemnities of the seventh month described in this chapter were very imposing. The seventh month of the ecclesiastical year was the first month of the civil year, and corresponded to Sept.-Oct. This was the Hebrew New Year. It was heralded by the blowing of trumpets, which constituted a solemn preparation for the sacred feasts which were held in greater numbers in this month than at any other part of the year.

There were special offerings for the first month, in addition to the usual monthly and daily offerings (6).

The great Day of Atonement fell on the tenth day of the seventh month (7–11). Its observances are fully noticed under Lev. xvi. But there seems to be an addition made here of the large burnt-offering (8), and also of the sin-offering to atone for the sins that mingled with the day's services (11). Our holiest service needs cleansing in the precious blood.

The feast of booths or tabernacles was held after the Day of Atonement (12–38). It lasted eight days, the first and last of which were Sabbaths; and a particular offering was appointed for each day, diminishing as each day passed by, as if God consulted the weakness of His children, who so soon tire. If the different days are lightly underlined in the Bible, the divine method will be more apparent. It is interesting to read Neh. viii. 14–17: also to remember that it was at the close of this week that our Lord Jesus spoke the marvellous words of John vii. 37. The annual offerings here enumerated as having been offered at the public expense amount to 1,241, besides the immense number of private offerings. Do we sufficiently recognize the daily and special claims of God on our time, our substance, and our persons?

Chap. XXX. Vows

Vows might concern the offering of some gift on the altar; the abstaining from particular articles of meat and drink; the observance of private fasting; or the doing something for the service of God beyond what was authoritatively required (Deut. xxiii. 21–23; Jud. xi. 30–35; 1 Sam. i. 11; Ps. cxxxii. 2; lxvi. 13, 14). A vow had to be audibly expressed; and it then became irrevocable. "Shall not break" (2: *See also* Ps. lv. 20). These vows in the case of women and children, however, were subject to the revision of husbands and parents (3–16).

It is very solemn when a soul devotes itself to God. Such an act of consecration should not be lightly entered upon. How terrible it is to hear people speaking frivolously about a solemn consecration service! When once the vow is made, at all cost it must be kept (Eccles. v. 1–6).

At the same time God always takes into account all those disabilities which are beyond our power to prevent, and occur to us from our association with others. "The Lord shall forgive" (5, 8, 12).

Jesus faithfully kept to His solemn undertaking to be our Surety, and to die for us. Though it cost Him bloody sweat, and death of agony, He swerved neither to the right nor left, but "set His face like a flint" (Isa. 1. 7), and finished the work of glorifying God, and saving us, which He had undertaken.

How solemn is our responsibility in hindering any whom we love from carrying out their pious schemes and wishes! We may have a right to disallow (5, 8). On the other hand, it is sometimes better to hold our peace (14). Let us allow the will of God to proceed in the souls of those whom we love, without meddling with it by a single word of praise or blame. In these things we shall be divinely directed. We think, however, that it is not the will of God that we, who are not under law, but grace, should bind ourselves by vows; but be led by the Spirit. "Swear not at all" is in our judgment a precept to this effect.

Chap. XXXI. The Midianites

The Midianites, under the direction of Balaam, were the principal instigators of the infamous scheme of seduction planned to entrap the Israelites into the double crime of idolatry and licentiousness; so that the Lord would be compelled to withdraw His help and presence (xxv.). Before Moses died, he gave orders for their extermination (2).

The word "delivered" (5) means draughted, or chosen. It is very remarkable to find Phinehas, the priest, who had commenced the process of judgment, commissioned to lead the troops. This was not one of the wars of Canaan, but a war necessitated by the evil passions and sinful outbreak of the people; and also of solemn judgment against the Midianites for their awful wickedness.

In this case the Midianite women were slain, because of their share in the seduction of Israel (15).

Though Israel was obeying God in this terrible act of judgment, they had contracted defilement (19), and needed cleansing (Num. xix. 11-13). We need this also, whenever we do God's work. All the spoils of war had also to be cleansed (21-23). We must all go through a process of purification; but not through fire, unless God knows we are able to bear it.

The booty was divided into two equal parts (26, &c.), the one for the whole people, the other for the soldiers; but from each a proportion was deducted for sacred purposes.

In token of God's wonderful care (48, &c.), the people gave of the spoils of jewellery an amount equal to £30,568 15s. for the use of the Tabernacle. The Midianites were fond of such display (Judges viii. 24).

It was a terrible judgment; and yet probably this nation had reached a pitch of wickedness which would have infested the world, and needed to be dealt with summarily. And probably God only anticipated by a few years the natural result of the awful vices which were rife in their midst. These young girls, who were taken into the Israelite homes as slaves, would be under very stringent regulations, and be brought up in the knowledge and worship of Jehovah.

CHAP. XXXII. **Reuben and Gad**

Reuben and Gad, being contiguous to each other in the camp, had many opportunities of conversing together, and therefore united in preferring the request for permission to settle on the East of Jordan, where the vast tracts of pasturage were eminently suited for their flocks. Many opinions have been expressed as to the rightness of their request. They have been taken to be half-and-half men, mere borderers, who were content with something short of God's purpose, and so stayed on the safe and comfortable side of Jordan. It is a great mistake to let the thought of good pasturage warp the action of obedience or faith.

At first Moses would not hear of their proposal (6–15), because it seemed to him that they were anxious to evade their fair share in the hardships of the conquest of Canaan.

But they explained their willingness to serve in the campaign, when they had rebuilt the cities recently captured, and had left their children under the care of some of their brethren. As only 40,000 passed over Jordan (*comp.* Num. xxvi. 7, 18, 34 with Josh. iv. 13) probably nearly 100,000 remained in charge of the new possessions. We are called to bear each other's burdens (Gal. vi. 2). After these solemn assurances, Moses was able to assent to their proposals, and formally announced the matter to the leaders of the people **(28–30)**. Let us not be content with anything less than Eph. ii. 6. This is our heavenly inheritance, across the river of death to self and sin. Let us be determined that it shall be possessed by us at all costs.

CHAP. XXXIII. **The Camping Places**

This is a catalogue of those camping places between Egypt and the Land of Promise, at which Israel made a prolonged sojourn. The record would confirm their faith in God's marvellous guidance and help, and would give them new courage on entering Canaan. This is practically the winding up of the story of the wilderness journeyings.

The burial of the firstborn throws a new light upon that terrible plague and the delay of Pharaoh in his pursuit **(4, R.V.)**.

The present road after losing sight of the sea for an interval, owing to a great mountain range, comes back to it again **(10)**. And here we have a remarkable testimony to the accuracy of this record. The arrival at Kadesh **(37)** is their *second* sojourn there (xx. 1). Between this and their former visit (xiii. 26; Deut. i. 46) occur the thirty-eight years of wandering.

The command for the expulsion of the Canaanites was very stringent **(51–56)**; and everything was to be destroyed which would serve to lead the Israelites into the atrocious sins of the heathen nations. We cannot be too careful in destroying prints, books, novels; anything which has been a curse to others or to us (*see* Acts xix. 19). Any failure to do this; any union with sinners; any permission of them or their ways—is sure to be terribly avenged on ourselves. It is ever so much better to root out evil with a strong hand, than to permit it in any form; for from small beginnings sin will inevitably grow till it dispossess us of our inheritance, or cause us serious discomfort.

CHAP. XXXIV. **The Boundaries**

In this chapter we have the boundaries of the inheritance of Israel on the west side of Jordan. The Israelites never actually possessed all this territory, except temporarily in the palmy days of David and

Solomon. They resemble many Christians, who are living far below their privileges, content with a portion only of that blessed state of enjoyment and usefulness which is ours in Christ. But there is surely coming a time when Israel shall literally inherit every inch of that land which is theirs in the counsels of God (Ezek. xlvii. 13–21; Rom. xi. 26–32).

The south border (3) was from the extremity of the Dead Sea, through Kadesh-barnea, to the ancient brook of Sihor, called "the river of Egypt."

The western border (6) was the Great Sea (the Mediterranean), great in comparison with the small inland lakes of their country.

The northern border (7) ran from the shore of the Mediterranean to the highest summits of the Lebanon range (here called Mount Hor, the great mountain), and away to Baalbek. *Compare* Ezek. xlviii. 1–8, 23–29.

The eastern border (10).—Hazar-enan is "the village of fountains," where probably the Jordan took its rise; and thus the boundary line was in all likelihood the river itself in its flow from its earliest springs to the Dead Sea.

The appointment of the princes, by name, who were to divide the land, in connection with Joshua, the military leader, and Eleazar, the priest (17–28), must have tended to raise the hopes of the people to certainty, and to prevent discord.

There are other limitations given of the Promised Land (Gen. xv. 18–21; Deut. i. 6–8, &c.), in some of which further boundaries are named. Those in this chapter were the least, whilst conquest was permitted to the further boundaries named. There are possibilities before us for which God has apprehended us, which we shall do well to apprehend. Never let us be content till we have possessed all that we may possess on this side of heaven (Phil. iii. 12).

Chap. XXXV. The Levites: Cities of Refuge

The Levites had no land assigned to them among the tribes, but were distributed throughout the country in forty-eight cities (6, 7). Around each city a distance of 1,000 cubits was measured for suburbs (3, 4). And around these suburbs a distance of 2,000 cubits more was measured, as a pasture land for cattle. It was well to distribute the Levites thus; because they would act as salt in the midst of the people, teaching the law, administering justice, settling disputes (Lev. x. 10, 11; Deut. xvii. 9; 2 Chron. xix. 8–10; Mal. ii. 4–7). How carefully God provides for those who do His work! He becomes responsible for their maintenance.

The cities of refuge, six in number (**6, 8**), were so distributed that they were easily accessible from all parts of the land. They offered sanctuary to all who had committed homicide, until a judicial investigation could be held as to whether it was done with evil intent, and was, therefore, murder; or was done by accident. This would be adjudicated by the magistrates and Levites resident in the cities. For murder the penalty was death (**30, 31**; Exod. xxi. 14; 1 Kings ii. 28–34). But for accidental homicide there was freedom, so long as the man-slayer could reach the refuge in time, and would stay within its limits (**24–28**). Jesus is our refuge city, in whom we must abide: there only is salvation (Heb. vi. 18).

The institution of blood-avenger was almost a necessity in those lands of scattered population and rudimentary organization. It is very ancient (Gen. iv. 14). It has led to great abuses. And here, without destroying the practice, it is placed under careful limitations. The justice of God is on the track of the sinner, even though he sins ignorantly: hence the need of sheltering in Jesus.

What a glorious promise is implied in verse **34**. *Compare* Ezek. xlviii. 35; Matt. xviii. 20; 2 Cor. vi. 16; Rev. xxi. 3.

CHAP. XXXVI. **Daughters of Zelophehad**

We are here led back to the enactment of chapter xxvii. The elders and leaders of the tribe of Manasseh feared that, if the daughters of Zelophehad married into other tribes, they would take with them the property which they had recently acquired, and thus the territory of the tribe would become broken up. It was a reasonable objection (**5**). Moses immediately appreciated it, and having consulted the word of the Lord, ordained that girls possessing an inheritance should ever after marry into their own tribe, so that the portions of the tribes would be kept intact (**8**).

God always does what is best for each of His children; but in such a manner that the good of the individual unit is consistent with the good of the whole community. How marvellous is it that whilst the weight of all the world rests upon the shoulders of Christ, yet

He is minutely interested in each poor and needy one! There is not a cry of the weakest for vindication that He does not heed (Ps. xl. 17).

The distinct injunction as to keeping to the inheritance (7) reminds us of 1 Cor. vii. 18–22. We are all so apt to rove and change. There is a spirit of unsettlement in us all. Let us be quite sure that we are where God would have us; and then stay there in His strength, and for His glory—until He clearly gives us an intimation to remove. "He shall choose our inheritance for us" (Ps. xlvii. 4).

"The plains of Moab" (13) constituted an extensive plateau on the north of the river Arnon, which had once belonged to the Moabites, till wrested from them by Sihon and Og, who now in their turn were dispossessed by Israel.

The Book of Deuteronomy

This Book, like the preceding ones, is called by the name given to it by the Greek translators. It means "the second law." This is a second edition of the Law, with additions and explanations enforcing its spiritual character; and was the more needful, as a new race had gathered round the aged Lawgiver. The book contains little of incident; but it is of great importance, because of its spiritual and hortatory character, which gave a model on which many later prophecies and addresses were formed. There are some four divisions:—

I. The first four chapters recapitulate the story of the wanderings from Horeb until the new generation had come to the confines of the Land of Promise—a story which was the text for solemn exhortation that they should not repeat their fathers' sins.

II. The following eight chapters rehearse the Law, with many earnest pleadings that they should keep it, in all its commandments and statutes. It was looked on as a covenant between God and the people; and their obedience was, therefore, a necessary condition to receiving the benefits to which God pledged Himself.

III. The following chapters (xiii.–xxvi.) give in detail the laws and regulations which should take place in the Land of Promise, and which they were to observe to do. The worship of God at the appointed place; the punishment of seducers to idolatry; the times and seasons of worship together with moral, judicial, and ceremonial laws—are carefully mentioned.

IV. In chaps. xxvii.–xxx. we read the blessings and curses attached to obedience and disobedience; and Moses described the solemn scenes of the blessing and cursing on Mounts Ebal and Gerizim. Then follow the memorable chapters that tell how Israel would be scattered from their land: the advent of the Chaldeans and of the Romans being described with graphic and vivid minuteness; with assurance of Israel's restoration on repentance.

The remainder of the Book (xxxi.–xxxiv.) contains the last address and song of the great Lawgiver, and the story of his death: a noble conclusion to one of the noblest books in Scripture. Our Lord frequently quoted from Deuteronomy, as we shall see. The key words are "Observe to do, for thy good always," which occur like a perpetual refrain. As we read we do well to remember John xiv. 21–24.

Chap. I. Moses' Retrospect

The scene in which Moses spoke these closing words was the plains of Moab. "On this side Jordan" is rendered in R.V. "beyond Jordan." "The Red Sea" should be "over against Suph," a deep valley in that immediate neighbourhood. In another month Moses would climb Pisgah to die.

The distance, given in days (*eleven*), is mentioned (2) to show that the great number of years spent in travelling from Horeb to the border of the Land of Promise was not owing to the length of the way, but to the necessary penalty of repeated sin. If we will not obey, our course as Christians cannot be straight or progressive.

The recapitulation of the story of the past (7–46) serves to introduce the various exhortations that succeed. We need not dwell on the stages *seriatim*; but on the words which may help our own life.

What a relief it is to turn from the failure of the noblest men to the all-sufficiency of the Great Burden-bearer! (12; Ps. lv. 22; lxviii. 19, R.V.; 1 Pet. v. 7). What Moses failed to do, God did (31).

When God sets before us a land, whatever be the difficulties, we have simply to go right forward and possess it; but it is a mistake to try to assure ourselves by sending spies (21, 22). A blind faith that goes forward without asking—just trusting—is the happiest. God permitted the people to send spies, because they were bent upon doing so; but it was a wrong step for them to have taken.

We need to keep just behind God; and then no enemy can stand before us for a single moment. The Good Shepherd precedes His sheep (John x. 4). The Great Overcomer overcomes in, and for, those who trust.

How careful we should be to walk with God! Disobedience to Him will lose the Land of Promise; will cut the sinews of our faith: and will hinder our prayers (35–46).

Chap. II. The Desert Wanderings

In verses 1 and 3 Moses comprised the whole of the thirty-eight years of wilderness wanderings. The Israelites had been refused passage on the western frontier of Edom, and had been obliged to retrace their steps slowly down the Arabah towards the Red Sea, and so they came round to the eastern and weaker frontier of Edom; and the Edomites, who had haughtily repelled them before (Num. xx. 14–21), were now inclined, in the good providence of God, to give them a free passage. The natives also kindly supplied them with bread, meat, fruits, and water (**6, 29**). Thus may God make even our enemies to be at peace with us (Prov. xvi. 7). They lack nothing who travel with God. He knows all our need (**7**; Luke xxii. 35).

Israel were forbidden to touch Moab or Ammon, because of their far-off connection with Lot (Gen. xix. 37, 38). So careful is God of His holy covenant; so true is He to His friends! For long generations He will remember and fulfil promises into which He has entered.

Zered was the southern border of Moab (**13**); and the people passed through that country until they came to its northern border, the river Arnon (**24**), which lay between Moab and the kingdom of the Amorites. Notice that, before ever Israel appeared on the scene, there had been great revolutions (**20, 21**): the hand of God had been compelled to destroy nations which had reached an excessive pitch of sin (Lev. xviii. 28).

A pacific offer was made, in all good faith, to Sihon; but he refused to meet it (**26–30**). God hardens hearts which have already hardened themselves against Him. The sun, which melts wax, hardens clay; but the fault is not with the sun, but with the clay.

CHAP. III. **Conquest of Bashan**

Had Og, the king of Bashan, remained within his city, the Israelites would have been foiled unless they received special Divine help. But he came out (**1**). Perhaps Josh. xxiv. 12 may afford us a clue. Swarms of hornets may so have harassed them in their towns as to drive them out into the plains. Oh, how reassuring to hear God's "Fear not!" as we enter the battle or undertake some new plan!

It is noticeable that recent discoveries confirm these records of the many stone cities of Bashan (**4**). There are an immense number of remains; and it is a wonder how so many people could have subsisted on so small a tract of country. Porter says that the doors and gates are of stone, some of them nearly 18 in. thick. Some 500 ruined places still tell the might of the Amorites. The Israelites thus acquired fertile and beautiful pasture-lands, as far as Hermon, and including Gilead.

158   THE FIVE BOOKS OF MOSES

The bedstead (11) would measure 13½ ft., and the stature of the king might therefore have been 11 or 12 ft. Some think "bedstead" means coffin or bier.

"Unto this day" (14) was evidently inserted by Ezra, or some other pious man who arranged and edited the books of Moses.

Moses, like Paul, besought the Lord to reverse His word (23; 2 Cor. xii. 8, 9). But there are some decisions which prayer cannot alter. It is of no use to pray against God's will; but we should yield our will to Him in such a manner as that He may will in us and through us to His own glory. And yet there was tender compensation in the vision and burial of Pisgah (27).

Chap. IV. **Statutes and Judgments**

Statutes refer more especially to ordinances respecting religion and rites of worship; judgments to civil matters (1). It is as wrong to add, as to diminish (2; Rev. xxii. 18). It is noticeable that the terrible judgment of Num. xxv. fell only on the guilty, whilst the innocent were spared (3, 4).

Faithful observance of Divine laws is productive of intelligence and wisdom (6). The two great national advantages are described as God's nearness (7), and the excellence of their holy law (8; Rom. iii. 2). It became them, therefore, firstly, faithfully to observe and obey; secondly, to imbue the hearts of their children.

An earnest remonstrance against idolatry (15–40). Perhaps the heathen temple of Bethpeor was in sight (46). As we read of what the Israelites were not to do, we can form an idea of the extensive prevalence of idolatry, which deified almost every element and object in nature (Rom. i. 23). This tendency is not extinct amongst us (Col. iii. 5; 1 John v. 21).

How true is the description of ourselves in verse 20! An iron furnace is one for smelting iron. In such a position were we once, in an Egypt of misery. Now God looks for joy and comfort out of us, as a man from his property (Deut. xxxii. 9; Titus ii. 14). God takes us out of the furnace of our foes; but He does not spare us the fire. He is Himself that (24). Those who will not yield are exposed to His judgments; whilst others are cleansed by contact with His holy nature, which is fire to their bonds, though it does not singe one hair of their heads (Dan. iii. 25). Let us beware of the "jealousy" of God's love, which will not consent to a divided heart, nor permit His "glory" to be given to graven images (**23, 24**; Isa. xlii. 8; xlviii. 11).

What tender love breathes through the following paragraph! (**29-40**). Should any backsliders read these words, let them make haste to return (Jer. iii. 12; Hos. xiv. 4).

CHAP. V. **The Ten Commandments**

All Israel were summoned to hear the words of Moses (**1**), because no one was excepted from their range. And the end of hearing should always be learning, keeping, and doing (James i. 22-25).

"Not with our fathers" (**3**) may mean not with the patriarchs, who had simply the covenant of circumcision; or it may mean that the covenant of Sinai was ratified not only with the generation which received it, but with all others represented in them.

"Face to face" (**4**).—Not in dark visions, as of old to the fathers (Job. iv. 12, 13), but openly and clearly, so that all the thousands of Israel might hear and understand. Our face-to-face vision is yet to come (1 Cor. xiii. 12; 1 John iii. 2; Rev. xxii. 4).

What a vivid idea is given us (**5**) of the work of a mediator (Gal. iii. 19); one who stands between God and men, speaking to God for man, and to man for God.

The repetition of the ten commandments here is very interesting (**6-21**). There is some slight alteration in the words. The things commanded are the same; but the reasons and setting are a little different. In Exod. xx. the ground for the *fourth* commandment is taken from the creation of the world: here from their deliverance from Egypt. Is there not, therefore, a suggestion of the reason why we keep the Lord's Day—that Jesus rose from the dead, leading captivity captive? In the *fifth* commandment the promise is added which is quoted in Eph. vi. 2, 3. The *last five* commandments are coupled together, as they were not in Exodus; which reminds us that they are all of a piece, and that we must take them all together (Rom. xiii. 9; Gal. v. 14; James ii. 10, 11).

"He added no more" (**22**); therefore the Law is perfect: He wrote it in stone; therefore it is permanent. How the conscience which has not experienced the power of the blood of Jesus shrinks from the holiness of God! (**24-27**). But such fear has no saving element in it. In spite of all, a man may go back to sin and calf-making. The yearning of God expressed in verse **29** is very touching. It repeats itself in many parts of the Bible. "Oh that thou hadst hearkened!" (Isa. xlviii. 18). "How often would I have gathered thy children" (Matt. xxiii. 37). But God is willing to give us such a heart as is here spoken of (Ezek. xxxvi. 26).

Remember that our well-being depends on our obedience (**29, 32**). All God's commandments have our truest welfare as their end and aim. He forbids those things which we should be eager to renounce, had we the same knowledge as He has. He enjoins those things which we would gladly do, could we see, as well as He does, the end from the beginning.

CHAP. VI. **Further Statutes**

Obedience to God's Word is the one condition of true prosperity and increase (**1–3**). Lands still flow with milk and honey for those who have learnt to obey; and though the literal longevity which was so dear to the Israelites is not ours, yet they live long in a few years whose lives are constantly yielded to the will of God. We live in deeds, not hours.

A better rendering (**4**) has been proposed: "Hear, O Israel: Jehovah is our God, Jehovah alone." The basis of religion is in the assent of the understanding to the unity of God's nature, and the love of the heart towards Him. These two verses (**4, 5**) are reckoned by pious Jews as amongst the choicest portions of Scripture. They write them on their phylacteries, and repeat them at least twice every day. In this they resemble the scribe (Mark xii. 32). We must love God with the love which He alone imparts—sincerely, strongly, superlatively, intelligently. Not that we can produce such a love by effort; but by asking the Holy Ghost to shed it abroad within (Gal. v. 22; Rom. v. 5).

Various methods are here prescribed for maintaining religion in heart and home. Firstly, by meditation (**6**). Secondly, by the religious training of children (**7**). Thirdly, by pious discourse and conversation (**7**). Fourthly, by the frequent reading of the Word (**6, 9**). When books were scarce, isolated texts inscribed on walls would be of great service: we too may use them; but we must never let reliance on texts take the place of diligent Bible study.

Needful cautions are given (**10–12**) lest prosperity should wean their hearts from God. We need to offer Agur's prayer (Prov. xxx. 8).

Verse **13** was quoted by our Lord in Matt. iv. 10.

Verse **16** was also quoted in the same temptation (Matt. iv. 7).

To swear by the name of God (**13**) is used for the open avowal and confession of Him (Isa. xlv. 23; Rom. xiv. 11).

It is only when we are yielding full obedience to the commandments of God that we can expect Him to fight for us (**18**). Constant failure indicates lack of consecration.

Let us never forget that we were slaves, and have been redeemed (**20, 21**); and are now called to be the slaves of Christ—as devoted to the new Master as once to the old.

Chap. VII. Separation Enjoined

Israel is strictly cautioned against all friendship and fellowship with the people and abominations of Canaan (**1–5**; Eph. v. 11). We must be merciless in our separation (**2**). So in the New Testament Christians are exhorted to marry only in the Lord; and equally stringent rules are given about worldly intercourse (1 Cor. vii. 39; 2 Cor. vi. 14–18). Where these commands are violated, misery is inevitable. God can drive out the sevenfold power of sin from the hearts of all those who will hand the battle over into His hands; and are willing to cut off and destroy whatever would suggest sin (Exod. xxiii. 24, 25; xxxiv. 13).

God's reasons for thus cautioning His people are given (**6–11**). Firstly, that He had chosen them to be His own (**6**). Secondly, the freeness of His grace, which had no cause outside itself (**7**). Thirdly, because of the holy covenant into which He had entered, as the faithful God, and from which He would not recede (**8**). What incentives were these to obedience! Surely, as He was only for them, they should be only for Him. And there is not one of these arguments that does not apply with even tenfold weight to ourselves.

The promises to obedience are enlarged upon (**12–15**) with touching copiousness and fervour. Love, blessing, multiplication, freedom from sickness, are freely promised. Let us claim them also!

Whatever be the strength of our inbred corruption, let us fearlessly go against it (**16–26**). He who redeemed us from the penalty can surely deliver us from the power of sin (Rom. v. 10; vi. 14). Let us well remember what God has done already (**18**). The work may not be accomplished in a single moment (**22**); but it shall be done. We, however, must give sin no quarter (**25**). Knox said, "Pull down the nests, and the rooks will disappear." We become like the objects on which we set our hearts, whether good or evil (**26**; 2 Cor. iii. 18).

CHAP. VIII. **Warnings and Promises**

Fresh incentives are here given to induce obedience (**1-9**). Israel were first asked to remember the wonderful past, which was calculated to reveal so clearly the evil and perverseness of their hearts, that they might be humbled and led to walk with care and watchfulness. They were bidden also to remember the supplies which had been given them—of manna, and clothes, and physical strength. Our Lord quoted from this paragraph in His conflict with Satan (Matt. iv. 4; Luke iv. 4). Surely we, too, may count upon participating in similar blessings. Then Moses expatiates on the goodness of the Land of Promise. Is it not our portion to pass through trial which is intended to reveal us to ourselves, and to give us fresh views of the loving care which is ever at hand to provide us with all we need? The sorrows of life are not meant as the punishments of rebels; but the chastenings of sons (**5**; Prov. iii. 11, 12; Heb. xii. 5, 6). Let us, however, not wander ever in the wilderness; but let us live by faith in that good land of promise, drinking of the ever-springing water of life, and eating of the rich provisions of God's love.

Prosperity is full of temptations to us all (**10-16**). It is much harder to walk with God in the sunshine of success than in the nipping frosts of failure. Have we forgotten Him in His gifts?

The cure for this forgetfulness is in giving constant glory and praise to the loving Giver of all (**17-20**). In everything give thanks. And let us remember that the mental and physical power which win us bread are the direct gifts of God; and therefore are capable of being withdrawn. Of all He will most strictly demand an account, when He comes to take an account of His servants (Matt. xxv. 19).

Chap. IX. Failures Recounted

Moses set himself anew to convince the people that it was not on account of any worthiness in them that God was prepared to do such great things, in driving out their enemies before them (1–4). Let God go before you, and drive out your inward foes—not for your worthiness, but for His great mercy. Boasting is for ever excluded from all share, whether in our justification or sanctification (6; and Rom. iii. 27).

One great reason why the land was given to Israel was on account of the wickedness of the previous inhabitants (5). The iniquity of the Amorites had become full (Gen. xv. 16). The contagion of their sin would have spread to infect the world; so they were mercilessly extirpated. The love of God to the race compelled Him to act severely toward those who were flagrantly sinning against their own nature.

During the remainder of the chapter (7–29), Moses reminded the people of their rebellions. It is well, when we are tempted to elation, to listen to that faithful monitor conscience, recording the evil past. We are apt to forget our provocations, especially when the smart of the rod is over: we need to remember, and forget not. We all have our Horebs, Taberahs, Massahs, Kibroth-hattaavahs, and Kadesh-barneas (22, 23).

Again and again would the people have been destroyed, had it not been for the intercessions of Moses on their behalf (18, 20, 25–29). Ah, how often had we been put down from our positions of usefulness and privilege, had it not been for the secret intercessions of One who has not fasted only, but died for us! Mark well the arguments advanced in this prayer by Moses (26–29): pleadings like these prevail with God. Let us make use of them—not for ourselves only, but for others. We need to emulate Moses in his life of intercession.

Chap. X. Enumeration of Mercies

Some commentators consider verses 6 and 7 to be misplaced, and to belong to the second chapter; whilst the Samaritan version adds a longer list of stations, giving the general outlines of the exodus.

But the main point is to notice the marks of God's unexhausted favour to His people, in spite of their provocations. First, He gave them a second transcript of His law (**1–4**). Next, He led them forward to Canaan. Thirdly, He selected one of their tribes to stand before Him always to minister (**8, 9**). What a vivid description of the position into which Jesus has introduced us! (Rev. i. 6). We may be well content to have no inheritance among men, if the Lord is ours in all His glorious fulness.

Here is our duty to God (**12–15**).—To fear Him with the fear born of love. To walk with Him in His ways. To love Him with the love His Spirit inspires. To serve Him with *all* our being. We are too prone to give Him less than all. If you cannot give all; ask Him to come and take all.

Here is our duty to ourselves (**16, 17**).—There is pain in the use of the knife (Col. ii. 11). But who can tell the blessedness with which Jesus fills the soul, which is willing to taste His death, and to pass through death into the risen life! We have to see to this side of it—to the incessant mortification of our self-life: Christ will see to the constant inpouring of His Divine life (Rom. viii. 13; 2 Cor. iv. 10).

Here is our duty to others.—God's care for the fatherless, the widow, and the stranger, is very remarkable (**18**). Remembering His tender love to others, we should show them the same, being imitators of God, "as dear children" (Eph. v. 1). Remembering God's love in times past to ourselves, we should deal with needy ones as He dealt with us (**19–22**). Be specially careful of strangers, lonely hearts, wanderers, and prodigals (Heb. xiii, 1, 2, 3).

CHAP. XI. **Exhortations**

With this chapter closes the introduction to the enumeration of statutes and judgments, which follows in the next chapters. One further plea for obedience backed by many arguments.

A recapitulation of the wondrous past (**2–7**). Do we often enough stir our hearts by recalling what God has done?

A description is given (**8–17**) of the fair land which God had prepared for His people; and of the blessings that would accrue to obedience (Isa. lxiv. 4; 1 Cor. ii. 9, &c.). We need to remember that a like obedience is demanded of us, and is the condition of fruitfulness and blessedness. Our Lord Jesus lays great emphasis on obedience (John xiv. 15, 21, 23; xv. 10). We do not obey to be saved; but being saved, we obey. What a contrast between the life of effort and that of trust is suggested by the description of the difference between the laborious irrigation of Egypt, and the blessed rains which God would send from heaven!

Again the people are exhorted to con the holy words of God **(18–25)**. They were to be their incessant meditation; and it was on this condition being fulfilled that God undertook to drive out their foes. *Then* **(23)**: we must be saturated with the word of God, if we would live an overcoming life.

One final appeal is made **(26–32)**; as the blessing and the curse are set clearly before the people. This choice was to be repeated to them in the Land of Promise. Further particulars were given afterwards (xxvii. 11; *comp.* Josh. viii, 33). We are constantly passing beneath these mountains. Be it ours to know the Gerizim of Matt v. 1–12. Blessing and blessedness come from the outstretched hands of the ascending Lord (Luke xxiv. 51).

Chap. XII. Wholesome Admonitions

There was to be a ruthless destruction of all that would recall the idolatrous practices of the Canaanites **(1–3)**. Their abominable rites, which were probably practised afterwards by the Druids, were always celebrated in groves of trees: every trace of such rites must be obliterated. We must abhor that which is evil; and put away everything that might excite evil desire, and lead us back to sin.

Great stress is laid upon the place where religious rites were to be celebrated **(5–15)**. When Israel were settled in Canaan, God would certainly choose a place for His habitation (Ps. cxxxii. 13, 14). Thither were they to bring all their sacrifices **(13)**, and there were they to perform all their vows. This habit would promote the unity of the nation (Ps. cxxii. 4); would prevent idolatrous practices from creeping in; and would remind the people that their sacrifices were only acceptable when offered on that one altar which prefigured the work of Christ (Heb. xiii. 10). Our best gifts are valueless apart from Jesus. *We* live in a different dispensation; no locality is specially sacred; but we need to present all through Jesus Christ (John iv. 21; Eph. v. 20; Heb. xiii. 15; 1 Pet. ii. 5).

Blood was carefully prohibited as food **(16, 23–25)**. It was looked on as having sacrificial value, and as embodying the life. It is very remarkable, therefore, that Jesus should say, "Except ye eat the flesh of the Son of Man, *and drink His blood,* ye have no life in you" (John vi. 33). This saying offended the Jews; but it is the privilege of every Christian thus to feed on Christ (Matt. xxvi. 27, 28; John vi. 53–60; 1 Cor. x. 16; xi. 25, 26). The tithes of verse **17, 18**, were not the ordinary ones which belonged to the Levites; but extraordinary ones, on which the people might feast.

Once more it is enjoined to eat the holy things in the holy place; and a stringent prohibition is given against propitiating the local deities (**26–32**). The one demand throughout was to acknowledge God as both First and Last; and then all manner of prosperity and gladness would result—joy (**7, 12, 18**); rest and safety (**10**); blessing (**15**); success (**20, 28**).

CHAP. XIII. **Idolatry Forbidden**

Moses here gives directions as to the treatment of any who might entice the people to idolatry.

False prophets who entice to idolatry (**1–5**).—We may fairly admit that bad men have been permitted to work signs and wonders—from the days of Moses, when the magicians mimicked his earlier miracles, to the time of Simon Magus: and the same may be expected until the revelation of that Wicked One, "whose coming is after the working of Satan, with all power and signs and lying wonders" (2 Thess. ii. 9). Doubtless Spiritualism belongs to the same class of evils. But we must always test wonderful and miraculous signs by their moral and spiritual tone. If they detract from the glory of Christ, or entice the soul away from Him, we may know that the wonder-workers and their works are not of God (**2**; 1 John iv. 1, 2).

Relatives who entice to idolatry (**6–11**).—How often do hindrances arise in our own homes! There is a deep meaning in Matt. x. 36. And how subtle Satan is in presenting temptations through those whom we least suspect, or most tenderly love! It would need very great moral courage to follow out the stringent demands of this paragraph (**9**). And yet there is a sense in which it is still applicable (Matt. x. 37). Let us be more careful of our most secret intercourse with companions and friends: "entice thee secretly" (**6**; Prov. i. 10).

Cities which entice to idolatry (**12–18**).—Belial stands for the devil

(2 Cor. vi. 15). How easily a few bad men lead a whole city astray! Are we equally in earnest to lead it right? Before we judge, we should enquire, make search, and ask diligently **(14)**. Love "hopeth all things," till she is convinced sorely against her will. Would that all God's rivals were expelled from our hearts!

Chap. XIV. **Children of God**

With what a marvellous description of our standing in Christ does this chapter open. We are the children of God (Gal. iii. 26; 1 John iii. 1). All are not Israel that are of Israel (Rom. ix. 6). All real children of God are Israel (Rom. ii. 28, 29; Gal. vi. 16). We are chosen and called to be holy (Eph. i. 4); and to be God's people of possession (Tit. ii. 14; 1 Pet. ii. 9). But our position naturally involves certain prohibitions and abstinence (1 Pet. i. 14-16). (1) Israel were not to lament over the dead with the idolatrous practices of the heathen; and perhaps that excessive grief, which would conflict with God's will, and unfit us for the duties of daily life, is prohibited to us (1 Thess. iv. 13).

There were reasons, which were far from being arbitrary, for the exclusion of certain animals from the dietary of the people **(6–20)**; and, probably, the same sanitary and physical reasons for prohibition would equally exist for us, did we live under the same conditions of climate. There is no law given us now as to food; we are free to eat as we will (Acts x. 9, 13; Rom. xiv. 14; 1 Tim. iv. 4). But for health's sake, under certain conditions of life, we might learn some useful lessons here. We must also, for spiritual reasons, abstain from many things in which others indulge; just as Israel could not eat of some food which was not forbidden to others.

The regulation as to turning produce into money, and the money back again into produce **(25)**, was a very wise and merciful one; and let us remark that joy was positively enjoined on them in their religious observances **(26)**. In every third year this second tithe was to be spent in the home, so that those might share who were unable to go up to the distant city; and on the kindly treatment of these their own blessing depended **(28, 29)**. "He that loveth, knoweth God."

Chap. XV. The Year of Release

The Jewish law was very merciful to the poor. The seventh year brought release from all debts between the children of Israel. Of course a debtor might, after the year of release had passed, pay money which he owed, even; but the creditor had no legal claim for repayment. And God promised that whatever Israel lost by obedience to this command should be made up to them by His blessing **(4, 5)**.

What a marvellous forecast of the special genius of the Jewish race is given in the sixth verse!

A provision was inserted next **(7–11)** to guard against the disinclination to lend money on the eve of the year of release. Men were bidden to lend or give, irrespective of any consideration of repayment: doubtless God would more than make up to them any losses resulting from obedience in this respect **(10)**. Let us beware of the envious, or evil eye **(9)**; the eye which would rather see the evil than the good of others, and grudges to part with its possessions. The spirit of these enactments has passed over into Christianity (Matt. v. 42; Luke vi. 38). We, too, must give, except when we see clearly that our giving will do moral injury to those whom we would help (2 Cor. ix. 7; James ii. 16; 1 John iii. 17).

Servants were to be released at the end of six years, as we saw (Ex. xxi. 1–6). But here is an addition, that the master was to give them a little stock to begin with **(13–15)**: first, because God had blessed him; secondly, because he had obtained better service from his brethren than had been possible from strangers. The bored ear **(17)** reminds us of Ps. xl. 6. How freely our Lord Jesus releases us! (Luke vii. 41, 42). Yet how closely He binds us to Himself!

We ought to give the *firstlings* of our time, and strength, and income to the service of God—giving Him only the best **(19–23)**.

Chap. XVI The Great Feasts

Three yearly Feasts were appointed: of the Passover, of Pentecost, and of Tabernacles. (*See also* Notes on Ex. xii.; Lev. xxiii.; Num. xxix.)

Passover **(1–8)**.—The use of unleavened bread, which was general throughout the whole land, and not only at Jerusalem, had a symbolic reference (1 Cor. v. 8). We must never forget the price by which we have been redeemed; or the love of our Redeemer in offering Himself for our sins. These we commemorate in the Lord's Supper. "This do in remembrance of Me."

Pentecost **(9–12)** means *fifty*, *i.e.*, just seven weeks. This Feast was a glad acknowledgment of God's goodness in the gathered harvest. Our religion ought to be much more radiant with joy than it commonly is (John xv. 11; xvi. 24; xvii. 13; 1 John i. 4). How the very name of this Feast thrills those who remember Acts ii. Surely the gift of the Holy Ghost day by day is a reason for unceasing joy.

The Feast of Tabernacles **(13–15)** recalls Neh. viii. 14: also John vii. 2, 39, and the holy rites associated with this Feast in the days of Christ, when the water was brought up with such gladness from Siloam. Let us see to it, when we rejoice, that we have set other hearts rejoicing also (Job. xxix. 13).

The giving by the people, in proportion to their means, was rigorously insisted upon **(17;** 1 Cor. xvi. 1, 2; 2 Cor. viii. 12). We who owe so much to Christ are, for the most part, too careless of this: the Jews must have given nearly a third of their income. Some Christians do not give a tenth—which is the lowest sum mentioned in Scripture. Under the Gospel no exact proportion of our income is specified; but surely love should constrain us to offer more than was demanded by the Law (*comp.* Mark xii. 41–44).

The administration of justice was strictly controlled **(18–20)**. Compare this command with the promises in Ps. lxxii.; Isa. xi. 1–5; xxxii. 1). Care was taken for preventing conformity to the idolatrous customs of the heathen; nor must Israel set up what God would hate **(21, 22)**. What is "altogether just" must be the law of all Christian living (Phil. iv. 8).

CHAP. XVII. **Courts of Judgment**

We must not give God anything which is at all blemished **(1)**. This was the sin denounced by Mal. i. 6–8. The Old Testament sacrifices were types of Christ, who was without blemish (1 Pet. i. 19).

We have seen that it was a crime, punishable by death, to seduce others to idolatry (xiii.); but it was also a crime to be seduced, so much so that, whether male or female, no mercy was shown (2-7). Death was inflicted at the city gate. How solemn must have been the responsibility of the witnesses! We are reminded of Acts. vii. 57, 58.

In every city, courts of judgment were erected, which are referred to by our Lord in Matt. v. 22; xxiii. 2. But there was a right of appeal to the judge or high priest (8-13); and perhaps the ultimate decision would be given by the Urim and Thummim. We, too, must go for judgment and guidance to our Great High Priest, who cannot fail us. Presumptuous sin (12, 13) brought death: hence the prayer of Ps. xix. 13.

The appointment of a king was not commanded; but it was foreseen that it would inevitably follow in the very nature of the case (14-20). And it did (1 Sam. viii.-xii.). Regulations are here given. He must be from among his brethren, that he might typify our King, who is our kinsman (Heb. ii. 11-14). He must not multiply horses, lest it should produce commerce with Egypt (Ps. xx. 7; Isa. xxxi. 1; Hos. xiv. 3). He must not have many wives (*see* 1 Kings xi. 1-4). He must not accumulate money (Job xxxi. 24, 25, 28; Psa. lii. 7; lxii. 10). How beautiful was that provision which insisted on his writing out the law of God with his own hand, and the demand that he should read therein continually, "all the days of his life" (19; Ps. 1. 2; Josh. i. 8). But it is not enough to read: we must be careful to keep. The Scriptures correct pride and prolong prosperity (20; Matt. vii. 24-27; Rev. xxii. 14).

CHAP. XVIII. **The Levites and their Portion**

The priests and Levites were liberated from all the cares of this world (1-8), that they might be free for their spiritual functions (Acts vi. 2; 2 Tim. ii. 4; 1 Cor. ix. 13; x. 18). Ah, happy are we if we can echo Lam. iii. 24. The priests who served the altar had their share of the peace offerings brought, whilst they were engaged in their course of service. If any Levite, out of his course, preferred officiating as a servant to the sanctuary to continuing in his own city, he received the same portion as his other officiating brethren, notwithstanding his possible possession of some private income (8).

The people were again warned (9-14) against all the various forms of evil which abounded around them. This was one of Saul's fatal sins (1 Sam. xxviii. 7–20; 1 Chron. x. 13; *see also* Isa. viii. 19). The various terms used here include every form of seeking aid from invisible and wicked spirits; and undoubtedly forbids "spiritualism" in all its forms. We may seek help from God; but we have no more right to seek wisdom from demons than strength for our daily work from such a source.

The thoughts of the people are directed to Christ, the true prophet (**15–22**; John i. 45; Acts. iii. 22, 23; vii. 37). Let us go to Him with all our hard questions; and let us be careful to keep our loyalty to Him intact. Oh, how serious is the sin of those who refuse Him! How awful the words, "I will require it of him!" (**19**; Heb. x. 28–31). The chapter ends with a caution against false prophets (Jer. xxiii. 25, 26; Ezek. xiii. 6, 7). Let us prove all things; eschewing the evil, holding fast to the good, not fearing any evil predicted by those who are not God-sent (*see* Matt. vii. 15–20; xxiv. 11; 2 Pet. ii. 1–3; 1 John iv. 1).

CHAP. XIX. **The Cities of Refuge**

Renewed directions were given (**1–13**) about the Cities of Refuge. (*See* Notes on Num. xxxv.) The law against murder had been distinctly declared from the time of the deluge (Gen. ix. 6). And in new unsettled districts it was absolutely essential to be very stringent in these matters. The duty of avenging death was imposed on the nearest of kin. But it was obviously just to make a distinction between wilful murder and homicide. Hence the appointment of Cities of Refuge (**2–7**).

Verse **14.**—When once we realize that our lot in life has been appointed and given by God, we become content with it, and do not seek to aggrandize ourselves at another's expense. Envy, jealousy, and similar sins have no power over the soul which is satisfied with God's provision on its behalf.

Verse **15–21.**—No man should be condemned on the evidence of one witness only (Num. xxxv. 30). The same law holds good under the Christian dispensation (*see* Matt. xviii. 16; 1 Tim. v. 19; Heb. x. 28). What a sign this is that man is not to be trusted! As the Decalogue suggests, we are all too prone to bear false witness. How careful should we be not to condemn a brother on one speaker's evidence! We should certainly have a story corroborated before we either believe or circulate it (Lev. xix. 16). It was a severe but fair arrangement that a false witness should suffer the punishment which would have fallen to the lot of the one accused (**18, 19**). Perhaps this is one of the perpetual enactments of God's government. Men suffer from what they have falsely prepared for others (Ps. lvii. 6). How good is our God to have given us such abundant assurance! (John viii. 18; Heb. vi. 17, 18).

CHAP. XX. **War Measures**

Here are directions given about war. First, *as to the public proclamation to be given to those going to war* (**1–9**). If they were at all reluctant to fight, they must be discharged. God would not be served by any but volunteers (Ps. cx. 3). And if there were sufficient reasons for absence, they were to be respected. How thoughtful God is of His own! These reasons were: (1) The entrance upon a new home. David penned Psalm xxx. on such an occasion. We should always dedicate a new dwelling. (2) The desire to eat of the vineyard which had been recently planted, and of which the owner must not eat for four years (Lev. xix. 23); and (3) the claims of a betrothed woman or a newly-married wife: in the latter case the husband was exempt for one year (xxiv. 5). Or a man might feel timid at the prospect of the fight, as in the case of Gideon's army (Jud. vii. 3); such an one must return, not only for his own sake, but because his fear might prove contagious. Oh for the lion-hearted courage which comes from the indwelling of the victorious Lion of the tribe of Judah!

Second, *as to the proclamation to be made to the cities attacked* (**10–12**). It was right and generous for Israel to give their foes the chance of submission. Is not that what God is doing with the unconverted still?—not willing that any should perish, and sending the ambassadors of peace (2 Cor. v. 20). We should always try to make up quarrels amicably before proceeding to extreme measures. Canaanites were excepted from this law; because so near, and therefore able to infect Israel. Let us not show mercy to any sin, or anything that might be likely to lead us astray (**17, 18**). It is very beautiful to notice the distinction as to fruit trees. Other trees might be destroyed for the purposes of the siege (**19, 20**); but these must be preserved for use afterwards. We are taught by Christ Himself to gather up the fragments, so that there may be no waste of what is good for food (John vi. 12).

CHAP. XXI. **Social Laws**

God often brings to justice the perpetrator of a murder who seems to have eluded Him (**1-9**). But not always; and, therefore, deeply to impress the dreadfulness of such a crime on the hearts of men, this elaborate ceremonial was instituted. Shall we not learn to be careful to have no complicity—before by connivance, or after by silence—with sin?

A soldier might marry his captive if he chose (**10-14**). But at least for a month she must mourn after the Jewish customs. The paring of the nails possibly included the tinging them with yellow ochre, a method of personal adornment much admired in the East. This delay was full of humanity to the slave, testing the strength of her master's affection, especially under the circumstances of her much altered appearance.

This enactment (**15-17**) is not made respecting polygamy; but in the case of a man having married two wives, one after the other; and the precept is directed against the undue influence of an unscrupulous stepmother.

No case of the infliction of this penalty (**18-21**) is mentioned in the history of Israel: the presumption, therefore, is that the very presence of this statute on the page of the Law was sufficient to secure the object aimed at; or, perhaps, parents were too long-suffering to make use of it.

"The curse of the tree" (**22**) is here clearly brought out (Gal. iii. 13). It was for this reason that Christ's body was taken down from the cross so hurriedly (John xix. 31). Let us contemplate the Saviour in this aspect as made a curse for us, that we might inherit the land of perpetual rest and blessedness.

CHAP. XXII. **Social Laws**—*Continued*

An important lesson of mutual love is given us here (**1-4**); not only for the sake of brute beasts, which might perish, if not properly cared for, but also for the sake of doing to others according to the golden rule. If the priest or the Levite had acted on this, the good Samaritan had never been required to succour the wounded traveller (Luke x. 34). We must not only help those who ask, but we "must not hide ourselves" from such as cannot ask (**3, 4**). This rule applies even to our enemies (*see* Exod. xxiii. 4, 5).

Disguises were often assumed in heathen temples (**5**); and such exchanges of dress would lead to levity and impurity of the worst sort.

On how tiny an act of humanity and obedience do God's great blessings rest! (**6, 7**). "That it may be well with thee." It was enough for the mother to lose her brood; and it was too great a stroke to deprive her of liberty also. Doth not God care for the birds—and for us? (Luke xii. 6).

As far as in us lies, we must see to it that we protect others from injury (**8**). It has been said that setting the example of total abstinence from strong drink is a necessary battlement for the defence of our young people.

A symbolical reference is made to this (**9**) in 2 Cor. vi. 14–18 (also **11**).

Verse **10**.—It would be unkind to the ass with its shorter step, and to the ox because it has a natural dislike to the ass with its foetid breath. The Lord's servants ought to be thoughtful even in very small matters.

These laws (**13–30**) were adapted to the Israelites in their teen position. The laws of Christ are, of course, a great advance upon them. Yet there are principles here which are of great value for all time. We must cultivate the habit of the most intense purity of thought: so only can we be kept from yielding to sudden gusts of passion. It is no slur on the Bible that it deals with these great human facts; which had better be considered under the sacred light of inspiration than from any prurient or curious motive. There are matters which we need to know about; and it is best to hear of them from Him who gave us this complex and beautiful nature, in which there is nothing common or unclean, unless we make it so.

CHAP. XXIII. Social Laws—*Continued*

An enumeration is given (**1–8**) of all who were excluded from incorporation into the Jewish state by circumcision or by marriage.

As no animal with blemish might be used in sacrifice, so no one with radical deformity, or the child of illegitimate birth, or a member of any of those nations which were regarded as special symbols of the flesh, were permitted to enter into those close relations with Israel, which are here intended by the phrase of entering the congregation of the Lord. The Israelites were to be a holy people (Exod. xix. 5). It was necessary to raise this partition wall against Ammonites and Moabites (3), because these nations lived so near the border. There was nothing to exclude them from becoming proselytes, and enjoying religious privileges, but only from identification with the chosen people. It is thought that this prohibition extended only to the males (Ruth iv. 10). "The tenth generation" means an indefinite period.

These injunctions for cleanliness (9–13) are very suggestive, because of the reason given (14). The Church of Christ is an armed host: but how careful should each body of Christians be, lest they lose the presence and power of the great Captain, Jesus!

Israel, like England, was to be the refuge for the slave (15, 16). The Church of Christ ought to welcome the poor, weak, and oppressed.

We must not think to condone for sin by bringing its proceeds into God's house (17, 18). Before He receives our gifts, He must know how they have been obtained.

"*Thy brother*" (19–20). Intended to bind Israelites in a strong common brotherhood.

Verses 21–23 apply specially to consecration vows (Eccles. v. 4; 2 Cor. ix. 7).

A provision is made for poor travellers and labourers (24, 25; Matt. xii. 1). We ought not to be niggardly over these small acts of generosity. God will always make up to us more than we lose; and nothing commends better the Gospel we professs than a literal obedience to 1 Pet. iv. 9. Always remember that there are times when it is kind not to give, but to withhold; lest men should be encouraged in courses of improvidence and crime.

Chap. XXIV. On Behalf of the Poor

These enactments as to divorce (1–4) were intended to meet habits which had been learnt in Egypt. Our Lord tells the Jews that these were temporary expedients "because of the hardness of their hearts"

(Matt. xix. 8). In His day these laws had led to great abuse by those who supposed that they gave permission for divorce on the most trivial grounds. Marriage is for life, unless broken by one special act of sin. Hence young men and women should see to it that they do not rush into the married state for a passing fancy; but with reverence, and earnest prayer for guidance and submission to God's leading.

Is there enough "cheering up" in our homes? **(5)**. How delicate the consideration for the poor!—protecting their means of livelihood **(6)**; prohibiting the scrutiny of their impoverished homes **(11)**; insisting on the return of their garments ere the cold night came on **(13)**.

Masters must not oppress their poor servants **(14, 15)**. Punctuality and promptness in paying are as obligatory now as ever (James v. 4).

"The stranger, the fatherless, and the widow." These injunctions **(17–22)** display the tenderness and loving-kindness of the Lord toward His poor and weak children (Deut. ix. 19; Ps. x. 14; lxviii. 5; cxlvi. 9; Jer. xlix. 11). The liberality of those who were in better circumstances was appealed to on the ground of their gratitude, because they were emancipated slaves. Every forgotten sheaf was to lie, and become the portion of the gleaner. Fruit trees were not to be gone over twice. What a rebuke to avarice and selfishness! What a glimpse we get of a bountiful and generous life (Prov. xi. 24). Do not we Christians come far short of a life like that sketched here? Perhaps we should be more prosperous in worldly circumstances if we lived thus (2 Cor. ix. 6–14).

Chap. XXV. **Social Laws**—*Continued*

Punishment was not to be excessive **(1–3)**. It is said that while this sentence was being carried out, the chief judge read in a loud voice, Deut. xxviii. 58, 59; and xxix. 9; concluding with Ps. lxxviii. 38. For fear of miscounting, one stroke was abated (2 Cor. xi. 24). In punishment we must not degrade **(3)**.

Whilst dumb animals serve us **(4)** they must be humanely treated and well fed (Prov. xii. 10; *see also* 1 Cor. ix. 9, 10).

The usage here referred to **(5–10)** was very ancient (Gen. xxxviii. 8); and seems to have originated in the desire to preserve the name and inheritance of the eldest son. This custom was made binding, to keep genealogies and inheritances distinct till the coming of the Messiah (Matt. i; *see also* Matt. xxii. 25). Refusal to conform to the rule was considered highly disgraceful (**7–10;** Ruth iv. 4).

Deceitful weights and measures are forbidden (**13–16**). Not only are the people prohibited from using them: they must not have them in the house, lest they should be tempted to use them. How hateful is the least deceit to our Heavenly Father! (Prov. xi. 1; xx. 10, 23; 1 Thess. iv. 6). Christ's law of love will constrain men to act faithfully and liberally one toward another (Matt. vii. 12; Luke vi. 38).

Verses **17–19**.—The treacherous action of Amalek (Exod. xvii. 8–16) is now referred to for the first time. There was no vindictiveness here; but an act of judicial punishment. The main crime lay in not fearing God (**18**). Amalek is the type of the flesh. Satan always takes advantage of us when we are faint and weary. Saul was entrusted with the execution of the sentence against Amalek (1 Sam. xv.). He failed to execute it thoroughly; and because he had rejected the word of the Lord, the Lord rejected him from being King over Israel (1 Sam. xv. 26). It is noteworthy that by the hand of an Amalekite Saul died (2 Sam. i. 8–11).

Chap. XXVI. The First-Fruits

This is the concluding chapter of the charge of the great Lawgiver.

Besides the sheaf of first-fruits offered for the whole land on the day after the Passover (Lev. xxiii. 10), each man was to take the first of all the fruit of his patrimony (**1–4**). Whatever ripened first, and therefore seemed most attractive to the husbandman, was to be put carefully aside for presentation to God. How well would it be, if we used our first flowers, or fruits, or earnings, for the service of God, by alleviating the sorrow and need of others around!

There is much beauty in this confession (**5–10**), beginning with the lowly origin of Israel (Hos. xii. 12). There is special reference to the career of Jacob, and to his going down to Egypt (Gen. xlii. 1, 2; xlvi. 3). There is also a recapitulation of the marvellous exodus, and a thankful acknowledgment of God's goodness in settling the nation in Canaan. How good is it to acknowledge that all we have is the gift of God's love to us (1 Chron. xxix. 14; Prov. iii. 6). But the mere giving is not enough, unless there be the reverent, devout

178   THE FIVE BOOKS OF MOSES

action of the soul going with its gifts—giving itself. "Thou shalt worship" **(10)**.

We have already considered the special tithe made at the end of three years (xiv. 28, 29). When this was made each Israelite was bound in these formal words to clear himself of all complicity with evil—no part used for any unhallowed purpose **(10–14)**. And they were not only to plead for blessing on themselves, but on their land and people **(15)**. We must be catholic in prayer (Ps. lxvii. 4–6).

Verses **16–19**.—What a covenant is this! and the new covenant, ratified by the blood of Jesus, is even better, because He is its surety. (Heb. viii. 6). All of each of us is for God; and all of God is for each of us. Before all worlds, God and we are bound together in an eternal union. And the outcome of it is—Holiness. God will be satisfied with nothing less (Eph. i. 4). And this will give us true dignity and pre-eminence.

Chap. XXVII. Gerizim and Ebal

It is probable that only the words of the Ten Commandments were to be inscribed on these sacred blocks **(1–10)**. But there, in the midst of the land, they were to stand as silent witnesses for God's truth and for national righteousness. There was to be a close connection between the overflowing plenty around and those majestic stones: when the latter were disregarded, then the land would become bare and sere (1 Kings xvii.). The prohibition of verse 5 was probably directed against the sculpture of any kind of image which might lead to idolatry; besides, to use any tool upon stones intended for an altar to God would pollute them (*see* Exod. xx. 25). Not only was the inscription on these stones to speak for God, but the altar in front would demand whole-hearted obedience and consecration. Well might Moses and the priests insist on obedience **(9, 10)**. These instructions were faithfully carried out (Josh. viii. 30–35).

In Ephraim's territory were two mountains, close together, with a narrow valley between; the one called Gerizim, the other Ebal **(11–26)**. The people were commanded to stand, six tribes on Ebal and six on Gerizim, answering with their "Amens," as the Levites pronounced the curses due to sin, and the blessings to righteousness. Only the curses are mentioned here. Is the reason—that those who are under the law are under the curse; that sinners can never win blessing by their obedience; that we must wait for Christ to come and sit on the Mount of Beatitudes, pronouncing His blessings? (Matt. v. 1–12). It is well for us to test ourselves by these enumerated items. We may be yielding to more evil than we realize; and it is well solemnly to ask ourselves whether we are incurring God's displeasure by walking carelessly in any of these respects. We may not be exposed to God's curse, which expended itself on our Substitute (Gal. iii. 13); but we may be losing our peace and power.

Almost beneath the shadow of Gerizim ("this mountain"—John iv. 20) Jesus sat, over fourteen centuries afterwards, on Jacob's Well, talking with the woman of Samaria.

CHAP. XXVIII. **Threatenings**

These verses (1–14) enumerate the blessings of obedience which will overtake us still, if we keep the commandments of Christ. Obedience will not save us, or wipe out the penalty of past sin; but it will enable us to appropriate without stint or hindrance all those blessings which are ours in Christ, awaiting our appropriation. We cannot enjoy our true position or privileges in Jesus, so long as we are consciously offending against the will of God. But when we are living up to our light, we can lay claim to the unsearchable riches of which we are heirs (Eph. i. 3; 2 Pet. i. 3, 4). These words are an inventory of blessings which are ours in Christ, including the bountiful supply of every want (3–5); victory (7); establishment (9); success in soul-winning (10); and all God's "good treasure" (Eph. iii, 16–20).

Here are the curses incurred by disobedience—many, grievous, terrible (15–44). They would pursue the sinner wherever he went, and in whatever he undertook. How marvellously is all the machinery of nature in arms against the man who is at enmity with God! "The stars in their courses" fight against him; though for a time he may seem to prosper in his evil way.

In these remarkable words (45–68) we have a description of the national captivities which, in consequence of their disobedience, were to befall the Hebrew people, first at the hands of Assyria and Babylon, but subsequently, and more especially, of Rome. Here are the Roman eagles (49); the horrors of the siege of Titus (53); the present dispersion of the Jews, which has lasted for eighteen centuries (**64**); the Jew-hate which has again and again broken out (**65**). All has come to pass; and here is a mighty proof of the truth of Scripture. But there is a ray of hope flung on the edge of this great thunder-cloud by the words of the Apostle (Rom. xi. 25–29). And for this the Jewish remnant is waiting, scattered in every land, at home in none; mingling with every people, but still distinct.

CHAP. XXIX. **Admonitions**

Strong inducements are here presented to the people to win their obedience (**1–9**). The great Lawgiver, however, bitterly laments that they were deficient in those spiritual sensibilities which are so necessary to the right appreciation of God's dealings. God would no doubt have imparted these spiritual gifts, if He had seen any desire on their part for them, or any will to receive and use them. "Keep therefore, and do; that ye may prosper" (Ps. i. 1–3; Josh. i. 8).

Again the covenant is renewed (**10–13**): that they, on their side, should obey; and that God would be their God in an especial sense. It would be well to study the opening chapters of Hosea, to know how much was involved in the respective words—"my Lord," "my Husband," and "My people" (Hosea i. 10, 11; ii. 1, 7, 16).

The case is here supposed (**14–21**) of a man who stood amid the crowd as the words of the covenant were recited, and who secretly resolved that he would continue to do as he chose, and to follow the imagination and caprice of his own nature; and the Heart-searcher said that such a man would be singled out of the midst of the nation to suffer in his sole person these curses. We are here reminded of that solemn scene when Achan was brought to view and punishment amid Israel's thousands (Josh. vii. 14–25).

(**22–28**).—What utter desolation sin entails!—not on men only, but on all that they touch; so that nature herself suffers (Rom. viii. 20). Is not the state of Palestine to-day a standing sign of God's dealings with the disobedient? "Because they have forsaken." God never forsakes till we forsake.

All the reasons of God's dealings are not disclosed to us (**29**); but enough is revealed to indicate the great principles of His procedure. Let us not be wise above what is revealed; but let us reverently study the written Word, asking for the illumination of the

Holy Spirit to open up to us the deep things of God (1 Cor. ii. 10). We must know—not in order to gratify curiosity, but—that we may *do* the Lord's will (John vii. 17; xiii. 17).

CHAP. XXX. For the Repentant

What infinite comfort for all backsliders there is in these words! **(1-10).** Notwithstanding the desperate condition into which sin might bring the people, forgiveness and restoration were proffered to them. Return; and God will turn. Obey; and God will gather. These promises were often fulfilled in the national history under the Judges (*see* Judges vi.; Ps. cvi. 44). But they are yet to be realized on a larger scale, when Israel look on Him whom they pierced, and mourn (Zech. xii. 10; Rev. i. 7). And there is here predicted a marvellous change, which is to pass over the chosen people, when God shall cleanse and regenerate their inmost heart **(6;** Rom. xi. 26, 27). And as the result of this blessed operation of the Divine Spirit, they should become obedient **(8).** We are reminded of Heb. viii. 10-12. Is not this inner circumcision (Col. ii. 11) what we all want, especially on entering the land of rest? (Josh. iv., v.).

In these ten verses Moses, twelve times over, calls God "*the Lord thy God;*" from which we learn that no sin on the part of God's children can break the holy relationship into which He has entered with them (Rom. viii, 38, 39).

The commands of God were so clear and simple that no one could plead their obscurity as a reason for disobedience **(11-14).** They were not in a strange foreign tongue; but in words which were constantly in their mouth. Not wrapt up in outward rites only, to be performed by priests; but imprinted in the heart of each worshipper. This is specially true of the Gospel (Rom. x. 8). We need not fetch Christ to us: He is risen, He is here, He is by our side for evermore.

What marvellous eloquence is in this last appeal **(15-20).** Surely we must each choose! If we choose life, we choose love; and love is length of days, and a settled rest of heart in God's promised heritage. Is not Jesus Christ our Life? "He is thy life" **(20;** Col. iii. 4).

Chap. XXXI. Be Strong!

Moses' life breaks into three forties: the first in Egypt; the second in the wilderness; the third as leader of the exodus. His natural force was not abated; but his career was closed by the Divine decree (**2**; xxxiv. 7). He, however, comforts the people by saying that though he could not go with them into the promised land, yet Israel would have the presence and care of God (**3**), with the assurance that He would precede them, destroy before them, and give their enemies into their hands. Does not God always treat His people thus? Expect it to-day! The courage of verse **6** may be ours, because of Heb. xiii. 5. Throughout the Bible, the watchword rings out, "Be strong!" (Hag. ii. 4; 2 Tim. ii. 1).

Verses **9–13**.—The solemn public reading of the Law took place every seventh year—the year of release; when the people were free from their ordinary toils: and at such times the women and children must be present that the rising generation might be informed of the way of the Lord. How important is it to use well our days of leisure (Neh. viii. 1–8); and to train the children (Deut. iv. 9; vi. 6, 7; xi. 19; 2 Tim. iii. 15).

Moses and Joshua had a sad prevision of Israel's unfaithfulness (**14–27**). The people would forsake God; and God would hide His face from them. A song was therefore to be prepared, which should be easily remembered, and serve as a standing witness for God, and against sin (*see* Eph. v. 19). How careful is God to do all that may be done to warn men of the evils of backsliding, and to leave the door open for their return!

There was a solemn assembly of elders and officers called to hear this sacred song, that they might teach it to others (**28–30**). Moses had no hope that the nation he loved so well would be turned from their evil ways. He had at least the consolation of having done his best. And herein is the comfort of the faithful but unsuccessful worker. God sends us to do His will; and it is sufficient for us to do this, earnestly and faithfully, leaving the results with Him. We must seek—not success, but—to be found faithful (Matt. xxv. 19–29; 1 Cor. iv. 2).

CHAP. XXXII. The Song of Moses

This sublime song has entered deeply into the texture of Scripture, and deserves to be carefully studied. It was Moses' swan-song. How eloquent had this man become under the touch of God's finger! (*comp*. Exod. iv. 10, 11). What exquisite imagery is employed!

The opening stanza (**1, 2**) appeals to angels and men as witnesses, and describes the effect of His words, which should fall as summer showers on the parched and weary earth (*see also* Isa. lv. 10, 11; Micah v. 7; Heb. vi. 7).

The glorious character of God is here published (**3, 4**). For the first time in Scripture He is compared to a Rock. (**4, 18;** *see also* 15, 18, 31; 1 Sam. ii. 2; 2 Sam. xxii. 2, 3, 32, 47; xxiii. 3; Psalm xviii. 2, 31, 46; xxviii. 1; xxxi. 2, 3; xlii. 9; lxi. 2; lxii. 2, 7; lxxviii. 35; lxxxix. 26; xciv. 22; xcv. 1; Isa. xvii. 10). His work is perfect: He makes no mistakes. His character is immoveable (Ps. xcii. 15).

What a contrast between the character of God and that of His people Israel! (**5, 6**). We should live as those who remember that they have been made, bought, established, and blessed by God.

An enumeration of God's gracious dealings with Israel is here given (**7–14**). Whenever our heart is hardening, and our steps straying, let us recapitulate the gracious attributes and dealings of God. What tender imagery we find in verses **10, 11**! God does sometimes seem hard in forcing us to take unwonted flights in the air; but it is only to teach us the luxury of flight: and He takes care of us, lest we fall (*comp*. ver. 10 with Zech. ii. 8; *see also* Ps. xvii. 8). Does not the fair land of Canaan typify those heavenly places where believers have a right to be? (Eph. ii. 6).

Israel's sins may be traced to their abuse of God's mercies (**15–18**). Luxury and prosperity are great temptations: they chose strange gods, and forgot God.

Oh, terrible judgments, which have been terribly verified! (**19–35**). Love will not spare the fire if it is needed. Yet what pity mingles with the wrath! (**29**).

God cannot cast off His people (**36–43**). He will turn again, and have comparison, and save them. He will repay His adversaries, and be merciful to His land and people.

Oh that we might set our hearts to all these exhortations and commands—that we may taste of that abundant life, which is the gift of God, and enjoyment of which depends upon scrupulous and loving obedience!

CHAP. XXXIII. **The Tribal Blessings**

The glorious being of God is the opening theme of this grand ode (**1–5**). There is here probably a reference to the giving of the Law, when, amid fire and the celestial cortège of tens of thousands of angels, God descended on Mount Sinai (*comp.* Ps. xviii. 7–9; Hab. iii. 3, 4; *see also* Jude 14, 15). All God's commands emanate from His love (**3**). How safe are His saints (**3**; John x. 28).

Reuben had lost the supremacy of the birthplace; but Moses begins with him (**6**): though he could not excel in the best things, yet he was not to perish. Simeon is left out, as Dan in Rev. vii.; possibly because through the last outbreak (Num. xxv. 14) this tribe had become reduced in numbers, and received a very small portion of the land (Josh. xix. 9).

The blessing pronounced upon Judah comprised prosperity in prayer, and work, and war (**7**). Some render the good wish on his behalf, "Bring him home in safety from his wars." There is much in this benediction which might be coveted by any section of Christian people.

Levi, as the priestly tribe, receives special blessing (**8–11**). The margin of R.V. gives a sweet turn to the opening verse: "Thy Thummim and Thy Urim are with him whom Thou lovest." Should not each of us seek guidance there? This perhaps corresponds to the white stone (Rev. ii. 17). The act of Exod. xxxii. 26 was never forgotten. We may forget: but God—never! (Matt. xxv. 37).

Benjamin (**12**) "God shall dwell among His mountains" is a possible rendering; referring, it may be, to the fact that nearly the whole of the Temple and Jerusalem stood within the confines of this tribe.

Joseph includes Ephraim and Manasseh (**17**). We have an enumeration of the wealth in the large and valuable portions of these great tribes (**13–17**). Authority among their brethren (**16**); victory over enemies (**17**); and numbers. What an exquisite reference is there in verse **16** to Exod. iii. 2!

Zebulun and Issachar, sons of Leah, were neighbours in Canaan (**18, 19**); and, being near the sea-board, south of Phenicia, became wealthy by commerce. The "calling of the peoples" may refer to the Gentile proselytes, who were influenced by these tribes (1 Kings v. 1-6; Mark vii. 26).

The rest of the tribes have blessings suggested by their position in the Land of Promise (20-25). Gad the leader of the eastern tribes; Dan warlike as a lion, a portion standing on the northern frontier, and a portion on the western coast; Naphtali possessing a good portion of the shore of the Sea of Gallilee; Asher, situated on the north-western border, and assured that its bars (defences) should be iron and brass.

There is no god like our God—above us (26); around us, as our Refuge; beneath us; before us, thrusting out our foes (27). Happy are we if we belong to God's true Israel! (Rom. ii. 28, 29; Gal. vi. 16).

Chap. XXXIV. Moses on Nebo

This chapter may have been added by Ezra, when he arranged the Old Testament Scriptures. How full of instruction it is! We learn much from it *dispensationally*; for the Law, as represented by Moses, can never take us into the Land of Promise and Rest. That is the special prerogative of Joshua (Jesus). And *morally*, what a solemn lesson is here: that though God forgives, yet we must suffer in this life the stern results of our misdeeds and mistakes (Num. xx. 12).

The loneliness of Moses' death.—Aaron was accompanied to Mount Hor; but Moses went alone, when his hour came. One by one we set sail to the unknown land (1).

The vision of his dying hour.—The Lord showed him the Land of Promise. It is a marvellous privilege to stand on the mountain-top of vision, with God's Spirit as our Teacher (4; 1 Cor. ii. 12). And often it seems as if the moment of death is the time of Apocalyptic glory.

The gentleness of his death.—"According to the word of the Lord" is rendered by the Rabbis, "with a kiss from the mouth of God." Is not this true of all saints? Precious in the sight of God is their death (Ps. cxvi. 15). And death only comes at such a time and in such a manner as He appoints (John xxi. 18, 19).

His burial.—The Lord hid his grave: possibly that it might not become the occasion of superstition and idolatry. We need not trouble as to our burying-place, so long as we are at home with God. And God will see to our dust. Angels shall guard it (Jude 9).

His successor was well qualified to take up his work. God is always able to find workmen, or to make them; but Joshua never could vie with the great leader (Num. xii. 8). Christ constantly appealed to the writings of Moses (Luke xx. 37; xxiv. 27; Mark x. 3; John v. 45, 46; vii. 19). And the title by which he is most frequently named in Scripture, is—"the servant of God" (1 Chron. vi. 49; 2 Chron. xxiv. 9; Neh. x. 29; Dan. ix. 11; Rev. xv. 3). The men whom God sends are those who have learnt implicitly to obey. What a contrast is there between the *buried* Lawgiver, and the *risen* ascended Saviour!

INDEX

Aaron, 63, 137, 140
Aaron's Rod, 137
Abel's Death, 11–12
Abimelech and Abraham, 26
Abimelech and Isaac, 32
Abram and Lot, 20
Abram Called Forth, 20
Abraham, God's Promise to, 21-2, 23
Abraham at Gerar, 26
Abraham's Death, 30–31
Admonitions to Israel, 113, 114, 165, 180
Altar of Burnt-Offering, The, 91
Altar of Incense, The, 85
Amalek, 73
Angel-Visitors, 24
Anointing Oil, The, 84
Arad, 141
Ark, Noah's—constructed, 13
Ark of the Covenant, 79, 132
Atonement Money, The, 84
Avenger of Blood, The, 153

Babel Built, 18
Babylon First Mentioned, 17
Balaam, 142, 143, 144
Balak, 142
Bashan, Conquest of, 157
Benjamin in Egypt, 46
Bereshith, 7
" Be Strong ! ", 182
Bethel, 33, 40
Bezaleel and Aholiab, 85, 89
Blasphemer, Death of, 118
Boundaries of the Land, The, 151
Bow in the Cloud, The, 16
Brazen Altar, The, 81
Brazen Serpent, The, 141
Burning Bush, The, 60
Burnt-Offerings, 97–8

Cain's Offering, 12
Caleb, 135
Camping Places, The, 151
Candlestick, The, 80
Chedorlaomer, 21
Cherubim, The, 80
Children of God, 167

Cities of Refuge, The, 152, 171
Clean and Unclean, 107
Cleansing, 110
Cloud Pillar, The, 131
Consecration of Priests, 83, 104
Corn in Egypt, 45
Courts of Judgment, 169
Creation, The, 8
Cup in the Sack, The, 47
Curtains of Tabernacle, 80

Daughters of Zelophehad, 146, 153
Day of Atonement, 117, 148
Death of the First-Born, 67
Deluge, The, 14
Desert Wanderings, 156
DEUTERONOMY, Book of, 155
Dinah's Fall, 39
Dove and the Ark, The, 15

Ebal, Mount, 178
Elim, 72
Esau, 31, 37
Esau and the Edomites, 41
Eve, Fall of, 10–11
Exhortations, 164
EXODUS, Book of, 55
Exodus, The, 68

Failures Recounted, 163
Fatherless, The, 176
Feasts, The, 117, 123, 168
First-Born of Egypt, Death of, 67
First-Born Sons, 69
First-Fruits, The, 177
First Passover, The, 68
Fragment of Genealogy, A, 63

GENESIS, Book of, 7
Gerizim, Mount, 178
Gershonites, The, 126
Gifts of the People, 89, 129
Golden Calf, The, 85
Great Cry in Egypt, The, 68

Hagar, 22
Haran, Jacob at, 36
Haran, Departure from, 36
Hardness of Pharaoh's Heart, 64
Hebrew Slave, The, 76

INDEX

High Priest's Robes, The, 82
Holiness, 77, 116
Holiness of God, The, 75
Holy Place, The, 111
Idolatry Forbidden, 114, 166
" In the beginning, God ", 8
Isaac Born, 27
Isaac on the Altar, 28
Isaac's Death, 40
Ishmael, 27

Jacob's Deception, 33–4
Jacob at Bethel, 33
Jacob and Esau 31, 37
Jacob Goes Down to Egypt, 49
Jacob and Pharaoh, 49
Jacob Blesses the Sons of Joseph, 50
Jacob's Dying Bed, 51
Jealousy, 128
Jehovah! 63
Jethro and Moses, 73
Joseph Born, 35
Joseph and his Brethren, 41
Joseph in Egypt, 43–6
Joseph's Death, 52–3
Joshua Appointed, 146
Jubilee, The, 118
Judah, 42

Kadesh, 140
Kohathites, The, 126
Korah, Dathan, and Abiram, 137

Ladder Chapter, The, 33
Lamps, The, 117
Laver, The, 84
Laws of Conduct, 76
Laws for the Priests, 115
Leah, 35
Leprosy, 61, 108–9, 127
Leper, Cleansing the, 109
" Let My People Go ! ", 62
Levites, The, 126, 130, 138, 152, 170
LEVITICUS, Book of, 95
" Lord thy God, The ", 181
Lot's Choice, 20
Lot Taken Captive, 21
Lot Brought Out of Sodom, 25

Man Created, 9
Magicians, The, 64
Manna, The, 72
Marah, 72
Meal-Offerings, 99, 136
Melchizedec, 21

Merarites, The, 126
Mercies Enumerated, 163
Mercy, 77
Mercy-Seat, The, 90
Midianites, The, 149
Miriam's Death, 140
Monotheism, 8
Month Abib, The, 69
Moses Born, 59
Moses' Rod, 61
Moses' Wife, 134
Moses' Retrospect, 156
Moses, Song of, 183
Moses' Death, 185
Murder Condemned, 16, 118
Murmurings, 72, 132, 135, 140

Nazarites, The, 128
Nimrod, 17
Nineveh, First Mention of, 17
Noah, Birth of, 13
Noah's Descendants, 17
NUMBERS, Book of, 124
Numbering the Tribes, 124, 145

Offerings, The, 97–103, 147
Og, King of Bashan, 157
Oil for the Lamp, 82
Oppression in Egypt, The, 58

Paradise, 9
Passover, The, 68, 69, 70, 117, 131
Patriarchs, Table of, 54
Peace-Offerings, 100
Peniel, 37
Pentecost, 117
Pharaoh's Dreams, 45
Phinehas, 144
Plagues of Egypt, The, 64–8, 94
Poor, The, 175
Priests, Consecration of, 83, 104
Priests, Food of the, 115
Priests, Laws for the, 115
Priests' Portion, The, 138
Priestly Sacrifices, 105
Purification, 108

Quails, The, 72, 133

Rachel at the Well, 34
Rachel's Death, 40
Raven Sent Forth, The, 15
Rebekah, 29
Redemption, 122, 126
Red Heifer, The, 139

INDEX

Red Sea, The—crossed, 70-1
Repentant, For the, 181
Restitution, 77, 127
Rest of God, The, 9
Retaliation, 77
Reuben and Gad, 150
Ribband of Blue, The, 136
River of God, The, 10
Rock, The, 183

Sabbath, The—instituted, 9
Sabbath, The, 72, 85, 88, 117
Sarah, Death of, 29
Second Adam, The, 12
Separation Enjoined, 161
Seventh Month, The, 147
Shechem, 39
Shewbread, The, 80, 117
Sihon, King of the Amorites, 141, 142
Silver Trumpets, The, 132
Sinai, 74, 78
Sin-Offerings, 100
Sins of Ignorance, 136
Social Laws, 173-7
Sodom and Gomorrah, 25
Song of Moses, The, 71
Spies, The, 134
Standards of the Tribes, 125
Statutes and Judgments, 158

" Strange Fire ", 106
Stranger, The, 136, 176

Tabernacle, The, 91, 92, 93, 127
Tabernacle Door, At the, 112
Tabernacles, Feast of, 117
Table of the Patriarchs, 54
Temptation, The, 10
Ten Commandments, The, 75, 85, 86, 159
Threatenings, 179
Tree of Life, The, 10
Trespass-Offerings, 101
Tribal Blessings, 184
Trumpets, Feast of, 117

Uncleanness, 130
Unclean, The, 127
Unleavened Bread, Feast of, 117

Vessels of the Tabernacle, 127
Vows, 148

War Measures, 172
Warnings, 121, 162
Widow, The, 176
" Without the Camp ", 86
Woman Formed, 10

Year of Release, The, 168

www.ingramcontent.com/pod-product-compliance
Lightning Source LLC
Chambersburg PA
CBHW071424160426
43195CB00013B/1798